Naturalism Beyond the Limits of Science

Naturalism Beyond the Limits of Science

How Scientific Methodology Can and Should Shape Philosophical Theorizing

NINA EMERY

OXFORD
UNIVERSITY PRESS

Oxford University Press is a department of the University of Oxford. It furthers
the University's objective of excellence in research, scholarship, and education
by publishing worldwide. Oxford is a registered trade mark of Oxford University
Press in the UK and certain other countries.

Published in the United States of America by Oxford University Press
198 Madison Avenue, New York, NY 10016, United States of America.

© Oxford University Press 2023

All rights reserved. No part of this publication may be reproduced, stored in
a retrieval system, or transmitted, in any form or by any means, without the
prior permission in writing of Oxford University Press, or as expressly permitted
by law, by license, or under terms agreed with the appropriate reproduction
rights organization. Inquiries concerning reproduction outside the scope of the
above should be sent to the Rights Department, Oxford University Press, at the
address above.

You must not circulate this work in any other form
and you must impose this same condition on any acquirer.

CIP data is on file at the Library of Congress
ISBN 978–0–19–765410–1

DOI: 10.1093/oso/9780197654101.001.0001

Printed by Integrated Books International, United States of America

For Rob, David, and Ava Hope.

Contents

Acknowledgments ix

Introduction 1

1. From Content Naturalism to Methodological Naturalism 10
   1.1 Content Naturalism 10
   1.2 Three Assumptions about Content 17
   1.3 The Content-Methodology Link 26
   1.4 Worries about the Argument 33
   1.5 Strong and Weak Versions of the Link 44

2. Content Naturalism as the Default View 45
   2.1 The Simple Case for Content Naturalism 46
   2.2 Worries about Content Naturalism 47
   2.3 Content Naturalism and Scientific Realism 54
   2.4 From Limited Content Naturalism to Methodological Naturalism 58

3. Why Methodological Naturalism Impacts Metaphysical Theorizing 66
   3.1 Underdetermination 67
   3.2 Extra-Empirical Principles in Science 72
   3.3 Extra-Empirical Principles in Metaphysics 78
   3.4 Consequences for the Practice of Metaphysics 91
   3.5 Two Alternative Ways of Thinking about Extra-Empirical Reasoning 92
   3.6 Recap 99

4. Case Study: Pattern Explanation and the Governing Account of Laws 101
   4.1 The Pattern-Explanation Principle 102
   4.2 Pattern Explanation as Metaphysically Robust Explanation 108
   4.3 What This Tells Us about Laws of Nature 111
   4.4 The Pattern-Explanation Principle, Inference to the Best Explanation, and Explanationism 114
   4.5 The Governing Account and Humeanism about Laws 118
   4.6 What Is Governance? 122

viii CONTENTS

5. Case Study: Mooreanism and Nihilism about Composition — 128
   5.1 Minimal Divergence — 129
   5.2 Mooreanism as a Part of Standard Scientific Practice — 133
   5.3 Objections and Replies — 138
   5.4 Minimal Divergence and Nihilism about Composite Objects — 144
   5.5 Recap — 151

6. Case Study: Excess Structure — 153
   6.1 How the Lack of a Privileged Reference Frame Creates Difficulty for Presentism — 155
   6.2 The Relativity-Inspired Objection to Actualism — 163
   6.3 Privileged Reference Frames and Privileged Modal Perspectives — 165
   6.4 Objections and Replies — 171
   6.5 Recap — 179

7. Context Dependence in Scientific Methodology — 180
   7.1 Context Dependence as Background Dependence — 184
   7.2 Level Dependence and Competing Methodologies — 192
   7.3 Ways of Responding to Level Dependence — 196
   7.4 Context Dependence More Generally — 203

8. Metaphysics Unmoored? — 205
   8.1 Unmoored Metaphysics without Genuine Conflicts — 207
   8.2 Unmoored Metaphysics with Genuine Conflicts — 214
   8.3 Fine-Grained Naturalism — 219

Conclusion — 222

References — 227
Index — 239

Acknowledgments

For their general mentorship, encouragement, and advice throughout this project, I'd like to thank Brad Skow, Ned Markosian, Laurie Paul, Ned Hall, and Jay Garfield. For being truly exceptional colleagues and friends, thank you to Katia Vavova, James Harold, Sam Mitchell, and Laura Sizer. Thanks also to the many Mount Holyoke students who have inspired me during the past few years, and in particular to Gabrielle Kerbel, Wenny Shen, Yuan Tian, Mika Stanard, and Sabryna Coppola.

For their support, camaraderie, inspiration, and excellent feedback, thank you to Mahrad Almotahari, Fatema Amijee, Paul Audi, Mark Balaguer, Helen Beebee, John Bengson, Harjit Bhogal, Lindsay Brainard, Phil Bricker, Amanda Bryant, Rebecca Chan, Ellen Clarke, Cruz Davis, Heather Demarest, Callum Duguid, Matt Duncan, Katie Elliot, Maegan Fairchild, Vera Flocke, Steven French, Stephen Harrop, Mike Townsen Hicks, Nick Jones, Li Kang, Sam Kimpton-Nye, Sam Levey, Barry Loewer, Heather Logue, Rebecca Mason, Michaela McSweeney, Chris Meacham, Elizabeth Miller, Will Morgan, Jill North, Zee Perry, David Plunkett, Alex Prescott-Couch, Kate Ritchie, Juha Saatsi, Raul Saucedo, Josh Schechter, Erica Schumener, Ted Sider, Elliot Sober, Jack Spencer, Jonathan Tallant, Peter Tan, Elanor Taylor, Henry Taylor, Aimee Thomasson, Jenn Wang, Mallory Webber, Bruno Whittle, Isaac Wilhelm, and Al Wilson. I'm certainly forgetting some folks. My apologies!

For feedback and encouragement, thank you to audiences at Amherst College, Dartmouth College, Leeds University, the University of Massachusetts at Amherst, the University of Wisconsin at Madison, the University of Maryland, the University of Vermont, and Vassar College. Thanks also to the organizers of and participants in the 2017 Early Career Metaphysics Workshop at Fordham, the fourth IAPT conference, the 2017 SPAWN conference at Syracuse, the FraMEPhys workshop at Birmingham in June 2019, the 2019 workshop on Humean Laws at Harvard, the Explanation Across the Boundaries Conference at Middlebury College, the 2019 MARI Graduate Conference at UMass, a MAPS meeting at NYU in April 2019, the 2019 MITing of the Minds conference at MIT, the 2019 Ranch Metaphysics

Conference, the 2019 NEW Metaphysics Workshop, the 2020 California Metaphysics Conference, the Modality Laws, and Causation Workshop at Simon Fraser University, a 2021 Eastern APA session on metaphysics and science, Boris Kment and Adam Elga's graduate seminar at Princeton in the fall of 2018, Daniel Wodak and Errol Lord's proseminar at Penn in 2019, Ned Markosian's metaphysics class at UMass in 2019, the April Fools Metaphysics Workshop that began in April 2020, the Rutgers metaphysics reading group in the spring of 2022, the metaphysics reading group organized by Jenn Wang in the spring of 2022, and the Women in Metaphysics group organized by Li Kang and Maegan Fairchild.

I received extremely helpful comments from two reviewers for Oxford University Press, which greatly improved the book. Thank you also to Peter Ohlin for supporting the project. Some of the material in this book is based on previously published work. An early version of Chapter 4 was published in *Ergo* as "The Governing Conception of Laws," an early version of Chapter 5 was published in *Inquiry* as "Mooreanism in Metaphysics from Mooreanism in Physics," and an early version of Chapter 6 was published in *Noûs* as "Actualism without Presentism: Not By Way of the Relativity Objection." Thank you to Michigan Publishing, Taylor and Francis, and Wiley-Blackwell for permission to include this material.

I wrote the majority of this book during the COVID-19 pandemic and without consistent, reliable (or, for a lot of the time, any) childcare. I owe an especially significant debt of gratitude to the small village of family and friends from near and far who helped me through this challenging time. To Jenny, David, Ellie, and Bob Emery, Corey Robinson, Sarah and Greg Sargent, Mary Beth and Larry Williams, Jasmine Kerrissey, Kurt Bahneman, Anna and Joe Trapani, Anna and Tim Cook, Emily Marsters, Pete Morse, Bekka Klausen, Sophie Horowitz, Katia Vavova (yes, that's twice!), and Alejandro Perez Carballo: thank you for watching my children, for the campfires and camping trips, for all the skiing and biking and running adventures, and for the text threads and late-night phone calls that made me laugh. Thanks also to Arlo and Charlie, my dogs, who kept me company through many, many hours of reading and writing.

Most of all thanks to my partner, Rob Williams, and to my children, David and Ava Hope, for the joy they bring, every single day.

Introduction

Almost every fall, I teach an undergraduate philosophy course called Metaphysics. On the first day of class, I tell my students that metaphysics is the study of what the world is like. I then contrast metaphysics with two other traditional sub-fields of philosophy with which they are usually familiar: ethics and epistemology. Whereas *metaphysics* is the study of what the world is like, *ethics* is the study of what the world should be like, and *epistemology* is the study of how we come to know things about the world. "Make sense?" I ask my students. They all nod. And off we go, investigating questions about the nature of time and space, what it means for a person to remain the same person over time, whether possible worlds exist, and more.

My own view, though, is that what I say to my students on that first day of class, both by way of a definition of metaphysics and by way of a distinction between metaphysics and other sub-fields of philosophy, is problematic. Although it is a fairly standard thing to say, once we examine it more closely, it does not actually make much sense at all. First of all, there isn't a clear distinction between metaphysics, epistemology, and ethics. Epistemology and ethics are full of questions about what the world is like. (Consider one of the central questions of epistemology: "What is knowledge?" Surely that is a question about what the world is like. And the same can be said of: "Are there objective facts about what is right and wrong?") A similar observation holds for other sub-fields of philosophy that this tripartite distinction leaves out. Philosophers who study aesthetics ask questions about the nature of beauty. Political philosophers ask "What is race?" and "What is gender?" Metaphysical questions certainly aren't the only kind of philosophical question, but they are woven through pretty much every area of philosophical inquiry.

Second, and more importantly, consider again the claim that metaphysics is the study of what the world is like. Stop worrying about the distinction between different sub-fields of philosophy and focus instead on this as a definition of a distinctive area of philosophical inquiry. And notice that we already *have* a field of inquiry that is inquiry into what the world is like—that field is science. As I am teaching my metaphysics class, there are all sorts of chemists and biologists and geologists and physicists elsewhere on campus, giving lectures and running labs and writing papers. What are they doing, if not trying to figure out what the world is like?

In this way, the simple definition of metaphysics that I started with raises an important question—the question of the relationship between metaphysics and science. And as it turns out—as we will see over and over again throughout what follows—this question is by no means easy to answer. (It's tough enough that I think it's worth eliding with my undergraduates, at least at first; they have an easier time grappling with questions about what is distinctive, and what is not, about metaphysical inquiry once they've actually done some metaphysics.) At the same time, however difficult it may be, the question of the relationship between metaphysics and science is not a question that professional philosophers can ignore. Until we're able to understand that relationship, we can't have a very deep understanding of what we are doing as metaphysicians, or—given the prevalence of metaphysical questions across philosophical sub-fields—as philosophers quite generally.

The relationship between science and metaphysics is especially interesting because while science is often taken to be a paradigm of successful human inquiry, many debates within metaphysics are thought to be hopelessly abstract, arcane, and poorly motivated. In my metaphysics class, for instance, one of the questions I ask my students is: Under exactly what circumstances do two (or more) things compose a further thing? Sure, we talk all the time about composite objects like coffee mugs or café tables, but are we just using a convenient shorthand for fundamental particles arranged in a coffee mug- or a café table-like way? Another question we focus on is about the nature of personal identity. People can survive dramatic changes in their physical and psychological characteristics. So what is it that makes a person the same person over time? Could you replace *all* of one person's memories with those of someone else without destroying the original person? These kinds of debates strike many of us—philosophers and non-philosophers alike—at least initially, as odd. But they too are questions about what the world is like. So, what is the difference, exactly, between asking, for instance, "Do possible worlds exist?" and asking "Does the Higgs boson exist?" Why does the latter strike us as vitally important while the former seems potentially misguided? It has always seemed to me that regardless of the answer, investigating this relationship is likely to give us a better understanding not just of metaphysics, but of the nature of scientific inquiry, and its limits, as well.

At first glance, it might seem like any investigation into the relationship between metaphysics and science is likely to face a worrying dilemma. On the one hand, if metaphysicians are just trying to do the same thing that scientists are doing, then what is the point of doing metaphysics at all? Shouldn't we just leave questions about what the world is like to the scientists? What can we add from the armchair? On the other hand, if metaphysicians are doing something substantially different from what scientists are doing, then metaphysics starts to seem like a pretty mysterious enterprise. What could it mean for us to be investigating what the world is like in a sense that is distinct from the sciences? What constraints are there on this kind of investigation? What reason do we have for thinking that it is a legitimate and worthwhile pursuit?

The goal of this book is to articulate and investigate a way of thinking about the relationship between metaphysics and science that avoids this apparent dilemma. The approach I will lay out will be a version of *naturalism*, which is to say, it will take scientific inquiry as the paradigm of successful inquiry into what the world is like. In that way, it may sound as if I am leaning toward the first horn of the dilemma described above. But, as I will argue, there is a way of being a naturalist that still leaves space for metaphysics as a robust, interesting, and well-founded field of inquiry that goes beyond the domain of science. Indeed, unlike most naturalistic philosophers, who tend to draw a sharp distinction between metaphysical debates that are adjacent to science (which they think of as legitimate) and metaphysical debates that are farther afield (of which they are suspicious), I argue that there is a way of being a naturalist that blurs this distinction and preserves the legitimacy of even the latter kind of metaphysical question. Metaphysical inquiry, according to the approach that I will focus on, will be modeled on and respectful of scientific inquiry, but metaphysics will not be subservient to science in any worrying sense.

Of course, merely saying that the view I focus on is a version of naturalism does not give it much content. To be a naturalist is to be in some sense guided by or respectful of our best science.[1] But there is going to be a wide range of different views that count as naturalistic on this definition, which

---

[1] The term 'naturalism' is used in many different ways in the literature. Here my broad-strokes definition of the term follows David Papineau, who says that the traditional goal of naturalists was to "ally philosophy more closely with science" (Papineau 2021). As another relatively typical definition consider Liston (2007), who says that naturalism is "a blanket term for numerous vague stances that include a pro-attitude toward science." Naturalism is often associated, at least historically, with a Quinean approach to epistemology (e.g., as described in Quine 1951), but does not obviously require any further Quinean commitments.

vary depending on what the "guiding" or "respecting" relation consists in and what its relata are. One might think, for instance, as Wilfred Sellars did, that "in the dimension of describing and explaining the world, science is the measure of all things" (1963, 173); but one need not take such a strong stance. And while it is the entities posited (or not posited) by our best science that are often the focus of philosophical attention, there are other aspects of our best science that one might take to be important as a guide to philosophical theorizing.

The specific version of naturalism that is the focus of this book is what I call *methodological naturalism*. According to this view, philosophers who are asking metaphysical questions should be guided by our best science in the following sense: they should, whenever possible, use the same methodology that scientists use.[2]

On the face of it, especially for those without a background in philosophy of science, methodological naturalism might seem like a non-starter. When one considers what the physicists and geologists and biologists across campus spend their time doing on a day-to-day basis, in comparison to the ways in which I, as a philosopher, spend my time, it might seem like there is little opportunity for overlap in our methodologies. This is especially true if you focus on the aspects of science that involve the collection of data in the laboratory. Think again of the paradigm examples of metaphysical debates that I mentioned above—debates about composition, personal identity, and possible worlds. Whatever else you want to say about them, these debates just don't seem like the kinds of debates that will be settled by the kind of data that scientists collect. What kind of data could distinguish, for instance, between the hypothesis that there is a coffee mug before me and the hypothesis that there is a group of particles arranged coffee-mug-wise? So how *could* metaphysicians make use of the same methodology that scientists use?

I'm going to say much more about this kind of worry in Chapter 3, but in service of making methodological naturalism at least initially plausible, here is a brief preview of the reasons that the pessimistic attitude just described is unwarranted. Although the methodology of science involves the collection of data, the data that scientists collect rarely uniquely determines a

---

[2] Here again I follow Papineau (2021), who says that methodological naturalism "claims some kind of general authority for the scientific method." Methodological naturalism also bears some kinship to Penelope Maddy's "second philosophy" (see Maddy 2007), though Maddy would certainly express concern with methodological naturalism as defined above on the grounds that it seems to presume a distinction between science and philosophy. I say more about this in section 1.2. Note that the term 'methodological naturalism' has quite a different meaning in philosophy of religion.

particular set of scientific commitments. Instead scientists combine the data that they have collected with some *extra-empirical reasoning*—some reasoning that goes beyond mere consistency with the data. In the paradigm cases that I focus on in this book, they take the data that they have collected and apply what I will call *extra-empirical principles*.[3] Examples of potential extra-empirical principles are principles like "Choose the simplest theory that is consistent with the data" or "Choose the theory that provides the best explanation of the data."[4] These principles allow us to choose between multiple theories—all of which are consistent with the data—on the basis of other features. And these kinds of extra-empirical principles are plausibly principles that metaphysicians can make use of as well. For while it is unclear how the empirical data that we collect would ultimately decide debates about composition or personal identity or possible worlds, a principle like "Choose the simplest theory that is consistent with the data" might very well do so.

The big-picture view, then, is that methodological naturalism is initially plausible because extra-empirical reasoning plays an important role in the methodology of science and the very same kind of extra-empirical reasoning has the potential to impact a wide range of metaphysical debates—including those that, on the face of it, don't have much to do with science at all. In this way, methodological naturalism holds out hope for an account of metaphysics that can be both respectful of science and yet go well beyond the domain of science. Even those of us who are full-fledged naturalists can meaningfully ask and answer questions about what the world is like that go beyond the limits of what is standardly thought of as scientific inquiry.

In the broad strokes laid down so far, methodological naturalism is not unfamiliar. It has made regular appearances in the literature, in particular at moments when metaphysics as a field has been under scrutiny of one form or another. Consider, for instance, W. V. O. Quine, writing at a time when logical positivism still held sway, who claimed:

> Our acceptance of an ontology is, I think, similar in principle to our acceptance of a scientific theory, say a system of physics: we adopt, at least insofar as we are reasonable, the simplest conceptual scheme into which the

---

[3] As I discuss in Chapter 3, extra-empirical reasoning can also take other forms, including reasoning that helps us determine what the data is and various applications of confirmation theory.

[4] The reader will note that in what follows I do not argue for either of these candidate extra-empirical principles as actually playing a role in scientific practice. I use them here just because they are relatively familiar.

disordered fragments of raw experience can be fitted and arranged. (Quine 1953, 16)

Or consider Theodore Sider, Dean Zimmerman, and John Hawthorne, who wrote their introduction to *Contemporary Debates in Metaphysics* at a time when there was increasing interest in various neo-Carnapian and other deflationary approaches to metaphysics, and who noted that focusing on "continuity with science can help dispel radical pessimism about metaphysics" (Sider et al. 2008, 8). As they write:

Scientists must regularly choose between many theories that are consistent with the observed data. Their choices are governed by criteria like simplicity, comprehensiveness, and elegance . . . Just like scientists, metaphysicians begin with observations, albeit quite mundane ones: there are objects, these objects have properties, they last over time, and so on. And just like scientists, metaphysicians go on to construct general theories based on these observations, even though the observations do not logically settle which theory is correct. In doing so, metaphysicians use standards for choosing theories that are like the standards used by scientists (simplicity, comprehensiveness, elegance, and so on). (8)[5]

As a final example, consider the following quote from L. A. Paul's paper "Metaphysics as Modeling," writing in the aftermath of the critique of contemporary metaphysics leveled by James Ladyman and Don Ross in their book *Every Thing Must Go*:

Scientific theorizing itself, even empirically-based science, relies on a priori reasoning involving simplicity, elegance and explanatory strength. Such considerations play an important role in the development of successful scientific theories, and the use of the a priori in metaphysics is similar to the use of the a priori in science. (Paul 2012, 19)

As Paul goes on to say, "The main point I want to make here is that if the method can lead us closer to the truth in science, it can lead us closer to the truth in metaphysics" (21).

---

[5] For other examples of this kind of defense of metaphysics see Swoyer (1983) and Sider (2011, 11).

All of these authors clearly have something like methodological naturalism in mind. But in my view, they do not go nearly far enough for either the continuity between metaphysical and scientific methodology to be especially convincing or that continuity to do much work in defending metaphysics from the various critiques it has faced. As we will see (and as has also been observed in the many contributions to the literature that take issue with Quine, Sider et al., Paul, and others of a similar mindset), a loose gesture toward the idea that some combination of simplicity, explanatory power, and elegance plays a role in scientific theorizing is just too quick.[6] A full treatment of methodological naturalism would more carefully investigate the extra-empirical reasoning that plays a role in scientific theorizing and the consequences that similar reasoning would have when applied to metaphysical debates. This is the project that I take up below.

One of the key contentions of this book is that once we engage in this investigation, it quickly becomes clear that the extra-empirical principles that play a role in scientific theorizing are both nuanced and surprising. Although metaphysicians might gesture to principles like "Choose the simplest theory that is compatible with the data" or "Choose the theory that best explains the data" as examples of extra-empirical principles, the role that such principles play in scientific theorizing is far from straightforward. Moreover, in cases where we can identify a clear extra-empirical principle that does play a role in scientific theory choice, it often has unexpected results for metaphysical debates. The position in these debates that is standardly assumed to be the most scientifically respectable may turn out to be ruled out by methodological naturalism, properly understood.

Methodological naturalism, therefore, is by no means as straightforward as the authors above seem to suggest. Indeed, once it is fully understood, methodological naturalism promises to have widespread and surprising consequences—both for particular first-order debates within metaphysics and also for more general approaches to how metaphysical inquiry is structured and carried out. At the same time—and this is one of the other key contentions of the book—it turns out that methodological naturalism is also quite difficult to avoid. Indeed, my view is that the vast majority of

---

[6] For general critiques of the idea that methodological naturalism justifies metaphysics as it is standardly practiced, see, for instance, Ladyman (2012), Kincaid (2013), Humphreys (2013), and Bueno and Shalkowski (2020). For focused critiques of particular applications of methodological naturalism, see Huemer (2009), Sober (2009), and Willard (2014) on simplicity as an extra-empirical principle; and Day and Kincaid (1994), Saatsi (2017), and Thomasson (ms) on inference to the best explanation as an extra-empirical principle.

philosophers—including, almost certainly, you, dear reader!—already have commitments that lead straightforwardly to methodological naturalism. And these commitments are so ingrained in the field that contemporary metaphysics would look quite different if they were to be given up.

All of this means that once methodological naturalism and its consequences are clearly spelled out, we find ourselves in quite an interesting position. On the one hand, accepting methodological naturalism has widespread and surprising consequences. On the other hand, we can't avoid methodological naturalism unless we are willing to revise certain commitments that are central to contemporary metaphysics. Although I ultimately leave it up to the reader to decide which of these two positions to take—accepting methodological naturalism or rejecting the commitments that lead to that view—the point is that regardless of which choice you make, the way that you think about metaphysics should change. In some ways, then, I am trading one dilemma for another. But while the dilemma we might have thought faced metaphysicians (that metaphysics is either subservient to science or misguided) is pernicious, the dilemma that I ultimately settle on (one must either accept the surprising consequences of methodological naturalism or reject and revise the central and long-standing commitments that lead to that view) is a productive one. Although I myself am inclined to accept methodological naturalism, the key result that I hope to emphasize is that either way there is a wealth of fruitful and interesting work ahead for metaphysicians.

Here is a more detailed plan for what follows. First, in Chapter 1, I argue that the vast majority of philosophers (including, almost certainly, those reading this book) already have commitments that lead straightforwardly to methodological naturalism. In Chapter 2, I give some reasons for thinking that given the choice between accepting methodological naturalism or revising the commitments that lead to methodological naturalism, the former should be the default view. I then turn to the claim that accepting methodological naturalism will have widespread and surprising consequences for metaphysical theorizing. I defend this claim first, in Chapter 3, in quite general terms, before turning, in Chapters 4, 5, and 6, to three specific case studies that demonstrate these consequences for particular first-order debates in metaphysics. These case studies include some of the metaphysical debates discussed above, including the debates over composition and possible worlds, but also range over metaphysical questions that tend to be of interest to more naturalistically inclined philosophers, including the question of what it means for something to be a law of nature, and the question of whether and how time differs from space. In Chapter 7, I take up a significant complication that I have largely avoided throughout the earlier discussion: the question of how methodological naturalism works if one thinks that scientific methodology is context dependent. (Perhaps the most obvious way in which this might happen is if one thinks that different sciences involve different methodologies.) Finally, in Chapter 8, I discuss the consequences of rejecting methodological naturalism and give some options for what the resulting version of metaphysical inquiry might look like and how it might be justified.

As will become obvious, all of this is just the beginning of a much larger project. In the conclusion of the book, therefore, I make a plea for further research into the extra-empirical aspects of theory choice in science—research that I argue needs to be done jointly by metaphysicians and philosophers of science and needs to involve significant input from historians of science, and scientists themselves. Without this research, we cannot fully understand the potential implications of methodological naturalism on a wide range of philosophical debates. Nor can we decide, ultimately, whether to be methodological naturalists. This book, then, is by no means a definitive guide to methodological naturalism—it is a start in which I hope others can find inspiration and a foundation on which others can build.

The fact that this book is just the beginning of a larger project is a way in which my ambitions are more limited in scope than they may first appear. Here is a way in which those ambitions are more expansive than the reader may be expecting. In what follows I will often write things like "Metaphysicians are committed to..." or "Metaphysicians should..." or "Metaphysicians who..." It is important to keep in mind, however, that as I use the term, a metaphysician is just a philosopher who investigates questions about what the world is like. And, as I noted above, questions about what the world is like show up in nearly all areas of philosophy. So just because you don't think of yourself as a metaphysician or don't write "metaphysics" as an area of specialization on your CV doesn't mean that you can avoid the central choice that this book sets up for the reader and the surprising consequences that follow regardless of how one responds to that choice. If your philosophical investigations involve trying to determine what the world is like—and I would expect that that applies to most, if not all, philosophers—then this book is for you.

1
From Content Naturalism to Methodological Naturalism

Methodological naturalism is the view that when investigating metaphysical questions, and insofar as it is possible, philosophers ought to follow the methodology of science.

> *Methodological naturalism.* Metaphysicians should, whenever possible, use the same methodology that scientists use.

My goal in this chapter is to argue that the vast majority of philosophers already have commitments that lead straightforwardly to methodological naturalism and, moreover, that giving up those commitments would lead to a significant revision in the way that contemporary philosophers think about metaphysical questions. The argument will proceed in two steps. First I will argue that the vast majority of philosophers are committed to a different kind of naturalism—what I call *content naturalism*—and that this commitment constrains their theorizing in substantive ways. Then I will argue that anyone who is committed to content naturalism should also be committed to methodological naturalism.

1.1 Content Naturalism

The argument that the vast majority of philosophers already have commitments that lead straightforwardly to methodological naturalism begins by focusing on a distinct type of naturalism:

> *Content naturalism.* We should not accept metaphysical theories that conflict with the content of our best scientific theories.[1]

---

[1] Note that content naturalism, as defined here, is quite permissive—it only requires consistency between metaphysical theories and scientific theories. For a stronger but obviously related view,

Consider a metaphysical theory that you find initially attractive. Perhaps it is the view that time passes. Or the view that the mind is something over and above the brain. Or the view that at least some facts about what is right or wrong are objective. Imagine someone telling you that, unfortunately, the theory you find attractive conflicts with a well-established scientific theory. There are a number of ways you might respond to this. You might give up the initially attractive metaphysical theory. You might try to revise that theory to avoid the conflict. You might argue that the person raising the potential conflict is wrong about what our best scientific theories in fact commit us to. Here's a question: Can you simply ignore this potential objection? Could you, for instance, admit that there is a genuine conflict, maintain your commitment to the initially attractive metaphysical theory, and say, "Well, so much the worse for science!" The vast majority of metaphysicians, I claim, would answer these questions with a resounding "no." Throughout the field, objections of this sort are taken extremely seriously, and virtually no one responds by ignoring them or by rejecting the relevant science. The reason for this is straightforward: the vast majority of philosophers are content naturalists.

Many of the consequences that follow from content naturalism are taken to be so obvious that they are not explicitly discussed in the literature. One way to bring them out is to consider historically prominent metaphysical views that have since fallen out of favor. Consider, for instance, the Aristotelian view that everything is made of four elements—earth, air, fire, and water. No one today would bother trying to defend this sort of view. Why not? Because it so obviously conflicts with well-established claims in physics and chemistry. Or consider the Cartesian view that the Earth is a cooled star.[2] Today this view isn't just unpopular; it isn't even discussed. Why? Because it conflicts straightforwardly with what we know from both geology and astronomy. Traditional Buddhist thought says that the heart is the seat of consciousness.[3] But given what we now know about biology and neuroscience, no one today tries to interpret this claim as literally true.

These examples involve conflicts with scientific posits that are so deeply ingrained that they are taken to be obvious. As such, it isn't easy to find

---

consider what I call "radical content naturalism" below. Note also that I say more below about what counts as our "best" science.

[2] See Descartes ([1647] 1983, 181).
[3] See the discussion in Sugunasiri (1995).

contemporary philosophers saying things like "The view that everything is made of either earth, air, fire, or water is attractive, but, sadly, it conflicts with chemistry. So, we have to give it up."[4] In the next three sub-sections, I will give three examples from contemporary metaphysics in which the role of content naturalism is more explicit. All three of these cases involve situations in which the relevant science is at least somewhat controversial, but of course, this is what we should expect if content naturalism is a commitment of nearly everyone involved in contemporary metaphysical debates: the only cases where there will be an explicit discussion of the consequences of content naturalism will be cases where those consequences are not entirely straightforward. At the end of this section I will also say a bit more about some of the nuances that will be relevant to deciding whether and how content naturalism applies to even harder cases. (For those readers who are wondering how we know what precisely counts as the content of a well-established scientific theory, this last sub-section will be especially important.)

Presentism and Special Relativity

Here is the first example of content naturalism at work in contemporary metaphysics. One of the central questions in the metaphysics of time is the question of whether there is anything objectively special about the present moment, or if the fact that the present seems special to us is just a matter of perspective. One view that is clearly committed to there being something objectively special about the present moment is *presentism*.

Presentism. Only presently existing entities exist.

---

[4] An uncontroversial example of a contemporary philosopher who rejects content naturalism is George Bealer, who claims, "Insofar as science and philosophy purport to answer the same central philosophical questions, in most cases the support that science could in principle provide for those answers is not as strong as that which philosophy could in principle provide for its answers. So, should there be conflicts, the authority of philosophy in most cases can be greater in principle" (Bealer 1996, 81).
 Note that many other standard examples of non-naturalists (including E. J. Lowe; see footnote 6 in Chapter 2) are controversial because they can be reinterpreted as saying merely that science contains metaphysical presuppositions. As I will argue in section 2.2, the view that science involves metaphysical presuppositions is compatible with content naturalism.

Many philosophers claim that presentism is intuitive, but few philosophers are themselves presentists.[5] Why? There are several objections to presentism, but one in particular is considered decisive: the objection from special relativity.[6] I will go through the objection from special relativity against presentism in detail in one of the case studies later in the book (see Chapter 6), but here is the rough idea. One of the key commitments of relativity theory is the following principle:

> *The conventionality of simultaneity.* There are pairs of events such that there is no fact of the matter as to whether those events happen at the same time.

And it is a short step from the conventionality of simultaneity to:

> *The conventionality of presentness.* There are some events such that there is no fact of the matter as to whether those events are present.[7]

And the conventionality of presentness seems incompatible with presentism. More carefully, consider the following, highly plausible, background commitment with respect to existence:

> *Determinate existence.* There is a fact of the matter as to what exists.

No one who accepts determinate existence can also accept both the conventionality of presentness and presentism.

Let's assume that this argument is sound. You cannot accept special relativity, presentism, and determinate existence. Let's further assume (as almost everyone involved in the debate does) that determinate existence is unassailable.[8] So either we need to reject presentism or we need to reject special relativity. The vast majority of philosophers take the choice to be obvious: we

---

[5] The 2020 PhilPapers survey put the number of philosophers that accept or lean toward presentism at 17.5%. See Bourget and Chalmers (forthcoming).

[6] See, for instance, Putnam (1967), Sider (2001), Saunders (2002). Defenders of presentism in light of the relativity objection include Hinchliff (2000) and Markosian (2004). See also helpful discussion in Hawley (2009).

[7] The move from the claim that there are pairs of events such that there is no fact of the matter as to whether those events happen at the same time to the relativity of presentness is discussed in detail in Chapter 6. Note that this way of spelling out the conflict between presentism and special relativity follows Markosian (2004) and Hawley (2009). Other ways of trying to spell out the conflict are discussed in Emery (2021).

[8] Although see Balaguer (ms).

should reject presentism. In his book *Four Dimensionalism*, Sider sums up his reasoning this way: "In cases of science versus metaphysics, historically the smart money has been on science . . . consistency with something fairly close to current physics is a constraint that must be met by any adequate theory of time" (Sider 2001, 42).

Moreover, among those metaphysicians who attempt to rescue presentism from this argument, virtually none of them do so by simply accepting the apparent conflict with special relativity. Instead they usually try to claim that the content of special relativity is different than it first appears. Lawrence Sklar, for instance, writes of the apparent conflict, "While our total worldview must, of course, be consistent with our best available scientific theories, it is a great mistake to read off a metaphysics superficially from the theory's overt appearance" (Sklar 1981, 131). (Note that even as Sklar holds out hope of avoiding the apparent conflict, he affirms, in the first part of the quoted sentence, his commitment to content naturalism.) Other philosophers try to modify presentism in order to avoid the conflict, or argue that once one replaces special relativity with a more advanced theory, the conflict disappears.[9] Perhaps these strategies work, and perhaps they don't. What is important for our purposes is that content naturalism seems to be an assumption that everyone involved in the debate shares; indeed it is an assumption that shapes the very way in which the debate plays out. If there is a conflict between special relativity and presentism, that is a problem for presentism, and no one appears to think that we can resolve that problem simply by rejecting or ignoring special relativity. This debate, then, is an example of content naturalism at work in contemporary metaphysics.

Racialism

Here is a second example. One of the core questions in the philosophy of race is the question "What is race?" This is a metaphysical question. When we ask "What is race?" we are asking what facts about the world determine facts about race. In particular, we are usually asking whether these facts are biological, social, political, or some combination thereof.

A historically prominent view of race, as articulated (though not defended) by Ron Mallon, was the view that races can be associated with

---

[9] See Hinchliff (2000) for the former strategy and Monton (2001) for the latter.

"underlying natural (and perhaps genetic) properties that (1) are heritable, biological features, (2) are shared by all and only the members of a race, and (3) explain behavioral, characterological, and cultural predispositions of individual persons and racial groups" (Mallon 2006, 528–529).[10] Following Kwame Anthony Appiah (1996), Mallon calls this view *racialism*.

Today there is widespread consensus that racialism is not just false; it isn't even a serious contender for a metaphysics of race. Why? Here is how Mallon tells the story:

> Over time, belief in racial essences came to be interpreted within the framework of modern molecular biology as a belief in underlying genetic difference, for only genes seemed appropriate candidates to play such an explanatory role. But studies of human genetic diversity suggest that genetic variation within racially identified populations is as great as or greater than diversity between populations. Thus, it is very unlikely that any interesting genetic "essence" will be shared by all and only members of a race. (Mallon 2006, 529)

According to Mallon, then, this is another case of content naturalism at work in contemporary metaphysics. Our best scientific theories were found to conflict with racialism, so racialism must be rejected. In very broad strokes, most philosophers of race are now either *eliminativists*—they think that there is no such thing as race—or they are *social constructionists*—they think that facts about race are socially constructed.[11]

There are some philosophers who still attempt to defend the view that race has a biological foundation, though one that is distinct from the kind of foundation proposed by racialists.[12] But all of these philosophers are explicit about building their accounts of race with contemporary biology in mind. And debates about whether these kinds of contemporary biological realist approaches are legitimate often devolve into debates about how to interpret the relevant science. Philosophers working in this area seem to be especially cognizant of the way in which scientific investigation undermined a once

---

[10] Note that it is highly plausible to think that the explanandum cited in (3) in fact never existed to be explained and that the assumption that it did was the result of underlying racism. Insofar as one takes this view of racialism, one can still accept Mallon's account of why racialism was rejected as a story about the rejection of (1) and (2).

[11] See Appiah (1996) and Zack (2002) for the former view and Mills (1998) (among many others) on the latter.

[12] See, for instance, Kitcher (1999), Andreason (1998, 2000), and Spencer (2019).

popular metaphysical account of race, and so they design their own accounts with contemporary science in mind.

Naive Realist Accounts of Perception

Here is a third and final example. According to a *naive realist* account of perception, when someone successfully perceives something, they are directly aware of that thing in a way that they could not be if that thing had not been the way it is in fact perceived. As should be obvious, naive realists have difficulty handling cases of hallucination. Many of them, as a result, endorse *disjunctivism*, which says that even though a particular hallucinatory perceptual experience H might be indistinguishable from a particular veridical perceptual experience V, H and V are in fact mental states of importantly different kinds. Hallucinating an oasis across the desert ahead might be indistinguishable from veridically perceiving an oasis across the desert ahead, but they are in fact importantly different states. The explanation of this important difference is that in the latter case your experience involves in fact perceiving the oasis ahead, whereas in the former case it does not.

One might, of course, take issue with the disjunctive nature of disjunctivism. (Perhaps on the grounds that it is overly complex or otherwise unmotivated.) But let's set that sort of worry aside and instead focus on what is often taken to be a far more serious charge against disjunctivism—the charge that it is incompatible with contemporary vision science. The issue, according to Tyler Burge, is that contemporary vision science establishes that our visual states "causally depend only on proximal stimulations, internal input, and antecedent psychological conditions" (Burge 2005, 22). It follows that when one hallucinates an oasis across the desert ahead and this is indistinguishable from perceiving an oasis ahead, one is in precisely the same visual state in both cases. Therefore, according to Burge, disjunctivism is "directly at odds" with our best science and we ought not be disjunctivists (29).

Now consider a prominent response to Burge, due to John McDowell.[13] As we might expect, given the discussion so far, McDowell does not dispute that it would indeed be bad for disjunctivism if it conflicted with our best science. But McDowell does not think that this conflict in fact obtains. He

---

[13] See McDowell (2010), the response in Burge (2011), and the response to Burge's response in McDowell (2013). The debate is helpfully summarized in Fish (2021). Thanks to Heather Logue for encouraging me to think about this example.

argues that there is an important difference between the states of a perceptual system and the states of a perceiver. Vision science is about the former, while disjunctivism is merely making claims about the latter. So while it might be true that the state of someone's perceptual system cannot depend on whether they are in fact related to, e.g., an oasis ahead, the state of the perceiver can so depend. In this way, McDowell thinks that naive realists can avoid the apparent conflict with vision science.

As with the examples above, I don't want to take a stand on whether McDowell's move is compelling. What I want to emphasize is just that here again we have a debate that is playing out precisely as we would expect if everyone involved were a content naturalist. Apparent conflicts between a candidate metaphysical view and our best science are taken seriously. And those who want to retain the candidate metaphysical view are at pains to try to reinterpret the relevant science so as to avoid the apparent conflict.

1.2 Three Assumptions about Content

Before moving on to the argument from content naturalism to methodological naturalism, let me take a moment here to address an initial worry that the reader might have about the claim that the vast majority of metaphysicians are content naturalists. Here is the worry:

> "We can't know for sure whether most philosophers endorse content naturalism unless we know for sure what counts as part of the content of one of our best scientific theories. But this is a vexed question!"

I'm happy to agree that sometimes it can be hard to determine what precisely the content of a scientific theory is and that it can also sometimes be hard to determine which of our scientific theories counts as best. This is very much the case, for instance, with respect to foundations of quantum mechanics. Although there is a well-established and uncontroversial formalism for this theory, depending on how you interpret this formalism, you may come to very different conclusions about the theory's content. According to some interpretations, for instance, the fundamental laws of quantum mechanics are indeterministic. According to other interpretations, they are not. That's quite a significant difference! In cases like this, where the content of our best science is so deeply unsettled, we should be very cautious about making use of content naturalism to rule out various possible metaphysical claims on the grounds that they conflict with this theory.[14]

Nonetheless I think that there are many cases in which there *is* widespread consensus about the content of our best science. It is part of the content of our best chemistry and physics that there are more than four elements, and part of the content of our best geology and astronomy that the Earth is not a cooled star, and part of the content of our best biology and neuroscience that whatever one means by "the seat of consciousness," the seat of consciousness is the brain.

Moreover in those cases where the content of our best science is not as clear, the way the relevant debates play out in the metaphysics literature actually gives further support to the idea that most metaphysicians endorse content naturalism. This has already been illustrated by the three case studies of content naturalism above. Here is another example: in *Objects and Persons*, Trenton Merricks (2001) argues that composite objects, including, for instance, helium atoms, do not exist. In response to this argument, E. J. Lowe complains that "philosophers shouldn't feel too comfortable about dictating to physicists, in this rather highhanded fashion" (Lowe 2003, 705). Merricks then responds by claiming that "the physicist's (or chemist's) authority requires nothing more than nucleons and electrons (or more fundamental entities) arranged heliumwise" (Merricks 2003, 727). What has happened here is that Lowe has raised an objection based on content naturalism—he thinks that Merricks's view may well turn out to conflict with our best science, and therefore that Merricks's view should be rejected. Merricks's response is *not* to question content naturalism. Instead he tries to avoid the objection by making a substantive claim about the content of our best science: on his view, the content of our best science doesn't involve any commitment to composite entities but only a commitment to fundamental entities arranged in various ways.[15]

---

[14] Monton (2011) argues that we should be extremely cautious in trying to draw *any* metaphysical conclusions from contemporary physics because contemporary physics in general is currently deeply unsettled.

[15] It is perhaps worth noting that there are two potentially independent parameters at play here. On the one hand one might hold fixed that a particular theory is our best scientific theory but argue that the content of that theory is different than we originally thought. On this approach, Merricks, for instance, might argue that the periodic table doesn't involve a commitment to helium, but only to fundamental entities arranged helium-wise. Alternatively one might argue that what we were thinking of as our best theory is not in fact our best theory. On this approach, Merricks might argue that strictly speaking the periodic table isn't part of our best scientific theory, but instead our best scientific theory includes a closely related table that describes the relationship between fundamental particles arranged in various different ways. As far as I can tell, nothing important hinges on which

So far I've admitted that there are cases in which it is hard to determine the content of our best scientific theories, and that those who have been charged with putting forward a metaphysical theory that conflicts with our best science can try to avoid that conflict by creatively interpreting what the content of our best science happens to be. At the same time, there must be limits to how far we can go with these creative interpretations. Otherwise content naturalism would have no force at all—and as we have seen, it has quite a bit of force in contemporary metaphysics. If it is so easy to avoid conflicts with our best science with these sorts of interpretive maneuvers, why is there so much consensus around the examples of content naturalism at work that were presented earlier in this chapter?

In what follows, I will set out three assumptions about the content of our best scientific theories. I intend these assumptions to be both relatively uncontroversial and in keeping with the way in which content naturalism is deployed by the vast majority of metaphysicians. The overall goal, in other words, is to identify a way of understanding the terms in content naturalism that correctly maps onto the way that content naturalism plays a role in shaping contemporary metaphysical debates. I'll leave the discussion of whether or not this version of content naturalism is something that contemporary metaphysicians *should* endorse to Chapter 2.

Scientific Content Includes Extra-Empirical Content

The first assumption that I will be making is that we cannot simply reinterpret the content of our best scientific theories in such a way that it is neutral on all claims that go beyond the data that scientists have collected in the laboratory. In other words, I will be assuming that the content of our best scientific theories can and usually does include *extra-empirical content*. Let an *empirically adequate theory* be one that accurately predicts all of the data that we have collected. On the view I am advocating for here, replacing what is standardly taken to be one of our best scientific theories with an empirically adequate alternative may well result in a change in the content the theory.

Here is an example of a case in which this assumption matters. Consider again the conflict between special relativity and presentism. That argument

way we interpret the examples herein, so I'm going to continue to elide the distinction between these two approaches.

turned on the fact that the conventionality of simultaneity was a key commitment of relativity theory. But when we look more closely at the reasoning that leads to the conventionality of simultaneity, we see that it follows from the combination of two claims (again, more about this in Chapter 6):

> *The relativity of simultaneity.* There are pairs of events such that in some inertial reference frames those events happen at the same time and in some inertial reference frames they do not.

> *No privileged reference frame.* If two or more inertial reference frames disagree about some feature of the world, then there is no fact of the matter with respect to that feature.

It is famously difficult to draw a distinction between the empirical and the extra-empirical. But the second of these claims should be a relatively uncontroversial example of an extra-empirical claim. Nothing in the data that scientists collected that led to the development of special relativity required them to accept this claim. Scientists did discover, during that time, that if there was a privileged reference frame, they could not detect it, but there were existing explanations for why this would be so.[16] The rejection of a privileged reference frame, therefore, is widely understood to be an application of some kind of extra-empirical principle that says that we ought to avoid excess structure in our theories.

Some philosophers who are attracted to presentism have tried to make use of the extra-empirical justification for the claim that there is no privileged reference frame in order to defend their view. In "A Defense of Presentism," for instance, Ned Markosian (2004) argues that presentists are justified in rejecting any version of special relativity that includes the claim that there is no privileged reference frame. A natural way of interpreting Markosian's position here is that he thinks metaphysicians should be content naturalists but he doesn't think that content naturalism has any impact on the debate over presentism, because our best science does not strictly speaking include a commitment to there being no privileged reference frame. Our best science instead involves a version of special relativity that is neutral on the question of whether there is a privileged reference frame or not—this version would include the relativity of simultaneity but not the conventionality of

---

[16] In particular, the electrodynamic theory developed by H. A. Lorentz suggested that accelerations relative to the privileged frame distorted measuring rods and clocks in a specific way that led to that frame being undetectable.

simultaneity, and thus would not lead to the conventionality of presentness. So, on Markosian's view, there is no conflict between presentism and special relativity.

In the context of the discussion here, there are two serious worries about this way of thinking about the content of our best science. The first is just that it requires being highly revisionary with respect to both the kinds of things that scientists say and the kinds of things that they write in papers and textbooks. If you consult any textbook on the subject or sit in on any physics class or ask any physicist, everyone will agree that part of what we are committed to when we endorse special relativity is that there is no privileged reference frame. Second, it's worth emphasizing that although this kind of position might in some sense liberate metaphysicians, it does so by undermining science. If we allow that the content of our best scientific theories does not include any extra-empirical content—any content that goes beyond what follows directly from the data—then science tells us almost nothing at all about what the world is like. As I will discuss further in Chapter 3, the data that scientists collect in the laboratory places few constraints on what there is or what it is like. It follows that if we claim that our best scientific theories are neutral with respect to any content that goes beyond what follows directly from that data, then, even if we are content naturalists, our best science will have few implications for metaphysics.

For my own part, I think that we should, where possible, avoid being revisionary, with respect to the claims upon which practicing scientists have found consensus.[17] Nor do I think we should accept a view on which science tells us almost nothing about what the world is like. But the key point to make in the current context is that if one were to adopt a view on which it was permissible to be highly revisionary with respect to the content of science or on which science tells us almost nothing about what the world is like, then content naturalism would place few if any constrains on our metaphysical theorizing. But as the examples earlier in this chapter show, contemporary metaphysicians do take content naturalism to place substantive constraints on what theories they can put forward. So insofar as we are interested in the

---

[17] On my view, the move that I attribute to Merricks in the previous section, which involves reinterpreting the content of our best science to avoid commitment to composite objects, is not as obviously revisionary as claiming there is no privileged reference frame. Scientists rarely state their claims about composite objects in such a way that makes it clear that they are not merely using a shorthand for talking about objects-arranged-composite-object-wise. Scientists do, by contrast, state their claims about there not being a privileged reference frame in such a way that it is clear that they recognize and reject the alternative interpretation that Markosian proposes.

version of content naturalism to which the vast majority of contemporary metaphysicians are committed, we should not claim that the only content of our best scientific theories that is relevant in deploying content naturalism is the content that is fixed by the data that we collect. Extra-empirical content is relevant as well.

One last point on this thread. The reader will note that it's entirely compatible with what I have said above that the extra-empirical content of a scientific theory is in some important sense properly thought of as philosophical content. I encounter that sort of view relatively often in conversation, and one can also see it in quotes like the following from Markosian: "It is important, when evaluating an argument from some scientific theory to a philosophical conclusion, to be aware of the fact that there is likely to be some philosophy built into the relevant scientific theory" (Markosian 2004, 74). In general I think it's fairly hard to draw a clean distinction between science on the one hand and philosophy on the other, and therefore I don't think it's very helpful to spend time debating whether, for instance, the claim that there is no privileged reference frame is a bit of science or a bit of philosophy. What I am arguing here is that the claim that there is no privileged reference frame is part of the content of our best scientific theories. Perhaps this means that our best scientific theories have some philosophy built into them.[18] That is entirely compatible with both content naturalism and the idea that the content of our best scientific theories includes extra-empirical content.

Content Naturalism versus Radical Content Naturalism

Here is the second assumption that I will be making about the content of our best scientific theories. I will be assuming that the content of all of our best scientific theories, taken together, does not include what I will call a *totality clause*. The content of our best scientific theories, in other words, is compatible with there being true claims about the world that *go beyond* that content. In the abstract, here is what this means. Suppose that the content of all of our best scientific theories, taken together, can be represented as a set of propositions, {P1, P2, . . . Pn}. I will be assuming that there is no member of that set that says that for any proposition Q, if Q is not a member of {P1,

---

[18] Another way that a scientific theory might have some philosophy built into it is via various kinds of metaphysical presuppositions. I discuss this point, and how it impacts content naturalism, in section 2.2.

P2, ... Pn}, then Q is false.[19] This means that content naturalists can endorse propositions that are not part of the content of our best scientific theories. They just need to make sure that those propositions do not conflict with our best science.

Here is another way to put the point. I will be assuming that there is an important difference between the following two views:

Content naturalism. We should not accept metaphysical theories that conflict with the content of our best scientific theories.

Radical content naturalism. We should not accept metaphysical theories that either conflict with or go beyond the content of our best scientific theories.

Some philosophers express views that, at least on their face, seem to involve a commitment to radical content naturalism. For instance, when David Lewis claims that the motivation for his program of Humean supervenience is to "resist philosophical arguments that there are more things in heaven and earth than physics has dreamt of" (Lewis 1994, 474), that looks like an appeal to radical content naturalism.[20] Or consider James van Cleve's (2008) objection to compositional nihilism (the view that there are no composite objects). Van Cleve argues that compositional nihilism requires there to be at least some *mereological simples*—entities that have no proper parts. But, he claims, while our best science is compatible with there being mereological simples, it is also compatible with there being no such simples. (Instead the world might be *gunky.*) Therefore, he concludes we should not be nihilists. This is a convincing argument only if you think that the nihilist is not permitted to simply posit mereological simples. Van Cleve seems to be assuming, then, that metaphysicians are not supposed to go beyond our best science. They are not supposed to posit entities with respect to which our best science is silent.[21]

---

[19] Note that putting the point this way is just for ease of exposition. Most philosophers of science like to think of scientific theories as sets of models. (I discuss this "semantic view" of models further in section 3.3.) If you think it follows from the claim that scientific theories are models that it doesn't make sense to claim that any scientific theory includes a totality clause, then all the better for the point I am making here.

[20] And a controversial one. Maudlin (2007), for instance, claims that the non-Humean entities that Lewis is hoping to avoid are in fact part of our best physics.

[21] Ladyman and Ross's commitment to the Principle of Naturalistic Closure presumably also commits them to radical content naturalism. See Ladyman and Ross (2007, 27ff.).

These examples notwithstanding, the problem with radical content naturalism, in the present context, is that if most philosophers were committed to that view, metaphysics would look dramatically different than it currently does.[22] Someone who accepts radical content naturalism should not endorse metaphysical claims that go beyond the content of our best scientific theories. At best, metaphysicians could do legitimate work by clarifying scientific claims or drawing connections between those claims and other areas of philosophy. Huge swaths of metaphysics, including many of the examples that we have been discussing, would make no sense.

For these reasons, I think it is clear that the vast majority of metaphysicians are not committed to radical content naturalism, but only to content naturalism, and I will focus my attention on the latter. (Note that in Chapter 2, I will also discuss a reason for thinking that metaphysicians *should* be content naturalists instead of radical content naturalists. In brief, the idea is that if you think that science involves any kind of metaphysical presuppositions, it is very difficult to be a radical content naturalist, for just in virtue of the fact that they are presuppositions, these claims would presumably need to be developed in advance of the relevant science and thus would involve going beyond established science. See the discussion in section 2.2.)

Content Naturalism as a Substantive Thesis

Here is the third and final assumption that I will make about the content of our best scientific theories. The content of our best scientific theories is such that it is possible to have genuine conflicts between metaphysics and science. In other words, I will be assuming that content naturalism, as defined above, is a substantive thesis.

To see why this is important, consider a view on which content naturalism is not substantive. Suppose that the content of our best scientific theories does not include straightforward claims like "There is no privileged reference frame" or "There are no underlying genetic essences that correspond to existing racial groups." Instead, when a scientific theory appears to include a

---

[22] Again, you might think that metaphysics *should* look dramatically different than it currently does. But the project in this section is to spell out the version of content naturalism to which the vast majority of contemporary metaphysicians are committed. What I am arguing here is that this version cannot be radical content naturalism, since if it were, metaphysics would look very different than it in fact does.

commitment to the claim that p, what it really includes, instead, is the commitment to some qualified claim like

according to science, p
p, *with respect to science*
p, *from a scientific perspective*

And suppose, in addition, that the acceptance of qualified claims like those listed above is perfectly compatible with accepting a metaphysical theory that includes the claim that ~p. The idea here is that when our best scientific theories say there is no privileged reference frame, for instance, and the presentist says that there *is* a privileged reference frame, this is like me claiming that Gabrielle is sitting to the right of Maliha, and Wenny claiming that Gabrielle is sitting to the left of Maliha, when Wenny and I are on opposite sides of the room—we don't have a genuine disagreement here at all. According to science there is no privileged reference frame, and according to metaphysics there is, and both of those claims are entirely compatible with one another.

Let's call the view I have just described a *relativized approach to scientific content*. If you adopt a relativized approach to scientific content you will think that the content of our best scientific theories is such that it is not possible to have genuine conflicts between metaphysical theories and scientific theories. You will be able to accept content naturalism, but you will think that content naturalism is trivially true.

Why is it appropriate to make the assumption that the content of our best scientific theories is not relativized in this way? Because all of the examples above demonstrate that the vast majority of metaphysicians are committed not only to content naturalism but also to content naturalism being a substantive thesis. If the presentist, for instance, were willing to adopt a relativized approach to scientific content, then when someone pointed out that presentism appears to conflict with special relativity, she would simply shrug. Not because she thinks that presentism trumps special relativity, or anything like that, but simply because she thinks the apparent conflict is not actually a conflict at all. But this is not how would-be presentists in fact respond to the charge that their theory is in conflict with special relativity. Instead, as the discussion above shows, they try to revise their theory or find a way to avoid the apparent conflict that is specific to the case at hand. The same goes for the other examples above.[23]

The key claim of the two preceding sections has been that the vast majority of metaphysicians, whether they have explicitly thought about it or not, are content naturalists. We see this in the way in which various metaphysical positions are not even considered viable candidates for investigation because they so obviously conflict with our best science. We also see it play out in live metaphysical debates, where the objection that a metaphysical theory is in conflict with the content of our best science is one of the most serious objections that advocates of that theory can face, and philosophers are willing to engage in all sorts of maneuvers to try to avoid this kind of objection—all sorts of maneuvers *except* outright rejecting or simply ignoring the relevant science. If metaphysicians were to give up their commitment to content naturalism, contemporary metaphysics would look very different than it currently does.

It is important to recognize that, so far, the discussion has been purely descriptive. I have claimed that the vast majority of metaphysicians are content naturalists. I haven't said anything about whether one *should* be a content naturalist. I will address that prescriptive claim in Chapter 2. First, though, let's get the connection between content naturalism and methodological naturalism on the table.

1.3 The Content-Methodology Link

The first step of the argument that the vast majority of philosophers already have commitments that lead straightforwardly to methodological naturalism was to establish that the vast majority of philosophers are content naturalists. The next step is to argue that if you are a content naturalist, you should also be a methodological naturalist. I call this *the content-methodology link*.

Before we begin, let me make one quick point by way of noting, and asking for patience with respect to, a common concern about the argument to come. Throughout the rest of this chapter (and indeed throughout much of the book to come) I am going to assume that there is such a thing as standard scientific methodology. That is to say, I'm going to assume that we can identify

---

[23] Thanks to Mark Balaguer for encouraging me to think more about a relativized approach to scientific content.

at least some core elements of the methodology of scientific theorizing that hold across science quite generally. My own view is that this assumption is highly plausible. Distinct sciences and distinct scientific theories differ from one another in many ways—but what sets them apart as a group from other forms of inquiry are general features of their methodology that they share in common. But as those with a background in philosophy of science will rightly recognize, this is still a substantive assumption. I say a bit more about what might happen if one were to give that assumption up in the objection and replies section at the end of this chapter, but a full discussion of the ways in which a more local or context-dependent approach to scientific methodology will impact methodological naturalism will have to wait until later in the book—specifically Chapter 7—when we have on the table the full scope of the argument for methodological naturalism and the case studies illustrating its impacts.

The Argument

Here's the basic idea behind the claim that if you are a content naturalist, then you should be a methodological naturalist: one can have no good reason for thinking that the *content* of our best scientific theories should constrain the content of our metaphysical theories if one does not also think that standard scientific *methodology* is a good guide to metaphysical theories. Scientific theories make a wide-ranging and heterogeneous group; what distinguishes that group is the methodology that was followed in producing those theories. And if standard scientific methodology is not relevant to producing good metaphysical theories, then why would we let the content of the theories that are produced using that methodology impact metaphysical theorizing?

On some occasions, when I have presented the paragraph above, that has been enough to convince my audience that anyone who is a content naturalist should also be a methodological naturalist. Those readers who find themselves in this camp should feel free to skip to the next chapter. For all the rest, I will present the argument in more detail.

In order to do so, we need to take a stand—at least for the moment—on what we take the goal of metaphysical theorizing to be. Let's assume, as a first pass, that the goal of metaphysical theorizing is putting forward true claims about what the world is like. Here is the argument:

P1$_T$ If you are a content naturalist who thinks that the goal of metaphysical theorizing is to put forward true claims about what the world is like, then you should think that the content of our best scientific theories is true.

P2$_T$ If you think that the content of our best scientific theories is true, then you should also think that standard scientific methodology is a good guide to the truth.

P3$_T$ If you are a content naturalist who thinks that the goal of metaphysical theorizing is to put forward true claims about what the world is like, then you should think that standard scientific methodology is a good guide to the truth.

C$_T$ If you are a content naturalist who thinks that the goal of metaphysical theorizing is to put forward true claims about what the world is like, then you should be a methodological naturalist.

Let's consider each of these premises in turn. First, P1$_T$. The idea behind this premise is simple. Consider someone who is a content naturalist and who thinks that the goal of metaphysical theorizing is to put forward true claims about what the world is like, but who *doesn't* think that the content of our best scientific theories is true. What could possibly justify this person's commitment to content naturalism? (Remember, as discussed in section 1.2 we are assuming that content naturalism is a substantive thesis. So they must have some justification for their position.) If the goal of metaphysical theorizing is to put forward true claims about what the world is like and the content of our best scientific theories is not true, then why would we care if there are conflicts between our favored metaphysical theories and our best scientific theories?

Now consider P2$_T$. Consider someone who thinks that the content of our best scientific theories is true but doesn't think that standard scientific methodology is a good guide to the truth. What could possibly be this person's reason for thinking that the content of our best scientific theories is true? Surely it is not just a fluke. After all, the content of our best scientific theories is a highly heterogeneous group of claims. Some of these claims accord with common sense or with historically familiar attitudes, but many of them do not. Some of these claims are such that we can verify them for ourselves using our observational capacities, but many of them are not. What is distinctive of the content of our best scientific theories is that they were produced using a certain methodology. Anyone who has the general epistemic attitude that the content of our best scientific theories is true, therefore, should think that the methodology that produces our best scientific theories leads to the truth.

P3$_T$ follows from P1$_T$ and P2$_T$. And the conclusion follows from P3$_T$ and the definition of methodological naturalism. If you think that the goal of metaphysical theorizing is to put forward true claims about what the world is like and you think that standard scientific methodology is a good guide to the truth, then, when possible, you ought to make use of that methodology. After all, that methodology, you've already agreed, is a good guide to the truth, and the truth is what you're after in your metaphysical theorizing.

What about those who don't think that the goal of metaphysical theorizing is to put forward *true* claims about what the world is like? Perhaps, instead, they think that the goal of metaphysical theorizing is to put forward claims about what the world is like that *roughly approximate the truth*, or that *are as close to the truth as is possible given our current capabilities*, or are *useful to creatures like us*. This list could be expanded in numerous ways. Either way, the argument from content naturalism to methodological naturalism will be the same. We will just need to take out all instances of 'claims about what the world is like that are true' and substitute in 'claims about what the world is like that roughly approximate the truth' or 'claims about what the world is like that are useful for creatures like us,' or what have you.

Here, then, is the argument in its most general form:

P1 If you are a content naturalist who thinks that the goal of metaphysical theorizing is to put forward claims about what the world is like that have epistemic feature F, then you should think that the content of our best scientific theories has epistemic feature F.[24]

P2 If you think that the content of our best scientific theories has epistemic feature F, then you should also think that standard scientific methodology is a good guide to epistemic feature F.

P3 If you are a content naturalist who thinks that the goal of metaphysical theorizing is to put forward claims about what the world is like that have epistemic feature F, then you should think that standard scientific methodology is a good guide to epistemic feature F.

C   If you are a content naturalist who thinks that the goal of metaphysical theorizing is to put forward claims about what the world is like

---

[24] Readers who are worried that 'useful for creatures like us' is not an epistemic feature of theories can insert 'epistemic or pragmatic feature' for each use of 'epistemic feature' here and throughout.

that have epistemic feature F, then you should be a methodological naturalist.

You may substitute in whatever you like for feature F. The argument for each premise will be the same as was given above. With respect to P1, if the goal of metaphysical theorizing is to put forward claims about what the world is like that have feature F, and the content of our best scientific theories doesn't have that feature, then why would we care if there are conflicts between our favored metaphysical theories and our best scientific theories? With respect to P2, if standard scientific methodology is not responsible for our best scientific theories having feature F, then what is? Is it an accident? P3 follows from P1 and P2. And C follows from P3 and the definition of methodological naturalism. If you think that the goal of metaphysical theorizing is to put forward claims about what the world is like that have feature F and you think that standard scientific methodology is a good guide to claims with feature F, then you should think that, whenever possible, metaphysicians should follow the same methodology that scientists use.

When we combine all of the versions of the argument that are generated by substituting in various different epistemic features for F in the argument schema P1–C, we get the following result:

The content-methodology link. If you are a content naturalist, then you should be a methodological naturalist.

What this way of presenting the argument shows is that the content-methodology link applies quite generally across different approaches to metaphysics. It is worth taking a moment to emphasize this point. In particular, it is worth taking a moment to emphasize that the argument above will apply even if one thinks of metaphysics as involving some form of conceptual analysis. Let me explain.

According to one way of thinking about metaphysics that traces back to philosophers like Gilbert Ryle, Ludwig Wittgenstein, and Rudolf Carnap, metaphysics is primarily a matter of conceptual analysis. What we are doing when we undertake a metaphysical project is seeking to understand the concepts that we as inquirers use to interact with the world. An important recent development in this approach has been the recognition that if you understand metaphysics as primarily about investigating the concepts that we use to interact with the world, then you can understand metaphysical projects as either purely descriptive or as in some way prescriptive.[25] Metaphysicians can be aiming to understand the concepts that we in fact use, or they can be aiming to determine which concepts we ought to be using. The latter idea has inspired quite a bit of exciting recent work that blurs the line between metaphysics and ethics. The metaphysics of race, as discussed above, is a good example. Sally Haslanger (2000), for instance, gives an account of race that explicitly takes into account our social and political goals.

One question we might ask about this approach is whether it still satisfies the original definition that I gave of metaphysics. If metaphysics is conceptual analysis, is it still the study of what the world is like? For the moment, at least, I want to set that question aside.[26] A more interesting question, from the current perspective, is whether those who think of metaphysics as conceptual analysis—either of the descriptive or the prescriptive variety—are committed to content naturalism. This is a question that, in my view, has not been clearly addressed in the literature, and I will say more about it in Chapter 8.[27] What I want to point out at present, however, is that the content-methodology link will still apply to these sorts of approaches to metaphysics. Insofar as the advocate of a conceptual approach to metaphysics—whether descriptive or prescriptive—is a content naturalist, then they should also be a methodological naturalist. I will go through only the prescriptive conceptual analysis case. (The reader should be able to figure out the descriptive conceptual analysis case for themselves.)

---

[25] For examples and discussion of the prescriptive approach, see Haslanger (2000 and 2006), Burgess and Plunkett (2013a and 2013b), Thomasson (2017), and the papers in Cappelen and Plunkett (2020). Haslanger uses the term 'ameliorative' instead of 'prescriptive' see, for instance, Haslanger (2006).

[26] As I say in Chapter 8, I think the prescriptive conceptual approach is pretty revisionary in this regard. I'm less sure what to say about the descriptive conceptual approach. Whether metaphysics that is primarily an analysis of our conceptual schemes counts as being about 'what the world is like' probably depends on what you think constitutes 'the world,' and I doubt there will be a productive debate around those terms.

[27] Consider, for instance, the following quote from Haslanger: "Work in the biological sciences has informed us that our practices of racial categorization don't map neatly onto any useful biological classification; but that doesn't settle much, if anything" (Haslanger 2000, 32). It is unclear, just from this quote, whether Haslanger thinks that the conflict between racialism and biology as described in section 1.1 doesn't prove much (or anything) because (a) of course we can't have a metaphysics of race that conflicts with biology, but even once we take that into account there are still many potential accounts of race on offer, (b) of course we can't have a metaphysics of race that conflicts with biology, but that's irrelevant because it should be fairly obvious that race is a social phenomenon, not a biological one, or (c) conflicts between our metaphysics of race and biology are in principle acceptable, but again, since it should be fairly obvious that race is a social phenomenon, that doesn't end up mattering much.

$P1_{C\text{-}P}$ If you are a content naturalist who thinks that the goal of metaphysical theorizing is to identify which concepts we ought to be using, then you should think that the content of our best scientific theories involves the concepts we ought to be using.

$P2_{C\text{-}P}$ If you think that the content of our best scientific theories involves the concepts we ought to be using, then you should also think that standard scientific methodology is a good guide to the concepts we ought to be using.

$P3_{C\text{-}P}$ If you are a content naturalist who thinks that the goal of metaphysical theorizing is to identify which concepts we ought to be using, then you should think that standard scientific methodology is a good guide to the concepts we ought to be using.

$C_{C\text{-}P}$ If you are a content naturalist who thinks that the goal of metaphysical theorizing is to identify which concepts we ought to be using, then you should be a methodological naturalist.

In what follows I will primarily focus on an approach to metaphysics that does not construe metaphysics as being a matter of conceptual analysis. In large part this is because I have a particular interest in those areas of metaphysics that involve questions about the nature of time, space, possibility, and probability. Although I find it relatively plausible to think that the metaphysics of race, for instance, is primarily a conceptual analysis task—and an extremely important one!—I, and many other metaphysicians, hold out hope that when we are asking questions about the metaphysics of time or the metaphysics of laws or the like, we aren't just analyzing the concepts of time or laws, we're trying to uncover what the temporal and nomological aspects of the world are like independently of how we think about and interact with those aspects. But again, it is important to note that although my interests and focus lie with this more "heavyweight" approach to metaphysics, the scope of my argument and the application of the content-methodology link is quite general.[28]

---

[28] The term 'heavyweight' comes from Thomasson (2017), as do the terms 'descriptive' versus 'prescriptive' conceptual analysis.

1.4 Worries about the Argument

Let's turn now to considering some worries that one might have about the argument for the content-methodology link. I'm going to split these worries into several groups. The first group of worries are what I think of as pseudo-worries. These are worries that I often hear raised in response to the argument, but that upon closer examination turn out not in fact to be worries about the argument at all. Instead they are worries that push us toward either denying the antecedent or denying the consequent of the content-methodology link. But denying either the antecedent or the consequent is entirely compatible with accepting the link itself. Nonetheless, some of the way in which these worries misfire can be instructive for what follows, so it will pay to take some time to discuss them here.

Distinct Methodological Domains

Here is a worry that I often hear voiced in response to the argument above:

> "Although I think that the methodology of science leads to the truth with respect to the domain of science, that doesn't mean that it also leads to truth with respect to the domain of metaphysics. For discovering truth about the domain of metaphysics, we need a distinct methodology."[29]

I myself am fairly suspicious of the idea that there is any kind of clear demarcation between the domain of science and the domain of metaphysics, but I am happy to grant the point for the purposes of responding to this objection.[30]

One thing that an advocate of this worry might be saying is that sometimes the methodology of science is quiet when it comes to choosing between metaphysical theories, and that in those cases, insofar as we wish to make a choice between competing metaphysical theories we need some additional methodological principles. I'm perfectly happy to accept this claim; it is compatible

---

[29] Note that this objection can be spelled out in terms of other epistemic features, like approximate truth, pragmatic value, etc., instead of truth. Everything I go on to say about the objection will still hold.

[30] Of course one could spell out this worry in such a way that the distinction between the two domains is vague or messy, as in Chakravartty (2017). In that case, one probably has in mind something closer to the distinct-but-overlapping worry that I describe and respond to next.

with content naturalism, with methodological naturalism, and with the content-methodology link. At most it raises questions about how impactful methodological naturalism will be. If, for instance, scientific methodology is nearly always silent on metaphysical debates, then metaphysicians can accept the consequent of the content-methodology link without any significant changes to their practice. I will address questions about the extent to which methodological naturalism will be impactful starting in Chapter 3.

Often when someone brings up this worry, however, they seem to have a more significant critique in mind. They think that the worry shows that we should not be methodological naturalists. When it comes to the domain of metaphysics, the methodology of science isn't just silent; it is potentially (or actually) misleading. The methodology of science just isn't the right sort of methodology for discovering truths about the domain of metaphysics.

But notice that this objection is not an objection to the content-methodology link. It is an objection to methodological naturalism. And rejecting methodological naturalism is perfectly compatible with accepting the content-methodology link as long as you also reject content naturalism. In order to have a genuine objection to the argument above we need an objection to methodological naturalism that is paired with a reason for continuing to be a content naturalist. And the worry above doesn't give us any reason for continuing to be a content naturalist. Indeed the natural response to the worry above is to reject content naturalism.[31] After all, if you don't think that scientific methodology leads to truth with respect to the domain of metaphysics, then presumably you shouldn't think that our scientific theories are true with respect to the domain of metaphysics, and then why would you care if your metaphysical theory conflicted with our best scientific theories?

This is why I classify this worry as a pseudo-worry. Upon closer examination, the worry doesn't give rise to an objection to the content-methodology link. It instead amounts to an argument for one of the two possible ways of responding to the link. (The two ways being to either accept both the antecedent and the consequent or reject both.)

Sometimes, in response to the line of thinking just outlined, I hear the following:

---

[31] Or take it to be trivially true. Recall, from section 1.2, that we are understanding scientific content in such a way that content naturalism, if true, is substantive.

"I don't think that scientific methodology leads to truth with the respect to the domain of metaphysics. But I think we should be content naturalists because I think we should have an overall consistent theory. And I think that our best scientific theories are true."

Here is the key question facing someone who is moved by this line of thinking: Do you think that the goal of metaphysics is merely to put forward claims about what the world is like that are true *with respect to the domain of metaphysics*? Or do you think that the goal of metaphysics is also to put forward claims about what the world is like that are true *full stop*? (Here by "true *full stop*" I just mean true without any qualification or domain restriction.) If you take the latter route, then the original argument for the content-methodology link still applies. If you take the former route, and you think that scientific methodology is not a good guide to truth with respect to the domain of metaphysics, then you have no reason to be a content naturalist.

Distinct but Overlapping Domains

Here is a more nuanced version of the worry just discussed:

"Science and metaphysics involve distinct but partially overlapping domains. The methodology of science leads to the truth throughout the domain of science, and that has implications for the areas of metaphysics that involve overlap with the domain of science. But this doesn't mean that the methodology of science will lead to truth *throughout* the domain of metaphysics. When it comes to discovering truth in the domain of metaphysics in general, we need a distinct methodology."

For the very same reasons described in response to the objection above, if the person who makes this argument has a good reason for rejecting methodological naturalism, she also has good reason for rejecting content naturalism. Instead, she should endorse the following view:

Overlapping content naturalism. We should not accept metaphysical theories *that are about the domain of science* if those theories conflict with the content of our best scientific theories.

It should be clear from the discussion in section 1.1 that the vast majority of metaphysicians do not endorse overlapping content naturalism—at least not in the general terms just described. If they did, then when they were faced with a potential conflict with our best scientific theories, they would simply shrug and say that the particular metaphysical theory they were putting forward was not supposed to be about the domain of science—it was supposed to be about the domain of metaphysics.

Of course, one might put forward a version of overlapping content naturalism that is spelled out in more detail—a version that says something more substantive, for instance, about the distinction between the domain of science and the domain of metaphysics. In principle, at least, it might be possible to give this distinction enough content that we can make sense of the fact that in the examples of content naturalism in section 1.1, no one saw fit to avoid the potential objection simply by arguing that their theory was within the domain of metaphysics. But that would not undermine the argument for the content-methodology link.

Here is another way to put this point. Overlapping content naturalism, as defined above, is one version of a more general strategy:

Domain-dependent content naturalism. When engaged in metaphysical debates that have feature F, we should not accept theories that conflict with the content of our best scientific theories.

The key thing to notice here is that insofar as your content naturalism is domain dependent in this way, the argument for the content-methodology link will still apply. It will just yield a methodological naturalism that is similarly domain dependent. So, if you endorse domain-dependent content naturalism, then you should also endorse domain-dependent methodological naturalism.

Domain-dependent methodological naturalism. When engaged in metaphysical debates that have feature F, metaphysicians should, whenever possible, follow the same methodology that scientists do.

Of course, depending on what F is, domain-dependent methodological naturalism may turn out to be not very interesting. If there are very few metaphysical debates that have feature F, then the applications of methodological naturalism will be quite limited. But notice that in that case, the relevant version of domain-dependent content naturalism is going to be very surprising. For if there are few metaphysical debates that have feature F, there are going to be few metaphysical debates that are constrained by science. On the other hand, if most metaphysical debates have feature F, then domain-dependent content naturalism won't be especially surprising—it will yield results pretty similar to content naturalism. But in this case the relevant version of domain-dependent methodological naturalism to which you end up committed will apply quite widely.

All of this is, of course, very abstract. The reader who is interested in this line of reasoning should note that in Chapter 2, I will consider several cases in which there is a more concrete and principled reason to adopt versions of content and methodological naturalism that are limited in scope. In those cases I will similarly argue that the versions of the content-methodology link that still apply will have substantive results.

This discussion does, however, introduce a bit of nuance that I have glossed over thus far. Above, I presented my overall argument in this book as giving readers a choice. Either they can reject content naturalism (in which case metaphysical theorizing should look quite different than it currently does) or they can accept content naturalism *and* methodological naturalism. As will become clear, especially toward the end of the book, I am also happy to have readers take a more fine-grained approach. In particular, it is entirely compatible with my argument that there are different types, or sub-fields, of metaphysics. For each type of metaphysics, the argument for the content-methodology link will apply: if one is a content naturalist, then one should be a methodological naturalist. But one might wish to respond to the content-methodology link in different ways for different sub-fields of metaphysics. For some sub-fields of metaphysics one might wish to reject content naturalism. For other sub-fields, one might accept content naturalism and methodological naturalism. In Chapter 8, I will give this kind of approach the name *fine-grained naturalism*. For all I've said so far here, it may not be clear why fine-grained naturalism will be attractive or how it would be developed in a principled way; I'm just noting it as an option.

Scientific Methodology as Value-Laden

Here is a third sort of worry that I think in fact qualifies as a pseudo-worry. Many philosophers of science think that scientific methodology is value-laden.[32] Sometimes this worry involves a focus on the claim that *theoretical virtues*—features like simplicity or explanatory power—play an important role in shaping our best scientific theories. These virtues, especially simplicity, strike some as obviously pragmatic. They make a theory easier to work with. But why think they make the theory true? This is a point familiar from Thomas Kuhn (1977), which also continues to arise in the contemporary literature. (Bueno and Shalkowski 2020, for instance, argue that these kinds of virtues should not be taken to be a guide to the truth, either in scientific or in metaphysical theorizing.)[33] In other cases, especially in feminist philosophy of science, this kind of worry involves the political, social, cultural, or economic interests either implicitly or explicitly shaping scientific theorizing (see, e.g., Longino 1996 and 2001).

As will be obvious below, I do think that theoretical virtues play a role in standard scientific methodology. I myself am less sure about political, cultural, or economic interests playing an important role—especially in the case of fundamental physics. But in any case, one might wonder: If scientific methodology is value-laden in either of these ways, shouldn't we resist methodological naturalism? Indeed these worries belong to a family of similar concerns, all of which have the following form. Scientific methodology has feature M, and feature M does not lead to good metaphysics, so we shouldn't be methodological naturalists. Here we can substitute in whatever we like for M—M could be 'relies on judgments about simplicity', for instance, or it could be 'is deeply androcentric', or 'changes over time', or 'is culturally relative'.

But note again that rejecting methodological naturalism is entirely compatible with my argument—you just need to reject content naturalism as well. And indeed this is what we should expect for someone who thinks that scientific methodology has feature M, where feature M does not lead to good metaphysics. If you think that our best scientific theories were produced using a feature that does not lead to good metaphysical theories, then why should you care if your favored metaphysical theory conflicts with our best science? So this worry isn't really a worry for the argument above. At most

---

[32] It is standard these days to think the values come into scientific practice at least in terms of what scientific projects are pursued and to what use scientific results are put. The kind of value-ladenness that is at issue here, and that is controversial, is whether values play a role in choosing between competing scientific theories.

[33] Note that I say more about Bueno and Shalkowski's argument in Chapter 3. Other recent papers that discuss the pragmatic nature of theoretical virtues are Ludwig (2015) (which focuses on the use of these virtues in science) and Bricker (2020) (which focuses on their use in metaphysics).

what it does is bring us back to the prescriptive question that we shelved at the end of section 1.1. In that section I argued that the vast majority of contemporary metaphysicians are content naturalists. But should they be? I will turn to this prescriptive question in the next chapter.

It is worth noting that some who have these sorts of concerns about the methodology of science may hope to replace *actual* scientific methodology with a better version that avoids the concerns in question. Call the latter version of scientific methodology *ideal scientific methodology*. Someone who takes this route should also then distinguish between the actual content of our well-established scientific theories, and the ideal content—the content that would result from following the ideal methodology. And they may well respond differently to the content-methodology link depending on whether one is talking about actual versus ideal science. They might, for instance, reject both content and methodological naturalism with respect to actual science, but accept both with respect to ideal science. In any case, however, there is no reason here for rejecting the link itself.

No Standard Methodology

Let's turn now to some worries that genuinely target the argument for the content-methodology link. I'll begin with a worry that targets P2. P2 introduces the notion of "standard scientific methodology." But is there such a thing? Above I considered worries that involved accepting that there was such a thing as standard scientific methodology, but arguing that it had some feature that made it suspect. This worry, by contrast, is arguing that there just is no such thing as standard scientific methodology.

The most plausible way of spelling out this worry is to say that there are different methodologies for different scientific contexts. One might, for instance, think there is a distinct methodology for distinct scientific levels— one methodology for physics, and another methodology for chemistry, and another methodology for biology, and so on.[34] Or perhaps scientific methodology is even more fine-grained than that.[35]

---

[34] At least some philosophers of science think this notion of levels is an oversimplification (see, e.g., Rueger and McGivern 2010 and Potochnik 2021). We can set that concern aside since I'm just using this as an example of one way in which scientific methodology is context-dependent.

[35] Readers familiar with the recent philosophy of science literature will likely think here of the kind of context-dependence found in John Norton's (2003, 2021) theory of material induction or Elliot Sober's (1990, 2009, 2015) account of simplicity or in work by Day and Kincaid (1994) or Khalifa

The question of how to think about content naturalism and methodological naturalism in light of a context-dependent approach to scientific methodology is a nuanced one, and for the most part, as indicated above, I am going to postpone my discussion of this approach until Chapter 7. There are a couple of key points that I want to note here, however, that may help those who are inclined toward this kind of approach get on board with the project in the next few chapters.

First and foremost, note that there is an important difference between saying that some aspects of scientific methodology are context-dependent and saying that all aspects of scientific methodology are context-dependent. One can hold that there are certain aspects of scientific methodology that vary from context to context while still accepting, for instance, that the aspects of scientific methodology that feature in the case studies in Chapters 4–6 are universal.

Second, note that insofar as there are aspects of scientific methodology that are context-dependent, there will be distinct content-methodology links for each distinct context that gives rise to a distinct methodology. There will be arguments, each of them parallel to the one provided above, for instance, that shows that if you are a content naturalist with respect to the content of physics, for instance, then you should be a methodological naturalist with respect to the methodology of physics, and if you are a content naturalist with respect to the content of biology, you should be a methodological naturalist with respect to the methodology of biology, and so on.

Third, perhaps the most significant concern one might have about methodological naturalism in light of context-dependent methodologies is the worry that the distinct methodologies might turn out to yield conflicting results. If the methodology of biology is distinct from the methodology of physics, and they yield conflicting results, then which methodology should the methodological naturalist use? I will say quite a bit more about this concern in Chapter 7. For the moment, however, let's just note that insofar as distinct scientific contexts give rise to conflicting methodologies, there is always the following option available to the methodological naturalist: she can adopt a multi-context approach to metaphysics that mirrors the one that is being posited in the sciences. Suppose, for instance, that you endorse the (very oversimplified) view that there are three distinct sciences (biology,

---

et al. (2017) on inference to the best explanation. Note that I say quite a bit more about these views and how they interact with methodological naturalism in Chapter 7.

chemistry, and physics) that give rise to three distinct methodologies. Then the methodological naturalist can accept a view on which there are also three distinct metaphysical contexts—the metaphysics corresponding to biology, the metaphysics corresponding to chemistry, and the metaphysics corresponding to physics. On this multi-level metaphysical view, it is the methodology of the relevant science at each level that guides metaphysical theorizing at that level. I say more about this option in Chapter 7.

As a final point with respect to the worry under discussion here, is also worth noting that sometimes philosophers of science appear to be making the stronger claim that there is no such thing as standard scientific methodology, when in fact they are really making a claim about scientific methodology being fairly minimal or in some other way different than usually assumed. Consider, for instance, the following quote from Ladyman and Ross:

> [T]here is no such thing as 'scientific method,' by which we mean: no particular set of positive rules for reasoning that all and only scientists do or should follow. There are of course many observed prohibitions (for example, 'do not induct on samples known to be selected in unrepresentative ways' and 'do not invent data'), but these apply to all sound reasoning, not to distinctively 'scientific' reasoning. Thus science is, according to us, demarcated from non-science solely by institutional norms: requirement for rigorous peer review before claims may be deposited in 'serious' registers of scientific belief, requirements governing representational rigour with respect to both theoretical claims and accounts of observations and experiments, and so on. (Ladyman and Ross 2007, 28)

As I understand the notion of standard scientific methodology, Ladyman and Ross are not in fact claiming that there is no such thing as standard scientific methodology. Rather they are asserting that (a) much of standard scientific methodology involves "prohibitions" as opposed to "positive rules," (b) much of standard scientific methodology is constituted by rules that are also used in other domains, and (c) what makes standard scientific methodology distinct is certain institutional norms. All three of those claims are entirely compatible with methodological naturalism. One might worry that the type of "representational rigour" that is the norm is science is difficult to achieve in metaphysics, but at most this is a worry about a potential disanalogy that undermines the impact of methodological naturalism, not an objection to methodological naturalism itself. (I say more about this potential disanalogy in Chapter 3.)

Alternative Methodology?

Here is a final objection to consider. Suppose I am a content naturalist who thinks that the goal of metaphysical theorizing is to put forward true claims about what the world is like, and I agree that scientific methodology is a good guide to the truth. However, I still want to resist methodological naturalism because I think that I have another, distinct methodology that leads to the truth in metaphysical debates. For this reason, I resist the move from P3 to C in the argument for the content-methodology link. Is this a reasonable way to resist the argument?

Before answering, it's important to distinguish this approach, which involves an *alternative methodology,* from a nearby but different approach, which involves a *supplemental methodology*. An advocate of an alternative methodology resists being a methodological naturalist because they think they can replace scientific methodology with an equally good methodology. An advocate of a supplemental methodology accepts methodological naturalism but proposes various supplemental principles that are applied if and only if scientific methodology doesn't settle some particular metaphysical question. (Of course insofar as one is open to a supplemental methodology one may then be inclined to question just how impactful methodological naturalism will be. After all, maybe the methodology of science leaves almost all metaphysical questions open, and thus the supplemental methodology of metaphysics is what is doing the vast majority of the work in the field. This is a concern that will be addressed in general terms in Chapter 3, and more concretely by the case studies in Chapters 4 through 6, which demonstrate specific debates where methodological naturalism has an impact.)

There will be two immediate challenges facing anyone who adopts an alternative methodology in response to the argument for the content-methodology link. First and foremost, they need to provide some reason for thinking that the alternative methodology that they propose will not generate results that conflict with those that are generated by scientific methodology. After all, if they are endorsing an alternative methodology and it is an open possibility that that methodology might yield results that conflict with the results of scientific methodology, then they should not be content naturalists—and remember, it is no objection to the argument above to give up methodological naturalism if you are also giving up content naturalism. (If you give up content naturalism, then the antecedent of the conclusion is false and the conclusion does in fact follow from P3.) Moreover, given the surprising ways in which science has developed in the past, providing a convincing reason to think that an alternative methodology won't generate conflicts with science is quite a tall order. And this is especially true if the alternative methodology looks anything like the methodology of those contemporary metaphysicians who do not spend a lot of time worrying about naturalism. The latter methodology is often supposed to include, for instance, appeals to intuition. But science has often turned out to lead in unintuitive directions.[36]

Second, an advocate of an alternative methodology surely needs to provide some positive reason for thinking that their alternative methodology is indeed a good guide to what the world is like. To some extent, the advocate of a supplemental methodology also faces this challenge, but it will be a particular worry for the advocate of an alternative methodology. The advocate of an alternative methodology, after all, recognizes that there is already a methodology available that is a good guide to what the world is like with respect to the questions that they are interested in, but they still choose to follow a distinct methodology. As such, it seems like it is especially incumbent on them to give us a reason for thinking that their alternative methodology is also a good guide to what the world is like. And this too, I think, will prove to be a significant challenge, especially if the alternative methodology is anything like the methodology of contemporary metaphysics. Insofar as the advocate of an alternative methodology appeals to intuition, for instance, they need to deal with familiar worries about the epistemology of intuitions.[37] Overall, then, I don't think that this is an especially promising route to take.

---

[36] Note that in Chapter 5, I will advocate for a very specific way in which scientific theorizing respects a certain kind of intuition, but my argument will be compatible with the idea that scientific theorizing often yields unintuitive results.

[37] See, for instance, the epistemic challenges for the methodology of "free-range" metaphysics raised in Bryant (2020).

1.5 Strong and Weak Versions of the Link

My assessment of the worries above is that none of them, once subject to careful scrutiny, is insurmountable. Thus I think the argument for the content-methodology link is sound, and I think my readers should too. Remember, accepting the content-methodology link doesn't require you to be a methodological naturalist. One response to the link is to reject methodological naturalism—but if the above argument is sound and you take this route, then you must reject content naturalism as well.

Suppose, however, that you, the reader, disagree with me. Perhaps because you think one of the worries above is stronger than I make it out to be. Or perhaps because you have a different worry in mind. In this case, let me just point out that in addition to the relatively strong, official version of the content-methodology link described above, there will also be a weaker version. Let's focus in particular on the following:

> *The weak content-methodology link.* If you are a content naturalist, there are good, though perhaps ultimately defeasible, reasons for you to be a methodological naturalist.

I contend that even if you merely accept the weak content-methodology link, you should, at least as a default, accept methodological naturalism. For it is still the case, as I will argue in the next chapter, that the default view should be to accept content naturalism, and (according to the weak content-methodology link) if one is a content naturalist then there are good, though perhaps ultimately defeasible, reasons for you to be a methodological naturalist. So even those who accept only this weak version of the content-methodology link should read on.

2
Content Naturalism as the Default View

In the previous chapter I argued that the vast majority of metaphysicians are committed to content naturalism, and that anyone who is committed to content naturalism should also be a methodological naturalist. Once this argument is made explicit, the reader has two options. She can either accept methodological naturalism, or she can revise her commitment to content naturalism. I don't intend this book to convince anyone one way or the other between these two options—both would lead to surprising and interesting consequences for the way we do metaphysics. I do, however, think that accepting content naturalism—and thus also accepting methodological naturalism—should be the default view. Consequently, the majority of the discussion in the chapters that follow will be about the consequences of accepting methodological naturalism. I will not return to the question of what follows if we instead choose to reject both methodological and content naturalism until Chapter 8.

Why think that accepting content naturalism—and thus also accepting methodological naturalism—should be the default view? This question is the focus of the present chapter. In what follows I will argue that content naturalism is a relatively natural and attractive position to take with respect to the relationship between metaphysics and science. Although in broad strokes this argument is fairly straightforward, there is also quite a bit of nuance in the background, especially with respect to recent literature in philosophy of science and the relationship between content naturalism and scientific realism.

But again, even if you are not persuaded by the reasoning in this chapter, you aren't thereby able to avoid the overall argument of this book. If I'm wrong, and content naturalism should not even be the default view, that, in and of itself, would be interesting and surprising. The routes by which we might avoid content naturalism are all such that they still lead to the result that metaphysical theorizing should look quite different than it currently does.

2.1 The Simple Case for Content Naturalism

Here is the simple case for content naturalism. First, notice that science has been highly successful in answering questions about what the world is like. I take it that this claim is fairly obvious to all of us who daily benefit from the lasers and microprocessors that are based on quantum phenomena, the GPS devices that make use of relativity theory, and the medical advances that were made possible by developments in chemistry, biology, and neuroscience.[1]

Second, notice that there is no clear demarcation between the domain of science and the domain of metaphysics. There are paradigm cases of scientific inquiry for which it would seem strange if not wholly inappropriate to consult a metaphysician (e.g., does the Higgs boson exist?) and paradigm cases of metaphysical inquiry for which it would seem strange if not wholly inappropriate to consult a scientist (e.g., if I put my memories in your body, is the resulting person you or me?), but there are also nebulous border regions between the two fields in which the questions that arise are not clearly within the purview of one field to the exclusion of the other. (For instance, what is the nature of space and time? What does it mean for something to be conscious? What kind of thing is a law of nature?)[2]

It follows from the combination of these two claims—that science is so successful and that there is no clear demarcation between metaphysics and science—that content naturalism should be the default view. The lack of a clear distinction between metaphysics and science suggests that metaphysics and science are about the same domain.[3] And if science and metaphysics are about the same domain (what the world is like) and science has proved itself highly successful in answering questions about that domain, then metaphysicians should not take on commitments that conflict with the content of our best scientific theories.[4]

---

[1] Note that I'm not making any assumptions here about what is meant by 'successful.' One might think of science as successful in the sense that it puts forward theories that are true, or in the sense that it puts forward theories that are approximately true, or in the sense that it puts forward theories that are useful for creatures like us in navigating the world. In this way I don't take the simple argument here to involve assuming scientific realism. Note that I discuss the question of the relationship between content naturalism and scientific realism in detail in section 2.2.

[2] We can also see the lack of a clear demarcation illustrated by the way in which many debates that were once clearly the provenance of philosophers later came to be seen as fair game for scientists.

[3] Note the difference between saying that the lack of a clear distinction *suggests* that science and metaphysics are about the same domain and saying that the lack of a clear distinction requires or entails that science and metaphysics are about the same domain. I'm making only the former claim.

[4] Note that the argument just given is importantly distinct from the *no miracles* argument for scientific realism. The no miracles argument (which goes back to Putnam 1975) has two premises. First,

2.2 Worries about Content Naturalism

Here are some initial worries that one might have about content naturalism. (Those readers who are concerned about the relationship between content naturalism and scientific realism should note that I discuss that worry in detail in section 2.2.)

Metaphysics as Subservient

In the introduction I set up a potential dilemma for metaphysicians: either metaphysics is subservient to science, or metaphysics is misguided. At first glance it might seem that to accept content naturalism is to take the first horn of the dilemma. As a result, some metaphysicians might balk at the idea of being content naturalists.

There are two key points to make in response to this worry. First, content naturalism requires that metaphysics be subservient in only one specific respect—metaphysical theories should not conflict with the content of our best science. It explicitly leaves open (a) the possibility that sometimes the content of our best science is not clear, (b) the possibility that sometimes there are multiple metaphysical theories that are compatible with the content of our best science, and (c) the possibility of putting forward metaphysical theories that go beyond our best science. So if content naturalism makes metaphysics subservient to science, it does so in a fairly limited way. It does not undermine the possibility of robust metaphysical inquiry that is distinct from our best science. And if there is a lot of interesting and legitimate work to do as metaphysicians, then why should metaphysicians care? As an analogy, I suspect that many scientists would agree that if a chemical or biological or neuroscientific theory is in conflict with our best physics, then we should give up the former, not the latter.[5] But few in this camp, I take it, would claim that the higher-level sciences, like chemistry, biology, and neuroscience, are subservient to physics in any worrying sense. What matters

---

that science is highly successful, and second that the best explanation of this success is that our best scientific theories are true. The argument just given relies only on the first of these premises.

[5] Ladyman and Ross (2007) describe a Primacy of Physics Constraint on scientific theorizing that is in agreement with this point.

is that there is still a wealth of important and interesting work to do in the higher-level sciences. We should think the same of metaphysics.

Metaphysical Presuppositions

One way that philosophers have sought to save metaphysics from the charge that it is subservient to science is to appeal to the idea that science relies on metaphysical presuppositions. This is an idea that can be traced back to Immanuel Kant and that was discussed by Kuhn (1962), who characterized periods of so-called *normal science* in part by the fact that they were periods during which a number of metaphysical assumptions were held fixed. The idea that science relies on metaphysical presuppositions also appears regularly in more recent literature.[6] Consider, for instance, Paul's claim:

> There is no way to make sense of the central concepts of classical field theory or quantum chromodynamics without using a concept of property. There is no way to make sense of the concept of mechanism in organic chemistry without using a concept of causation. There is no way to make sense of the central concepts deployed by biological representations of the citric acid cycle without using a concept of persistence. In such cases, we start with the metaphysical concepts as the conditions under which we understand the scientific concepts. (Paul 2012, 6)

Or, alternatively, consider Hasok Chang's discussion of what he calls the *principle of the single-value,* which states that "a real physical property can have no more than one definite value in a given situation" (Chang 2008, 123ff.). According to Chang, the principle of the single-value is a metaphysical principle without which standard kinds of scientific testing would not make sense.[7]

---

[6] In addition to the citations in the main body, see also Friedman (2001), Chang (2008), Robus (2015), and Esfeld (2018). In some of his writings, E. J. Lowe also emphasizes this point. See, for instance, Lowe (2002), where he writes, "[M]etaphysics goes deeper than any merely empirical science, even physics, because it provides the very framework with which such sciences are conceived" (Lowe 2002, vi). As I read Jenann Ismael's work on deterministic chance it also involves a claim that might be interpreted as a very specific kind of metaphysical presupposition. She writes that "a probability measure over the space of physically possible trajectories is an indispensable component of any theory—deterministic or otherwise— that can be used as a basis for prediction or receive confirmation from the evidence" (Ismael 2009, 89).

[7] Sometimes philosophers refer to the kinds of extra-empirical principles that I will talk about in detail later in this book as "metaphysical presuppositions." A good example of this is Sklar, who

Is the idea that science in some way presupposes metaphysics an issue for the content naturalist? I don't think so. I am happy to agree that we need the concept of causation to make sense of the concept of mechanism in chemistry and that we need the principle of the single-value to make sense of the way in which we test many scientific theories. I'm also happy to allow (though I myself am not totally convinced on this point) that the concept of causation and the principle of the single-value are distinctively *metaphysical* (as opposed to scientific). Even so, I don't think there is any particular issue for the content naturalist here.

The key thing to notice is that content naturalism, as I laid it out above, leaves room for metaphysicians to put forward and endorse claims that go beyond the content of our best science. This is what I think is happening when we (maybe largely implicitly) develop the concept of causation and then deploy it in chemistry, or when we (again, maybe implicitly) accept the principle of the single-value and then rely on that principle when testing various scientific theories. These are metaphysical commitments that, at least when they are first taken on, go beyond the content of our best science. (Later, of course, our scientific theories may develop in a way that relies on them.)

A view that would not—or at least not easily—be compatible with the idea that science relies on metaphysical presuppositions would be radical content naturalism, as described in Chapter 1. According to the radical content naturalist, we should not accept metaphysical theories that either conflict with or go beyond the content of our best scientific theories. Radical content naturalism would indeed make it mysterious how we ever develop the concept of causation (assuming that we need to understand that concept before we can put forward any scientific theories that make use of it) or accept the principle of the single-value (assuming that we need that principle in order to test our best scientific theories and no scientific theory can itself justify that

---

argues that some kind of verificationist principle like "don't posit entities that don't have any observable consequences" was a "metaphysical presupposition" of Einstein's relativity theory (Sklar 1981, 131ff.). On the face of it, this kind of principle seems to me more like an epistemological principle than a metaphysical presupposition, but maybe the idea is that the only reason why you would endorse this verificationist principle is if you were making a certain kind of assumption about what the world is like, namely that the world is such that following the relevant principle will lead to successful scientific theories. In any case, as with the two examples in the main text, if this kind of principle really is a metaphysical presupposition of science, then it might make trouble for the radical content naturalist, but it doesn't create any issues for content naturalism as I have defined it.

principle). But again, my argument throughout concerns only content naturalism, not radical content naturalism.[8]

No Clear Distinction between Metaphysics and Science

Many philosophers of science rightly note that it is hard to draw a clear distinction between science, on the one hand, and philosophy, on the other.[9] There are at least two reasons for this view. First, the view might be inspired by the metaphysical presuppositions of scientific theories that were mentioned just above. Second, as I noted in my discussion of the simple case for content naturalism, there are many questions about what the world is like that occupy a gray zone between science and metaphysics.

In conversation, I sometimes hear the following worry voiced: if there is no clear distinction between science and metaphysics, then content naturalism doesn't make sense. How can philosophers tell whether they are supposed to respect a bit of theory if there isn't any way to determine whether that bit of theory is a piece of science or not?

I do not think that there is a genuine concern here. Just because the distinction between science and metaphysics (or more generally between science and non-science) is vague doesn't mean that there aren't clear cases of scientific theories—cases where there is widespread consensus that the theory in question is indeed an instance of scientific theorizing. At the very least, then, we can use content naturalism in these cases. In cases where it is unclear whether the theory in question is a genuine scientific theory, it may well be unclear whether content naturalism applies. But that's okay. I've already admitted, in Chapter 1, that there are cases in which, even if we are confident that the theory before us is one of our best scientific theories, we are not confident as to what the *content* of that theory is. So I've already accepted that there will be at least some cases in which it is unclear whether content naturalism applies. This is not an impediment to endorsing content naturalism and applying it in the cases where it is clear that it does in fact apply.

---

[8] As far as I can see, the most promising way for the radical content naturalist to defend against the worry that their theory is incompatible with science having metaphysical presuppositions would be to try to argue that those presuppositions aren't actually metaphysical, but in fact are reasonably considered part of science.
[9] See Maddy (2001 and 2007) and Chakravartty (2017).

Underdetermination of Metaphysics by Science

Here is another worry that is related to the discussion in Chapter 1 of cases in which we might have questions regarding the content of a scientific theory. Here, however, the idea is that the content of scientific theories, in at least some cases, is just too minimal to allow us to decide which of two or more metaphysical theories is correct. A prominent example of someone who expresses this concern is Steven French, who writes, "[There is] a problem for this programme of 'reading metaphysics off current physics,' to put it crudely, which arises from what might be called the 'underdetermination' of metaphysics by physics" (French 1998, 93). French has in mind in particular the argument that it follows from quantum theory that quantum entities (e.g., electrons) do not qualify as genuine individuals.[10] This argument, French thinks, is too quick; there are a number of ways of saving the claim that electrons and the like are individuals, as long as you are willing to take on various further metaphysical commitments (e.g., accepting primitive individuality or giving up the identity of indiscernibles). "Quantum mechanics," French writes, "is compatible with two distinct metaphysical 'packages,' one in which the objects are regarded as individuals and one in which they are not. Thus, we have a form of 'underdetermination' of the metaphysics by the physics" (French 2000). One might try to leverage this kind of example into a general worry about content naturalism. If metaphysical claims are underdetermined by the physics, then content naturalism, even if plausible, won't have much force.[11]

While I'm sympathetic to this point in the particular case that French has in mind, I don't think that it arises all that often—or at least not often enough to undermine the claim that content naturalism is a substantive thesis. I think there are quite a number of metaphysical debates where the content of our best science *does* clearly and straightforwardly determine that some of the otherwise open positions in those debates are ruled out. These aren't debates that we spend a lot of time thinking about—but that's because we have so deeply internalized content naturalism. The kinds of metaphysical debate that take up the most space in the literature are ones where the content of our

---

[10] At issue is what French (2000) calls the Indistinguishability Postulate, which says that there is no way of distinguishing between two quantum states if the only thing that is different between the two states is that the individual particles have exchanged properties.

[11] Another example: Slater (2017) considers three cases in which biology seems to lead directly to metaphysical conclusions, and then argues that two of the three cases are far more complex than they at first appear.

best scientific theories either does not seem to be relevant or else seems to underdetermine the answer to the relevant metaphysical question. This fact about what metaphysicians spend their time thinking and writing about is what we should expect if most metaphysicians are content naturalists.

In addition, it's worth recognizing that there is a distinction between (a) claiming that we should endorse content naturalism and (b) claiming that content naturalism settles all (or most, or even many) debates in metaphysics. In this chapter, I am trying to establish only (a). Even if you accept (a) but not any version of (b), it follows from the argument in Chapter 1 that you should be a methodological naturalist.

Metaphysics as the Study of the Possible

According to some metaphysicians, metaphysics is the study of what is possible. One prominent advocate of this view is Lowe, who writes that "[e]mpirical science at most tells us what is the case, not what must or may be . . . Metaphysics deals in possibilities" (Lowe 1998, 11).[12] Insofar as one endorses this view, it's not immediately obvious why metaphysicians should care about science, or so one might think. This worry is a version of the worry discussed in section 1.4 according to which metaphysics and science are really about distinct domains.

The first thing to say in response to this worry is that I am skeptical that it is accurate as a description of actual metaphysical practice. Consider the three examples of content naturalism presented in Chapter 1. None of the metaphysical theses at stake there was, at least on the face of it, a modal claim. The question of whether only presently existing things exist, for instance, seems to be a claim about the actual world. We might argue further that if presentism is true, it is true across all metaphysically possible worlds. But there is no reason to interpret all metaphysicians who are interested in temporal ontology as making such a strong claim. The point is even stronger when it comes to the question of what race is. This is surely a question about our actual world. We care about race first and foremost because of the implications that it has for our actual lives, not because of the way in which it may or may not vary across the space of metaphysical possibility.

---

[12] See also Morganti (2013). Callender (2011) claims that this view about the difference in the aims of science and metaphysics is pervasive in contemporary metaphysics. This view is also discussed and critiqued in French and McKenzie (2012) and French and McKenzie (2016).

Second, and more importantly, notice that even if one thinks that metaphysical theories are theories about what is metaphysically possible and scientific theories are theories about what is actual, there can still be genuine conflicts between metaphysics and science. In particular, if our best scientific theories tell us that p is actual, and we have a candidate metaphysical theory that says that p is metaphysically impossible, then that candidate metaphysical theory conflicts with the content of our best science. Consider, for instance, what appears to be a plausible principle of mereology: that it is not possible for two distinct things to occupy exactly the same location at exactly the same time.[13] This principle—call it the *no co-location principle*—is clearly a modal claim. But, as it turns out, a fairly straightforward interpretation of quantum theory tells us that there are actual particles—namely bosons—that violate this principle. In this way, our best science appears to conflict with a modal claim that many metaphysicians have wanted to accept.[14]

At most, then, what one ends up with on this view is an example of what I called in Chapter 1 domain-dependent content naturalism, namely:

Modality-restricted content naturalism. When engaged in metaphysical debates that have consequences for what is actual or what is nomologically possible, we should not accept theories that conflict with the content of our best scientific theories.

Modality-restricted content naturalism allows that when you are making claims that are exclusively about what is merely metaphysically possible, then you need not accept content naturalism. But, as demonstrated above, these debates are few and far between.[15] And remember, the content-methodology link will still apply to modality-restricted content naturalism. Someone who accepts modality-restricted content naturalism will be committed to:

Modality-restricted methodological naturalism. When engaged in metaphysical debates that have consequences for what is actual or what is

---

[13] The more precise way to put this is as follows: Necessarily, if x and y have exact locations that overlap, then x and y themselves overlap. See Gilmore (2018).

[14] Note that, as with the examples in Chapter 1, the conflict here is contentious. Some philosophers respond to the apparent conflict by giving up the no co-location principle, but others argue that the straightforward interpretation of quantum theory that leads to a conflict with the no co-location principle is incorrect. For the former approach, see Hawthorne and Uzquiano (2011). For the latter, see Schaffer (2009b).

[15] One example would be debates about whether time travel is metaphysically possible.

nomologically possible, metaphysicians should, whenever possible, follow the methodology of science.

And modality-restricted methodological naturalism will encompass most metaphysical debates, because most metaphysical debates have consequences for what is actual or nomologically possible.

Here is another way to put the point. Someone who endorses this kind of view has bifurcated metaphysics into two sub-fields and is endorsing a kind of fine-grained naturalism as defined in section 1.3. There is, on the one hand, metaphysics of the actual (and nomologically possible) and, on the other hand, metaphysics of the merely (metaphysically) possible. The content-methodology link applies to both types of metaphysics, but potentially in different ways. When it comes to the metaphysics of the actual (and nomologically possible), one should presumably be both a content and a methodological naturalist. When it comes to the metaphysics of the merely (metaphysically) possible, we may instead wish to reject both content and methodological naturalism.

2.3 Content Naturalism and Scientific Realism

Throughout the discussion above, those readers who are familiar with the recent literature in the philosophy of science will likely have been wondering about the relationship between content naturalism and scientific realism. In particular, readers may be wondering whether one should be a content naturalist *only if* you are also a scientific realist.[16] This question is fairly nuanced, and answering it will require some digression into the relevant philosophy of science literature. Those readers who are already committed to scientific realism may wish to skip to the next chapter.

Although it is an oversimplification, I will focus on the broad-strokes distinction between the following two views:

Realism about science. Our best scientific theories are true theories about what the world is like.[17]

Pragmatism about science. Our best scientific theories are theories that are useful for creatures like us in navigating the world.

---

[16] See the discussion in Hawley (2006).
[17] Following van Fraassen (1980), much of the debate in this area has been about whether our best scientific theories should be read as literally true insofar as they make claims about unobservable

I'll say something about more fine-grained distinctions within these two camps in a moment. But for now, let's focus on the question of whether content naturalism is incompatible with pragmatism about science. The answer is: it depends. It depends, in particular, on which of the corresponding views about metaphysics one adopts. Consider:

Realism about metaphysics. The aim of metaphysics is to put forward theories about what the world is like that are true.

Pragmatism about metaphysics. The aim of metaphysics is to put forward theories about what the world is like that are merely useful for creatures like us.[18]

If there is a mismatch between one's view about science and one's view about metaphysics—if, for instance, one is a pragmatist about metaphysics but a realist about science, or if one is a realist about metaphysics but a pragmatist about science—then it would be odd to be a content naturalist. After all, someone who endorses this kind of mismatch thinks that science and metaphysics have significantly different goals—so why should they care if their scientific claims and their metaphysical claims conflict?

But if one is either a realist about both science and metaphysics, or a pragmatist about both science and metaphysics, then the simple case that I gave above for being a content naturalist still applies. So my view is: no—content naturalism doesn't presuppose realism about science. What it does presuppose is some congruence between how one thinks about the goals of science and how one thinks about the goals of metaphysics.[19]

In the contemporary philosophy of science literature, much of the discussion is about whether to endorse full-fledged scientific realism, as defined

entities. So you will also sometimes see definitions of scientific realism like the following: "A preliminary definition of scientific realism is that it is the claim that we have knowledge of the unobservable entities and processes posited by our best scientific theories" (Ladyman 2012, 33).

[18] In conversation I often have philosophers express skepticism that pragmatism about metaphysics is at all plausible. For a specific example of this kind of pragmatism that is related to the case study in Chapter 4, consider recent work by metaphysicians who argue for a Humean interpretation of laws of nature that focuses on what laws need to be in order to be useful for creatures like us. See, for instance, Dorst (2019) and the essays in Hicks et al. (forthcoming).

[19] The same goes for related worries about whether content naturalism presupposes a certain degree of epistemic commitment on behalf of scientists with respect to their theories—e.g., that scientists believe their theories as opposed to merely provisionally accepting them, or something like that. Content naturalism doesn't require that you think scientists believe their theories, but it does require some congruence between the epistemic attitude that you think scientists have toward their best theories and the epistemic attitude that you think metaphysicians have toward their best theories. If

above, or a more restricted version of the realist position, which says that only *some* of the claims that our best scientific theories put forward are true. Here's a prominent example of a more restricted realist position:

Structural realism about science. The parts of our best scientific theories that are about the structure of the world are true.[20]

Now, I'm intentionally not going to say very much about what counts as the structure of the world; different understandings of that concept will correspond to different versions of structural realism, but those differences won't have any significant impact on what I say below. But in very broad strokes the idea is that there is a contrast between the *things* that a theory posits—elements or electrons or black holes or what have you—and the *structure* that the theory posits. The latter is supposed to capture the causal, nomological, and modal relationships within the theory and is closely connected to the mathematical structure of the theory's formalism.

Advocates of restricted versions of realism—like structural realism—find them attractive for several reasons. Perhaps most notably, they are supposed to allow for a response to the so-called *pessimistic meta-induction argument* against scientific realism.[21] The pessimistic meta-induction starts from the observation that most of the scientific theories that we have had in the past—including scientific theories that were, in their time, wildly successful—have turned out not to be true. So, induction would suggest that our current scientific theories are also not true. One way of responding to the pessimistic meta-induction is to argue for a significant restriction on what parts of the content of our best scientific theories we should be realists about. The idea behind this maneuver is that there are certain kinds of claims that have tended to remain true, even after radical theory change (e.g., claims about structure). So if we restrict our realism to those kinds of claims, we can avoid the pessimistic meta-induction.

How do these restricted forms of realism affect the plausibility of content naturalism? Let's begin by noticing that here, too, there will be versions of

---

you thought that scientists only *provisionally accepted* their best theories, but metaphysicians *believed* their best theories, it wouldn't make sense to be a content naturalist.

[20] This version of restricted realism is supposed to evoke the view introduced by Worrall (1989) and developed by Ladyman (1998), among others. Another example of a restricted realist position would be Bas van Fraassen's (1980) constructive empiricism.
[21] See Laudan (1981).

metaphysical realism that mirror the relevant versions of scientific realism. Consider:

> *Structural realism about metaphysics.* The aim of metaphysics is to put forward theories about what the world is like where the parts of those theories that are about the structure of the world are true.

As with the discussion of realism versus pragmatism, there won't be any challenge for content naturalism stemming from the distinction between these different types of realism as long as one adopts similar versions of restricted scientific realism and restricted metaphysical realism. Insofar as one applies the same restrictions to both one's scientific and one's metaphysical realism, then everything that was said above about why content naturalism should be the default view still applies.

But what if there is a mismatch? What if, for instance, one is a straightforward realist about metaphysics but only a structural realist about science? In this case, it probably doesn't make sense to adopt content naturalism as defined above. Instead you should adopt a limited version of content naturalism, along the following lines:

> *Structural content naturalism.* We should not accept metaphysical theories that conflict with the structural content of our best scientific theories.

I will say a bit more in the next section about how my argument from content naturalism to methodological naturalism will apply to limited versions of content naturalism, but I warn the reader that the discussion therein is both abstract and complex, and that those who are attracted to full-fledged realism about both metaphysics and science may wish to simply skip ahead to the next chapter. For the most part, throughout the rest of the book, I will present the discussion in terms that are amenable to full-fledged realists. These are the views that I myself am inclined toward, and they are the views in which the discussion below is most easily framed. Moreover, I think it is clear that although they play an important role in the recent literature on philosophy of science, the limited forms of content naturalism under discussion here are not especially widespread among metaphysicians. If they were, then when metaphysicians were faced with a potential conflict between an attractive metaphysical theory and the content of our best science, there would be more resistance. Before giving up the attractive metaphysical theory, philosophers would first try to understand that theory as being about the part of the world regarding which we don't take the dictates of science to be relevant. In this way, even if one wishes to resist content naturalism as defined in Chapter 1 by accepting a limited form of content naturalism, one would still need to acknowledge that much of metaphysical theorizing should look quite different than it usually does.

2.4 From Limited Content Naturalism to Methodological Naturalism

Here is a further point that should rein in the hopes of someone who wishes to avoid the consequences of my argument by shifting from content naturalism to limited content naturalism. Even if one merely endorses limited content naturalism, a version of the argument for the content-methodology link will still apply.

Consider the specific version of limited content naturalism we discussed above:

> *Structural content naturalism.* Metaphysicians should not accept theories that conflict with the content of our best scientific theories that concerns the structure of the world.

To see how the argument for the content-methodology link applies, we need to first distinguish between two attitudes that a limited content naturalist might have about the methodology that produces our best science. On the one hand, they might think that methodology is *separable*. For the particular case at hand, a separable methodology would be one in which there is a distinct part of the methodology—call it the *structural methodology*—that produces the structural content of a theory, and a distinct part—call it the *extra-structural methodology*—that produces the content that goes beyond the structural content.

If the methodology is separable in this way, then it is straightforward to apply the argument for the content-methodology link to limited content naturalism. The version of the argument that applies will be as follows:

P1'   If you are a structural content naturalist and you think that the goal of metaphysical theorizing is to put forward claims about what the world is like that have epistemic feature F, then you should think that the structural content of our best scientific theories has epistemic feature F.

P2'   Anyone who thinks that the structural content of our best scientific theories has epistemic feature F should also think that the structural methodology is a good guide to epistemic feature F.

P3'   If you are a limited content naturalist and you think that the goal of metaphysical theorizing is to put forward claims about what the world is like that have epistemic feature F, then you should think that the structural methodology is a good guide to epistemic feature F.

C'   If you are a limited content naturalist and you think that the goal of metaphysical theorizing is to put forward claims about what the world is like that have epistemic feature F, then you should be a structural methodological naturalist.

Where structural methodological naturalism is defined as follows:

Structural methodological naturalism. When choosing between candidate theories, metaphysicians should, whenever possible, use the structural methodology that scientists use.

More generally, suppose you adopt a limited form of content naturalism and think the methodology is separable. Call the *limited methodology* the methodology that produces the parts of the theory with respect to which we should be content naturalists. An argument similar to the one above will then commit you to:

Limited methodological naturalism. When choosing between candidate theories, metaphysicians should, whenever possible, use the limited methodology that scientists use.

The foregoing discussion has been abstract. Here is a concrete example of a version of limited methodological naturalism that is related to the recent literature. Consider Juha Saatsi's (2017) critique of what he calls *explanationism*, the view that metaphysicians are justified in appealing to inference to the best explanation because scientists do so as well. Saatsi's argument is complex.[22] But one key strand in the argument is the following: Saatsi thinks that explanationists are working with an oversimplified understanding of the history of science. On his view, if one looks closely at the kinds of cases that inspire the pessimistic meta-induction argument mentioned above—if one looks closely, in other words, at the cases in which highly successful theories later turned out to be false—it often turns out that the parts of those theories that turned out to be false are precisely those parts that were underwritten using inference to the best explanation. "Again and again in the history of science," he writes, "it is precisely the metaphysical and ontological assumptions concerning the nature of gravity and other forces, light, disease, life, genes, etc.—the assumptions that were underwriting the best scientific understanding of the relevant phenomena—that have subsequently turned out to be false" (Saatsi 2017, 12). On his view, this history suggests that inference to the best explanation "cannot reliably function as a guide to the fundamental nature of things" (12).

I don't want to take a stand here on whether Saatsi's interpretation of the historical record is accurate. My own view is that quite a bit depends on what constitutes inference to the best explanation, and that this is a remarkably slippery concept in both science and metaphysics. There is also quite a bit of philosophical nuance in what Saatsi means by an aspect of a theory being 'underwritten by' inference to the best explanation (IBE). In any case, if you agree with Saatsi, then you should not be a content naturalist. You should be a limited content naturalist, and your content naturalism will be explicitly limited by the type of methodology that is involved.

Non-IBE content naturalism. We should not accept metaphysical theories that conflict with the content of our best scientific theories—except where that content has been underwritten by inference to the best explanation.

And note that this way of arriving at a limited form of content naturalism is one on which the methodology is explicitly separable. Those who endorse non-IBE content naturalism should therefore endorse a corresponding version of methodological naturalism:

---

[22] Note that I say more about a different part of his argument in Chapter 4, when I discuss a methodological principle that is related to (though distinct from) inference to the best explanation.

Non-IBE methodological naturalism. When choosing between candidate theories, metaphysicians should, whenever possible, use the methodology that scientists use except inference to the best explanation.

Here non-IBE methodological naturalism is a version of limited methodological naturalism.

To what extent will non-IBE methodological naturalism yield different results from the wholesale version of methodological naturalism that I will be focused on in the majority of this book? We can't answer this question clearly until we take a stand on precisely what constitutes inference to the best explanation, and in particular the type of inference to the best explanation that is supposed to be playing the role that Saatsi identifies across the historical scientific record. This is likely to involve some fairly substantive and controversial commitments. Casual gestures toward inference to the best explanation in both science and metaphysics make it out to be a fairly expansive idea. Indeed, it sometimes seems that one can reinterpret nearly any appeal to extra-empirical features of a theory to be an appeal to inference to the best explanation.[23] But presumably a notion of inference to the best explanation that correctly corresponds to all and only the aspects of previously successful scientific theories that later turned out to be false will need to be quite specific. This suggests that there will be a number of substantive aspects of scientific methodology that are still relevant to metaphysical theorizing, and therefore that non-IBE methodological naturalism will still have interesting and surprising consequences.

Insofar as one instead attempted to defend the idea that the sense of inference to the best explanation that is playing a role in non-IBE methodological naturalism is fairly expansive—perhaps so expansive that it captures all or most of the extra-empirical reasoning that happens in science—that would suggest that non-IBE methodological naturalism is not likely to have any substantive impact on metaphysical theorizing. But notice that if one takes this view, then the version of content naturalism that one is adopting—non-IBE content naturalism—will have only very limited consequences for metaphysical theorizing. When a metaphysician is faced with an objection that suggests that their favored metaphysical theory conflicts with their best science, they shouldn't be immediately concerned. After all, those conflicts

---

[23] Beebe (2009), for instance, contains a list of 15 distinct kinds of explanatory consideration, including, e.g., ontological parsimony, that could be relevant to inference to the best explanation.

will be relevant only insofar as inference to the best explanation is not underwriting the relevant science. And given that we're assuming that the notion of inference to the best explanation that is relevant here is fairly expansive, there will be quite a lot of wiggle room for metaphysicians who are faced with a potential conflict.

For this reason, although the specifics that follow from my argument may differ insofar as one shifts from content naturalism and methodological naturalism to non-IBE content naturalism and non-IBE methodological naturalism, the consequences will still be substantive. Either the way in which non-IBE methodological naturalism is restricted is quite specific, in which case applying this version of methodological naturalism should still yield interesting and surprising results, or the way in which non-IBE content naturalism is restricted is quite general, in which case there are far more avenues open to metaphysicians whose theories appear to conflict with our best science than are usually recognized.

All that by way of thinking about a plausible case in which one might want to be a limited content naturalist and is inclined to think that the relevant methodology is separable. What if the methodology is non-separable? Here things are trickier. There will still be a version of the argument that applies in this case, but it will have a more limited conclusion. Let's call the content that the limited content naturalist thinks metaphysicians must respect the L-content.

P1" If you are an L-content naturalist and you think that the goal of metaphysical theorizing is to put forward claims about what the world is like that have epistemic feature F, then you should think that the L-content of our best scientific theories has epistemic feature F.

P2" Anyone who thinks that the L-content of our best scientific theories has epistemic feature F should also think that standard scientific methodology is a good guide to epistemic feature F with respect to L-content.

P3" If you are an L-content naturalist and you think that the goal of metaphysical theorizing is to put forward claims about what the world is like that have epistemic feature F, then you should think that standard scientific methodology is a good guide to epistemic feature F with respect to L-content.

C" If you are an L-content naturalist and you think that the goal of metaphysical theorizing is to put forward claims about what the world is like that have epistemic feature F, then you should also be an L-methodological naturalist.

Where L-methodological naturalism is defined as follows:

L-methodological naturalism. When choosing between metaphysical theories that differ with respect to their L-content, we should, whenever possible, use the same methodology that scientists use.

The difference between L-methodological naturalism and limited methodological naturalism is subtle but strikes me as potentially important. Limited methodological naturalism applies to all metaphysical theorizing, but only some of the methodology of science is relevant. The shift to L-methodological naturalism, by contrast, is likely to place some significant constraints on the application of methodological naturalism. Suppose, for instance, that you are a structural content naturalist. You think that metaphysicians should not accept theories that conflict with the content of our best scientific theories when that content concerns the structure of the world. Even if you think standard scientific methodology is not separable, you should still think that methodology, in its entirety, is a good guide to claims about what the world is like in terms of its structure. So insofar as we are debating metaphysical theories that involve different structural claims, we should also, whenever possible, follow the methodology that scientists use. In other words, we should adopt:

S-methodological naturalism. When choosing between candidate metaphysical theories that differ with respect to their structural content, metaphysicians should, whenever possible, use the same methodology that scientists use.

To what extent does S-methodological naturalism differ from the more expansive version of methodological naturalism that I will focus on in what follows? It depends on how one understands the relevant notions of structure. Consider, for instance, debates about composite objects or about merely possible worlds. Are those debates about the structural content of a theory? At first glance, maybe not. These are paradigm cases in which we are debating whether to add a certain kind of thing to our metaphysics. On the other hand, if you think that composite objects exist, then you are committed to a certain kind of relation, the composition relation, that nihilists about composite objects can deny. Perhaps that is part of the structural content of the theory? Similarly, if you think that merely possible worlds exist, then logical space has an enormous amount of structure that it lacks if one thinks there are no such things.

I don't mean to imply that there hasn't been a great deal of important and interesting work already done regarding the notion of structure—there certainly has been. My point is just that the notion is hard to pin down precisely. And notice that the situation here will, at least in broad strokes, mirror the discussion above regarding inference to the best explanation. On the one hand, one might have a fairly expansive notion of structural content in mind. Quite a lot of the content of our best scientific theories counts as structural content. In that case, one should expect that S-methodological naturalism will still have interesting and substantive results for a wide range of metaphysical debates, for many metaphysical debates will also differ with respect to their structural content. On the other hand, one might have a fairly restrictive notion of structural content in mind. Very little of the content of our best scientific theories counts as structural content. In that case, one should expect that S-methodological naturalism will have only limited impact on metaphysical theorizing—for one should expect that very few metaphysical debates differ with respect to their structural content. But at the same time, this highly restrictive notion of structural content will mean that the version of limited content naturalism that one endorses is very limited. So by shifting from content naturalism to the relevant version of limited content naturalism, one is going to open up quite a bit of room for metaphysicians to maneuver when it comes to potential conflicts with science. If they only need to respect the structural content of science, and the structural content of science is extremely limited, then the content of science places few limitations on the content of metaphysics. The shift, therefore, from content naturalism to one of these limited versions of content naturalism will itself have significant consequences for metaphysical theorizing.

The upshot, then, is that the relationship between limited forms of content naturalism and the content-methodology link argued for in Chapter 1 is complex. It may be that metaphysicians who wish to avoid the consequences of methodological naturalism that are discussed in the next several chapters can do so by moving from content naturalism to limited content naturalism, but their work will be cut out for them, and they will still be committed to a view on which metaphysical theorizing should look quite different than it currently does. In any case, in what follows, I will shelve the discussion of limited content naturalism and focus on content naturalism proper.

Recap

Before moving on to a discussion of the consequences of methodological naturalism, let me recap briefly what I take this section to have established. I have argued that content naturalism ought to be the default position. There may be ways of avoiding content naturalism, but in order for some such approach to be well-motivated it needs to be premised on quite a bit of controversial and nuanced worked in history and philosophy of science. Moreover, depending on the precise way in which one's avoidance of content naturalism is motivated, it is likely to still give rise to some limited version of the content-methodology link.

When combined with the content-methodology link, the argument in this chapter shows that methodological naturalism ought to be the default view. But there is also a more subtle conclusion that can be drawn from this discussion. In Chapter 1, I argued that metaphysicians either need to accept methodological naturalism or give up content naturalism. It is easy to anticipate that accepting methodological naturalism will require metaphysicians to pay quite a bit more attention to history and philosophy of science. Rejecting content naturalism, therefore, might have come across as the best option for those metaphysicians who don't wish to engage substantially with science. But as the above discussion shows, someone who wishes to avoid a commitment to content naturalism is also going to take a fairly nuanced and controversial stand regarding to what extent and in what way science can be considered successful, what kinds of metaphysical presuppositions can be found in scientific theories, the limits of the scientific domain, and more. If I'm right about the content-methodology link, then, there just isn't any way to do metaphysics without also engaging seriously with history and philosophy of science.

3
Why Methodological Naturalism Impacts Metaphysical Theorizing

In the previous chapters I argued that metaphysicians who accept content naturalism should also accept methodological naturalism, and that accepting content naturalism should be the default view. In this chapter I'm going to argue that if we accept methodological naturalism, we should expect it to have a significant impact on metaphysical theorizing. I will do this in several steps. The first step is to argue that our scientific commitments are regularly underdetermined by the data that scientists collect. The second step is to argue that when this kind of underdetermination is present, scientists often choose which commitments to take on using various extra-empirical principles. The third step is to argue that we should expect the kinds of extra-empirical principles that scientists use to have a widespread impact when applied to metaphysical debates.[1]

The reader should note that throughout most of this chapter I'm going to focus on a particular way in which extra-empirical reasoning plays a role in science—via extra-empirical principles that reference particular theoretical virtues. But I am open to, and my overall project is compatible with, there also being other types of extra-empirical reasoning. Toward the end of this chapter, I will briefly consider two such ways.

---

[1] My sense is that the claim that our scientific commitments are underdetermined by the data is fairly widespread among contemporary philosophers and it is often asserted without a lot of argument, including by philosophers of science (as opposed to analytic metaphysicians) and by those who aren't ultimately endorsing anything like methodological naturalism. See, for instance, Ivanova and Farr, who write, "Scientists often need to choose between competing explanations of the same observations and the only way they can do so is by employing non-empirical factors in their decision making, such as aesthetic considerations like simplicity and elegance" (2020, 4).

3.1 Underdetermination

The first step in my argument is to show that our scientific commitments are regularly underdetermined by the data.[2] I will begin by giving a series of examples from actual scientific practice—some historical and some contemporary. I will then discuss some examples of scientific underdetermination that are inspired by philosophical considerations.

Underdetermination in Actual Scientific Practice

Let's start with a historical case. Consider debates about the nature of the solar system in the early 17th century. More specifically, consider the situation in 1610, when Kepler had just published his *Astronomia Nova*, which included his first two planetary laws, and Galileo had just published *Sidereus Nuncius*, which included his observations of the surface of our moon and of the moons of Jupiter.

At the time there were three types of theories regarding the nature of the solar system. On the one hand, there was the old Ptolemaic model, which said that the sun and the planets orbited the Earth. On the other hand, there was the heliocentric model, first advocated by Copernicus in the mid-16th century, which said that the Earth, and all the other planets, orbited the sun. Copernicus's version of this model had all of the planets moving uniformly in circular orbits. Kepler's version had the planets moving in elliptical orbits in keeping with his two laws of planetary motion. There was also a hybrid approach, due to Tycho Brahe, according to which Mercury and Venus orbited the sun, and then the sun and the other planets all orbited the Earth.

The reader with even a passing familiarity with this historical episode will be eager to point out that these theories were not on a par. Most famously, the Ptolemaic model required epicycles in the planetary orbits in order to explain occasional periods of retrograde motion (periods during which the planets seemed to move backward relative to their usual trajectory). I will say more about this in section 3.2. The key thing to note for now, however, is that all of these theories were *empirically adequate*—they were all able to accurately

---

[2] This kind of underdetermination is what Stanford (2017) calls 'contrastive underdetermination,' which is distinct from (though related to) the notion of 'confirmation holism.' See also Bonk (2008). Readers familiar with the literature should note that I say more about the distinction between weak and strong underdetermination in section 3.3.

predict the data that scientists observed. It wasn't always straightforward to make them compatible with the data—hence the Ptolemaic epicycles—but it was possible.[3] Insofar as a scientist working at this time chose one of the three models, as, for instance, both Kepler and Galileo did when they endorsed the heliocentric model, they were making a choice that was underdetermined by the data. Indeed, as Rabin (2019) points out, throughout the 16th and early 17th centuries, even those scientists who refused to endorse the heliocentric model for theological reasons often used Copernicus's theory when making certain astronomical calculations because it was easier.[4] Why could they do this, while still adhering to the Ptolemaic or the Tychonic model? Because the data that they had was compatible with either theory. Their view was that although the heliocentric model was inaccurate with respect to what the world was like, it was still empirically adequate.

Here is a second case. Consider special relativity as developed by Einstein in 1905. As discussed in Chapter 1, two key components of special relativity are the following:

The relativity of simultaneity. There are pairs of events such that in some inertial reference frames those events happen at the same time and in some inertial reference frames they do not.

No privileged reference frame. If two or more inertial reference frames disagree about some feature of the world, then there is no fact of the matter with respect to that feature.

And these two claims combined result in:

The conventionality of simultaneity. There are pairs of events such that there is no fact of the matter as to whether those events happen at the same time.

The conventionality of simultaneity is clearly a part of special relativity as developed by Einstein. But, as I pointed out in Chapter 1, the claim that there is no privileged reference frame is not a claim that follows from the data that Einstein had available to him. The data that was available to Einstein showed

---

[3] As I say more about in section 3.2, Copernicus's heliocentric model also involved epicycles—he used them to explain why it looked like the planets didn't move uniformly, even though, on his view, they did.

[4] See Rabin (2019), especially section 2.6.

that if there was a preferred reference frame, then it was not detectable. But that doesn't mean that there could not be such a frame. Indeed, Einstein could have explained the undetectability of the privileged reference frame using Lorentz's electrodynamics, in which measuring rods and clocks that are accelerated with respect to the privileged reference frame are distorted in a way that makes it impossible for us to detect which reference frame is privileged and which reference frame is not. Let's use the term *the Lorentzian alternative to refer to a view that* combines the relativity of simultaneity, the claim that there *is* a privileged reference frame, and Lorentz's electrodynamics as an explanation of the fact that we cannot detect which frame is privileged.[5]

Again, here, the reader is likely to be eager to point out that special relativity as developed by Einstein seems *better* than the Lorentzian alternative—the inclusion of an undetectable privileged reference frame in the latter seems ad hoc.[6] But what is important for our purposes is just to notice that special relativity and the Lorentzian alternative are both empirically adequate. When Einstein put forward special relativity, then, he was making a choice that was underdetermined by the data.

Examples like the two just given, whether historical or contemporary, can suggest that underdetermination is mainly a threat in highly abstract theoretical physics or cosmology.[7] This is not so. Consider the aspect of geology that involves investigating aspects of the internal composition and structure of the Earth that aren't directly observable. Here are two of the ways in which geologists go about this kind of investigation (as discussed by Belot 2015):

Gravimetry. Geologists collect data about the gravitational field at points on the surface of the Earth and then draw conclusions of the distribution of mass density within the Earth.

Neutrino tomography. Geologists collect data about the rate of attenuation of beams of neutrinos as they pass through the Earth at various points. They

---

[5] As Acuña (2014) discusses, it may be more accurate to describe this as the Lorentz-Poincaré alternative, since Poincaré made substantive contributions to the version of Lorentz's view that was empirically adequate.

[6] See Acuña (2014) for a detailed account of the possible ways of arguing for Einstein's view over the Lorentzian alternative, though note that I disagree with Acuña's argument that ultimately the choice of the former over the latter cannot be justified on *any* non-empirical grounds.

[7] Another cosmological example is found in Earman (1993). Earman shows how general relativity allows for universes with significantly different global topological features but in which there is no evidence inside the light cone of even an idealized observer that would allow that observer to determine which of the topological features is actually instantiated in the universe that they live in.

then draw conclusions about the nuclear density of the matter through which those neutrino beams have passed.

In both of these cases, for any particular set of data that geologists have collected, there are many conclusions that they could draw about the distribution of mass density or nuclear density in the interior of the Earth. (Just as an easy example, one could posit that the rate of attenuation of neutrino beams that one has observed is primarily the result of a very thin layer of material with extremely high nuclear density surrounded by material with relatively low nuclear density, or one could posit that the very same rate of attenuation is the result of a relatively homogeneous distribution of matter, all with roughly the same nuclear density.) What this shows is that there are many theories of the Earth's internal structure that are empirically adequate. But this does not stop geologists from drawing conclusions about the relevant kinds of internal structure. Indeed they do so all the time. The conclusions that these geologists draw, therefore, are underdetermined by the data that they collect.

Philosophical Arguments for Underdetermination

In addition to examples like those listed above, philosophers have also pointed out that there are many other cases of underdetermination that scientists don't explicitly discuss. These cases involve the kinds of scenarios that have traditionally raised skeptical concerns—they involve scenarios in which the data is precisely the same as the data that we actually have, but the world is very different than we usually take it to be.[8]

Consider, for instance, the choice between the following pairs of claims:

U1 The universe is 13.8 billion years old, started with the Big Bang, and underwent a period of rapid expansion in the first few moments.

U2 The universe was created by an all-powerful being much more recently, but this being wanted to be sure that humans had plenty of

---

[8] Kukla (1996) contains several algorithms for generating empirically equivalent theories. For instance, according to Kukla, for any theory T there is an empirically equivalent theory T*, where T* is the theory that the world behaves according to T when observed but differently when not observed. There is also an empirically equivalent theory T**, where T** is the theory that the world is different from T but a powerful being is manipulating us to make us think that T is true.

things to investigate, so she created the world in such a way that it seemed to be much older and filled with all sorts of interesting and challenging cosmological questions.

H1 Blood is pumped throughout my body by my heart.
H2 I don't have a body or a heart. All there is is my brain, floating in a nearly empty region of space. It was created when just the right sorts of particles happened, just by chance, to align in just the right sort of way to create a brain that would give rise to an experience like the one that I am having right now, which includes seeming to remember things like learning that blood is pumped throughout my body by my heart.

E1 Humans evolved from primates.
E2 There are no such thing as primates. I am part of a computer simulation run by an advanced civilization. The programmers included evidence of primates, and evidence that humans evolved from primates, in the simulation to see what psychological affect it would have on those who are part of the simulation.

In each of these cases, the first claim in the pair is something that is a standard commitment of our best science. The second claim, however, is also compatible with all of the data that we have collected—it is empirically adequate. (Or it would be if it were spelled out in more detail.) When scientists choose between these pairs of theories, then, they are making a choice that is underdetermined by the evidence.

There are numerous places in the literature where you can find philosophers expressing concern about these kinds of examples of underdetermination. Ladyman (2012), for instance, calls them "artificial" and "parasitic." But note that there is an important distinction between the following two claims. On the one hand, you might claim that the above pairs of hypotheses are not genuine cases of underdetermination. On the other hand, you might claim that although these cases *are* genuine cases of underdetermination, they are easily handled because there is something obviously bad about one of the hypotheses in the pair. The fact that scientists don't spend a lot of time worrying about hypotheses like U2, H2, or E2 shows that at least one of these claims is true, but it doesn't tell us which one.

Take, for instance, Ladyman's claim that hypotheses like U2, H2, and E2 are "entirely parasitic in their empirical content on the beliefs they are proposed to call into question" (Ladyman 2012, 44). Ladyman argues that this shows that there is no need to take the kind of underdetermination that they give rise to seriously. But notice that one way of developing this idea is to say that these are genuine cases of underdetermination, they are just cases in which U2, H2, and E2 are ruled out on the basis of their being parasitic in the relevant sense.[9]

My own view is that we should treat these as genuine cases of underdetermination, but cases which are relatively easily handled. In part, this just seems obvious—on a straightforward definition of empirical adequacy, both of the hypotheses in each pair are empirically adequate (or could easily be made empirically adequate if they were spelled out fully). As a result, these are genuine cases of underdetermination. Indeed, the only reason I can think of for trying to resist these cases as genuine cases of underdetermination is if you were worried that there was no way of designing extra-empirical principles that rule out U2, H2, and E2, and thus that dramatic skeptical consequences would follow. But I do not think that we should be so worried. Indeed in Chapter 5, I argue for a specific account of the feature that U2, H2, E2 (and similar hypotheses) have that allows scientists to either dismiss them quickly or never actively consider them at all. So the reader who finds these kinds of cases discomfiting is encouraged to pay particular attention to that chapter. In the meantime, we should remain optimistic that we can admit that these are genuine cases of underdetermination without descending into outright skepticism.

3.2 Extra-Empirical Principles in Science

Here's where we stand so far. Scientists regularly face cases of underdetermination—cases where there is more than one theory that is compatible with the data. It follows that insofar as they make a choice between empirically adequate theories in these cases, they are a making a choice for

---

[9] Ladyman doesn't elaborate on what he means by 'parasitic,' but presumably the idea is that quite a bit of the content of U2 is unspecified, and the way that we would go about specifying that content would be to read it off of U1. But note that U2 looks parasitic in this way only because we already believe U1. If we instead started with a belief in U2, U1 could just as reasonably be accused of being parasitic.

some reason that goes beyond compatibility with the data. They are making a choice, in other words, based on some extra-empirical reasoning.[10]

It's worth noting, of course, that sometimes scientists do not choose between empirically adequate rivals. In Newtonian physics, for instance, there is no way to detect whether the universe as a whole is moving with some constant velocity or whether it is at rest. Any and all theories of the universe's motion will be empirically adequate, as long as they do not say that the universe is accelerating. In response to this situation, physicists just ignored the question of whether the universe is moving and how fast. There was no reason for choosing one particular empirically adequate theory of this type over another, so they didn't make a choice.

In many other cases, however, including the examples in section 3.1, scientists *do* make a choice. Galileo chose the heliocentric model of the solar system over the Ptolemaic model. Einstein chose special relativity over the Lorentzian alternative. Geologists put forward specific theories about the internal structure of the Earth. Virtually all contemporary scientists accept U1, H1, and E1 instead of U2, H2, and E2. Since all of these cases involved competing theories that are (or were at the time the choice was made) empirically adequate, scientists must be engaging in some extra-empirical reasoning when they make these choices.[11]

A natural starting point to take here is to think of extra-empirical reasoning as involving principles that satisfy the following schema:

Extra-empirical principle schema. When choosing between two or more empirically adequate theories, choose the theory that has feature F.

---

[10] Readers who are wondering about the distinction between two theories both being compatible with the data and two theories being equally well-confirmed by the data, note that I discuss confirmation theory (and reasons for thinking confirmation theory also involves extra-empirical reasoning) near the end of this chapter. It is also worth noting that the distinction between empirical and extra-empirical reasoning might admit of borderline cases. A good example of an aspect of scientific practice that might be a borderline case is the process of data cleaning, through which inaccurate and duplicate data is removed from a data set and messy data is reorganized. Thanks to Peter Tan for this example.

[11] Using the word 'reasoning' here suggests that scientists explicitly recognize these competing theories and, moreover, recognize them as genuine competitors. But this need not be so. It might be that in some cases of underdetermination scientists never fully recognize the theories, or recognize them but ignore them as irrelevant. Note that the literature on the relationship between underdetermination includes an extensive debate on whether underdetermination is genuine in cases where the alternatives are unconceived, but this is primarily relevant to those who are using underdetermination in order to argue against scientific realism (see, e.g., Stanford 2006 and Chakravartty 2008).

Where F ranges over various features that a theory might have that go beyond empirical adequacy. These features may well include the familiar theoretical virtues—like simplicity, explanatory power, elegance—and combinations thereof. But more generally, F ranges over any feature of theories that go beyond empirical adequacy.

One of the main contentions of this book is that figuring out which extra-empirical principles play an important role in standard scientific methodology is a challenging and complex process. Scientists receive little to no explicit training in the extra-empirical aspects of the scientific method, and when they try to explicitly articulate what kinds of extra-empirical criteria are relevant, they often disagree. Moreover many of the cases where there is clear consensus about the application of some extra-empirical principle are historical, and it's quite difficult to tease apart what exactly was going on in each case.

Consider again the choice between the Ptolemaic, the heliocentric, and the Tychonic models of the solar system in the early 17th century. An oft-repeated story is that the heliocentric model was chosen because it was simpler—it didn't require the kind of epicycles that were such a famous feature of the Ptolemaic system. But Copernicus's own version of the heliocentric model actually had more epicycles than Ptolemy's. Copernicus included them because he was attempting to hang on to one of the central principles of Aristotelian physics which said that heavenly bodies always moved in uniform circles. It wasn't until Kepler's theory that there was a heliocentric model without epicycles. And depending on the specific notion of simplicity that one has in mind, one could even make the argument that Kepler's theory was not obviously any simpler than Ptolemy's or Copernicus's—after all, Kepler's theory involved moving from thinking about circular orbits to elliptical orbits, and allowed that planets travel with non-uniform speed. So insofar as one wants to defend Copernicus's or Galileo's choice of the heliocentric model—both of which occurred before the development of Kepler's theory—as instances of standard scientific practice, those choices cannot have involved any straightforward appeal to simplicity.[12] And even after Kepler's theory was developed, it isn't entirely obvious how to evaluate the relative simplicity of the competing models.

---

[12] Cohen (1985, 55) says that Galileo accepted the heliocentric model sometime before 1597, i.e., before he made his observations with the telescope and before Kepler published his laws.

Perhaps the only obvious way in which Copernicus's version of the heliocentric model was better than Ptolemy's is that it allowed Copernicus to calculate certain physical quantities that could not be calculated in Ptolemy's model—in particular the distance between each planet and the sun and the period with which each planet orbited the sun.[13] This suggests that perhaps the extra-empirical principle that was motivating Copernicus and Galileo involved choosing among empirically adequate theories on the basis of *empirical fecundity*—the extent to which a theory generates novel predictions, even if those predictions are untestable at the time. But then one would need to wrestle with the historical fact that if one sets aside Copernicus and Galileo, few other scientists accepted the heliocentric model until after Kepler published his laws. If empirical fecundity is an important aspect of extra-empirical scientific reasoning, why didn't more scientists get on board with the heliocentric model at an earlier date?[14]

All of this is by way of demonstrating that extracting clear extra-empirical principles from scientific practice is going to be challenging, even in relatively well-known cases like this one.[15] Indeed, I won't spend much time discussing this particular case of underdetermination in what follows because I think the historical nuances are just too complex. Depending on whose choice of the heliocentric model over alternatives you are interested in—Copernicus's in the early 16th century? Galileo's in the late 16th century? The majority of early astronomers, at some point in time that isn't entirely clear?—as well as what background claims you make about the context in which those choices took place and what features of the models you focus on, you can argue that the choice of the heliocentric model over alternatives was the result of an extra-empirical principle that features pretty much any theoretical virtue you like.[16]

At the same time, the challenge of extracting clear extra-empirical principles is not one that methodological naturalists can ignore. Insofar as you are committed to the view that metaphysicians should, whenever possible,

---

[13] Cohen (1985, chapter 3).

[14] One possible answer is that it was politically dangerous to endorse the heliocentric model, given the theological ramifications. My point is just that there is quite a bit of nuance here.

[15] Note that I discuss the choice of special relativity over empirically adequate alternatives in more detail in Chapter 6.

[16] As I will say more about in section 5.3, one thing that I do think this case clearly demonstrates is that scientists do not take unification with existing physics to be a requirement when choosing between empirically adequate theories. All versions of the heliocentric model under discussion here involved a dramatic split with existing Aristotelian physics. Bueno and Shalkowski (2020) have a nice discussion of this point.

use the same methodology that scientists use, and insofar as you intend to continue doing metaphysics, it is incumbent on you to have a clear account of scientific methodology, and specifically of the extra-empirical principles that scientists deploy. The purpose of the case studies in the next three chapters is to give some examples of how this challenge might begin to be met, and some models for how to carry out further investigation.

Although it may be obvious by this point, it is worth emphasizing that in attempting to meet this challenge we cannot simply gesture toward some loose combination of theoretical virtues as playing a role in scientific theory choice and consider our work done. Consider again the quotes in the introduction, where Paul says, "Scientific theorizing... relies on a priori reasoning involving simplicity, elegance and explanatory strength" (Paul 2012, 19) and Sider, Hawthorne, and Zimmerman describe the extra-empirical standards used by scientists as "simplicity, comprehensiveness, elegance, and so on" (Sider et al. 2008, 8). As I read them, Paul and Sider et al. are suggesting that scientists make use of extra-empirical principles that involve appeals to theoretical virtues, but leaving the work of figuring out what precisely these principles are for another time. This is precisely the kind of work to which I am trying to contribute with the case studies in the next three chapters. Another way of reading these quotes, however, is as saying that there is nothing more to extra-empirical reasoning in science than a loose appeal to some vague combination of theoretical virtues. On this kind of view, standard scientific practice involves the following extra-empirical principle:

Theoretical virtues. When choosing between two or more empirically adequate theories, choose the theory that is best with respect to some combination of simplicity, elegance, and explanatory power, and other theoretical virtues.

Theoretical virtues might sound attractive, but this principle cannot be all there is to extra-empirical reasoning in standard scientific practice for the simple reason that it is not precise enough. There are of course cases in which there is no widespread agreement about which of several competing empirically adequate theories is best. (The current situation with respect to non-relativistic quantum mechanics is an excellent example of this.) But at least sometimes standard scientific practice involves a clear consensus around one particular theory. And the kind of loose appeal to theoretical virtues involved in the principle above cannot underwrite this kind of consensus. Unless you say something more about what kind of simplicity, elegance, and explanatory power is relevant, what other theoretical virtues play a role, and in what way all of these should be combined, you can justify nearly any possible theory choice on the basis of an appeal to theoretical virtues.

As a demonstration of this point, consider Otavio Bueno and Scott Shalkowski's (2020) recent paper "Trouble with Theoretical Virtues," in which they argue that if one applies the above *theoretical virtues* principle in a straightforward way to several historical scientific cases, you get the wrong result—you get the result, for instance, that physicists should have stuck with the Ptolemaic model instead of shifting to a heliocentric model, and that they similarly should have continued to endorse Newtonian physics instead of accepting non-relativistic quantum mechanics in the early to mid-20th century.

About the choice between the Ptolemaic and the heliocentric models, for instance, Bueno and Shalkowski write:

> The standard ways of assessing the relative virtuousness of their respective theories would not support Copernicus's over Ptolemy's, despite the falsity of the latter. Ptolemy's astronomy was the first ever unification of physics and astronomy... The resulting theory was [also] explanatory (it systematically accounted for the motion of planets as orbiting in circles around a stationary Earth, thus preserving appearances), and simple (since all celestial motion was circular). (Bueno and Shalkowski 2020, 462)

And about the choice between Newtonian mechanics and quantum mechanics, they write:

> After all, (non-relativistic) quantum mechanics does not satisfy the theoretical virtues, despite the impressive empirical success of the theory. The theory is not simple, since it is highly counterintuitive, and requires a number of distinctive mathematical procedures. It introduced a new disunity into physics, since it is inconsistent with relativity theory. Even though it successfully predicted a number of new phenomena, its explanatory power is suspect, given its multiple, incompatible interpretations. (463)

What is important to notice in the present context is that in these passages Bueno and Shalkowski are making substantive assumptions about the relevant notions of simplicity, explanatoriness, and unification, and about the way in which these theories combine. Consider, for instance, the suggestion in the first passage that explanatoriness is satisfied merely by preserving appearances, or the suggestion in the second passage that simplicity is importantly related to intuitiveness. I'm not saying that either of these claims is incorrect, but I think they involve substantive assumptions, which someone who wished to use theoretical virtues to defend the actual historical choices of physicists could reject. Or consider Bueno and Shalkowski's observations about the way in which the existing physical theories in both of these cases were plausibly more unified than the new physical theories that were eventually adopted. Here too, an advocate of theoretical virtues might be able to avoid the argument by focusing on a different type of unification, but notice that they could also simply accept Bueno and Shalkowski's claims about unification but argue that in the relative weighting of simplicity, explanatoriness, and unification, unification counts for little—it's largely a tiebreaker.

The point, again, isn't that Bueno and Shalkowski are wrong about the verdicts that theoretical virtues returns in these cases—it's that theoretical virtues can be interpreted in a wide range of ways, some of which will return the verdicts that Bueno and Shalkowski identify, and some of which will not.[17] Whatever the principles are that govern extra-empirical reasoning in science, therefore, must be more precise. All of which is to say that methodological naturalists have quite a bit of interesting work ahead of them.

3.3 Extra-Empirical Principles in Metaphysics

So far in this chapter I have argued that scientists often choose between theories when that choice is underdetermined by the data, and that when they do so, their choice involves some extra-empirical reasoning. The final step of my argument is to establish that we should expect the extra-empirical methodology that scientists use—whatever it turns out to be—to have a

---

[17] This was Kuhn's view of his own list of theoretical virtues. He wrote that "two men fully committed to the same list of criteria for choice may nevertheless reach different conclusions" (Kuhn 1977, 358). See Schindler (2022) for further discussion.

The concern that I am raising about theoretical virtues is similar to a concern raised by Pablo Acuña. Acuña writes, "Theoretical virtues, such as simplicity and explanatory power, are usually context-dependent," and also that "there is no clear and universally accepted hierarchy between non-empirical features: is simplicity more important than explanatory power or vice versa?" (2014, 296). But whereas Acuña takes these points to be an argument against extra-empirical reasoning playing any important role in scientific theorizing, I see them only as reasons to think that extra-empirical reasoning must be more specific than what is captured by theoretical virtues.

widespread impact on metaphysical theorizing. To some extent, the proof of this claim will be found in Chapters 4–6 when I go through three specific case studies. But let me say something general at this point about why this expectation is reasonable.

Overall, I take the point here to be fairly straightforward. On the way of thinking about things that was spelled out above, standard scientific practice involves an appeal to principles that satisfied the following schema:

Extra-empirical principle schema. When choosing between two or more empirically adequate theories, choose the claim that has feature F.

Where F is some theoretical virtue or combination of virtues like simplicity, explanatory power, or elegance—but where those virtues are carefully defined and defended and their hierarchy is made explicit. The key observation that is relevant at this point, then, is that many, if not all, metaphysical debates involve choosing between competing claims that *also* differ with respect to similar kinds of extra-empirical features. If we adopt principles that involve prioritizing (or de-prioritizing) theories with particular combinations of these features, we should expect that to have a widespread impact on metaphysical theorizing.

This, I take it, is enough to make it reasonable to expect methodological naturalism to have a significant impact on metaphysical theorizing. But there are at least three points at which philosophers who are not inclined toward methodological naturalism might try to identify disanalogies between metaphysics and science that would undermine this expectation. I will discuss these potential disanalogies below.

Before I do, let me emphasize the difference between what I am arguing for in this chapter and several nearby, but distinct claims, which are not my target. What I am arguing for in this chapter is that because of the role that extra-empirical reasoning plays in scientific methodology, it is reasonable to expect methodological naturalism to impact metaphysical theorizing in interesting and substantive ways. This is importantly different from either of the following claims:

For some particular theoretical virtue (or set of virtues) T, T works in science in roughly the way that most metaphysicians think that it does.

> For some particular theoretical virtue (or set of virtues) T, the way that T plays a role in scientific methodology licenses the standard way in which metaphysicians appeal to T.

The recent literature contains a number of compelling critiques that target these kinds of claims.[18] But these critiques are entirely compatible with the position that I am defending here. My own view is that contemporary metaphysicians are often mistaken about what methodological naturalism entails because they haven't thought carefully enough about scientific methodology. That is not a count against methodological naturalism. Instead it is a reason for thinking that methodological naturalism, once it is properly applied, has the potential to yield surprising results.

In addition, note that nothing in my argument commits me to the claim that methodological naturalism will give us the resources to decisively settle *all* or even most metaphysical debates. This is certainly not the case given our current, relatively underdeveloped understanding of the extra-empirical criteria that play a role in science. Nor do I think that there's any reason to expect that a more careful examination of the history of science is likely to yield a set of criteria that will choose a clear winner in all metaphysical debates—that would be overly optimistic. But similarly, to suspect, given just what has been said so far, that the relevant extra-empirical criteria will rarely or even never impact metaphysical theorizing is to be overly pessimistic. My own view, as demonstrated in Chapters 4–6, is that methodological naturalism will yield substantive and surprising results when correctly applied to a range of contemporary metaphysical debates. But I'm entirely open to the idea that methodological naturalism will also leave some metaphysics debates unsettled.[19]

Empirical Vetting as a Potential Disanalogy

Let's turn now to three potential disanalogies between scientific and metaphysical theorizing that might be used to block the impacts of methodological

---

[18] See, e.g., Saatsi (2017) and Thomasson (ms) on metaphysicians' appeals to inference to the best explanation (which I will say more about in Chapter 4) and Sober (2009), Huemer (2009), and Willard (2014) on metaphysicians' appeals to simplicity.

[19] In this way I am happy to accept the kind of epistemic dismissivism advocated in Bennett (2009) as a live possibility in at least some cases (although I disagree with Bennett about whether this kind of dismissivism should be applied to the debate about the existence of composite objects, as will be clear in Chapter 5).

naturalism. Consider first the following concern raised in James Ladyman's paper, "Science, Metaphysics and Method":

> [Paradigm examples of metaphysical debates] are decoupled from anything but the most general and common empirical content and bear no relationship to any research programmes in current science. These disconnections break the continuum between high theory and metaphysics. (Ladyman 2012, 48)

Here is a way of making this concern into an objection to the argument that I have presented in this chapter. First, let's use the term *empirical vetting* to describe a process by which a group of candidate theories is narrowed down to a smaller group of empirically adequate candidate theories by the process of collecting empirical data and using that data to eliminate members of the initial group. Next, let's suppose that the way in which extra-empirical reasoning plays a role in science is via principles that satisfy the following schema:

> *Extra-empirical principle schema (with empirical vetting).* When choosing between two or more empirically adequate theories, all of which have been empirically vetted, choose the claim that has feature F.

Here again, F ranges over extra-empirical features of theories. F may involve familiar theoretical virtues like simplicity, explanatory power, elegance, for instance—but insofar as it does, those virtues are carefully defined and their hierarchy is made explicit.

Last, let's assume that metaphysical debates involve candidate theories that are not empirically vetted. It follows that the extra-empirical principles that play a role in scientific theorizing just do not apply in metaphysics.

In reply to this potential worry let me first note that in order to be sure that there really is an objection here, we need to confirm that the empirically adequate alternatives in scientific debates are, in general, empirically vetted, while the empirically adequate alternatives in metaphysical debates are not. In order to do so, we would require a more precise notion of empirical vetting. Certainly, some metaphysical debates seem sensitive to empirical data. This is most obvious in the case of metaphysical debates that are adjacent to science, like metaphysical debates about space and time or the nature of consciousness. A particularly good example would be the way in which data about the frequency and nature of illusions and hallucinations plays a role in shaping theories of perception. But even metaphysical debates that are less adjacent to science are still sensitive to some empirical data—if only the way that things seem to us. Think about how much easier compositional nihilism would be to defend if it didn't look to us like the world was full of composite objects. Or how much more difficult it would be to argue that time travel is metaphysically impossible if we in fact experienced the world as Billy Pilgrim does in *Slaughterhouse-Five*. The data that is relevant to metaphysical debates is usually relatively easy to collect and to incorporate in the initial design of one's metaphysical theory.[20] But that doesn't mean that it isn't playing some role. Even Ladyman himself seems to acknowledge this. When he writes that metaphysical debates are "decoupled from anything but the most general and common empirical content," he seems to be admitting that metaphysical debates are sensitive to *some* empirical data—it's just data that is "general and common." So in order for there to be an objection here we would need to spell out the notion of empirical vetting in such a way that general and common empirical data is not sufficient.

It is also worth noting that some scientific debates plausibly do not count as empirically vetted—especially when it comes to contemporary physics. Richard Dawid, for instance, has argued that "physics is losing contact with empirical testing. While microphysics was driven by a continuous stream of empirical data throughout most of the twentieth century, recent decades have witnessed the increasing importance of theories whose characteristic predictions lie far beyond the reach of contemporary experimental testing" (Dawid 2013, 1). And Dawid has gone on to argue for a particular account of how what he calls "non-empirical theory assessment" (or, in more recent work, "meta empirical theory assessment"; see Dawid 2022) can and should work in contemporary physics. There are of course alternatives ways of thinking about the status of contemporary physics, as well as criticisms of both Dawid's specific proposal and the idea of non-empirical theory assessment in general.[21] The point here is just that it is far from a given that all scientific debates will count as empirically vetted, especially if we haven't clearly specified what empirical vetting consists in.

---

[20] Although see, for instance, attempts by philosophers who deny that time passes to explain why it seems to us that time passes. (An especially clear example is Paul 2010, but there are many others who take a similar line.)

[21] See the papers in Dardashti et al. (2019) as well as Dawid (2022) for discussion.

Perhaps more importantly, it's also worth thinking about why a certain extra-empirical principle would be a guide to the truth (or to useful theories, or whatever epistemic feature you think is relevant) *only* when choosing between empirically vetted rivals. This is a tough question, and answering it fully would probably require taking a clear stand on the deeper epistemic justification of whatever extra-empirical principles are relevant. In the meantime, the question is where the burden of proof lies. Consider, for instance, the following quote from Katherine Hawley:

> After all, it would be peculiar if metaphysical claims could be subject to non-empirical reasons, but only when they also had empirical confirmation or disconfirmation. For example, if a metaphysical theory's being simple counts defeasibly in its favour, then presumably it does so whether or not the theory is also subject to scientific investigation. (Hawley 2006, 453)

Here I am in agreement with Hawley. If some extra-empirical criteria count in a theory's favor after empirical vetting, the default position should be that those criteria count in a theory's favor in general.

For those who remain worried about empirical vetting, let me extend a potential concession, inspired by the discussion in Alyssa Ney's paper "Neo-Positivist Metaphysics." Ney agrees that, even if there is little empirical vetting, "there doesn't seem to be justification for saying that while such virtues are truth-conducive in the case of science, they are not truth-conducive in the case of metaphysics." But she remains worried about the degree of confirmation that we end up with in the metaphysical case. She writes:

> Suppose that observation gave us some very small reason for thinking that some planet's orbit was in the shape of a circle around its sun, and it gave some equally tiny reason for thinking that the planet's orbit was in some distinct, complicated shape S, and it gave us some equally tiny reason for thinking the planet's orbit was in another complicated shape S', and so on for very many hypotheses. Like I said, our empirical evidence is very, very small for each hypothesis. Let's grant that out of all of these many shapes, the circle is the simplest. I don't see that this would give us reason to think that we now have established this scientific hypothesis that the shape of the planet's orbit is circular. This isn't to say that the simplicity of the circle hypothesis doesn't increase its confirmation with respect to its rivals. But it seems a large stretch to say that when the empirical evidence is so small,

we can appeal to the theoretical virtues and this will allow us to settle hypotheses. (Ney 2012, 74–75)

Ney presents this case as a concern for the methodological naturalist, but I see it in a more positive light. Above I argued that it is not so clear that the degree of empirical vetting is dramatically different in metaphysics than it is in science. But even if you disagree with me about this, what Ney's example suggests is that you should still think that methodological naturalism will give us *some* reason for accepting one metaphysical theory over another; those reasons will just be relatively weak. They won't, as she puts it, "settle" the debate. But my sense is that metaphysical debates are rarely considered "settled" anyway. Metaphysicians put forward reasons for preferring one view rather than another, but they rarely take those reasons to be decisive. So even if we accept Ney's view, methodological naturalism can still have an impact on metaphysical theorizing.

Strong Underdetermination as a Potential Disanalogy

In "Science, Metaphysics and Method," Ladyman (2012) also claims that there is an important disanalogy in the type of underdetermination that shows up in scientific theorizing and the type of underdetermination that shows up in metaphysical theorizing. The distinction is between *weak* and *strong* underdetermination.[22]

> *Weak underdetermination.* A scientific claim is weakly underdetermined by the data if the data that scientists have collected up to now is also compatible with an alternative claim.

> *Strong underdetermination.* A scientific claim is strongly underdetermined by the data if any possible set of data that scientists could collect would also be compatible with an alternative claim.

---

[22] This distinction is sometimes also expressed as a distinction between 'transient' and 'permanent' underdetermination. See Sklar (1981).

Ladyman claims that cases of underdetermination between candidate metaphysical theories are always strong, while cases of underdetermination between candidate scientific theories are always weak.[23]

Here is how one could use this potential disanalogy to block the argument that we should expect the extra-empirical principles that play a role in scientific theorizing to also have an impact on metaphysical theorizing. Suppose that the way in which extra-empirical reasoning plays a role in science is via principles that satisfy the following schema:

Extra-empirical principle schema (with weakness). When choosing between two or more weakly empirically adequate theories, choose the claim that has feature F.

Then, assuming it is true that choices between metaphysical theories are all strongly underdetermined, none of the extra-empirical principles that play a role in scientific theorizing will have any effect on metaphysical theorizing.

There are a number of things to say in response to this worry. First, it is worth emphasizing that we don't actually have a clear distinction here unless we say something more about how to understand the relevant sense of 'could' in the definition of strong underdetermination.[24] Consider, as a particularly confounding case, the fact that there are experiments—indeed experiments that are quite straightforward to describe—that would allow us to experimentally distinguish between the orthodox interpretation of non-relativistic quantum mechanics, according to which the collapse of the wavefunction is caused by measurement, and the Ghirardi-Rimini-Weber (GRW) interpretation, according to which collapse is spontaneous.[25] These experiments would, however, take something like 10^8 years to complete and would need

---

[23] Ladyman (2012, 43ff.). Note that Ladyman also tries to point to a disanalogy between metaphysical and scientific theories on the grounds that the former are global and the latter are merely local. I admit to being pretty befuddled by this local/global distinction. Consider Lewis's (1986) modal realism—the view that concrete possible worlds exist. Or van Cleve's (2008) universalism about composition—the view that any two or more things compose a further thing. Compare these views with Maxwell's theory of electromagnetism, or with Darwin's evolutionary theory. In what way are the former global, while the latter are not?

[24] Ladyman recognizes this. See Ladyman (2012, 43).

[25] All you need is a double slit experiment with both slits open but in which it takes the electrons 10^8 years to reach the detection screen and in which the electrons don't interact with anything else during this time. According to the orthodox interpretation, since there is no measurement taking place during the experiment, the electrons will be in a superposition when they hit the detection screen. This will give rise to an interference pattern. According to the GRW interpretation, there is a very high probability that the superposition will spontaneously collapse during the experiment, so there will be no interference pattern.

to be fully isolated from their surroundings during that time. Should we consider the choice between GRW and the orthodox interpretation to be weakly or strongly underdetermined? This is a really hard question to answer.

Second, and more importantly, it is not obvious that all cases of scientific underdetermination are merely weak, while all cases of metaphysical underdetermination are strong. Regarding investigations of the Earth's internal structure that make use of gravimetry, for instance, Belot writes that "corresponding to any given configuration of the gravitational field external to the Earth is a vast (infinite-dimensional) family of possible internal structures (some of which will differ very dramatically from one another)" (2015). He goes on:

> Of course, in the case of the Earth and other planets, we have ways of finding out about internal structure other than by making measurements at the surface (in principle, if not in practice). But the techniques considered above [e.g. gravimetry] can be used to study the internal structure of the Sun and other stars . . . And in the stellar case there is considerable plausibility to the idea that we never will (and never could) have any way of investigating internal structure directly. (459)

In other words, Belot takes the choice between certain competing models of the internal structure of the sun and other stars that are developed using gravimetric data to be strongly underdetermined.[26] And of course the point is even more obvious for cases of underdetermination like the choice between U1 and U2 (or H1 and H2 or E1 and E2). These cases are strongly underdetermined.

Especially in the latter group of cases, it might be tempting to try to argue that these instances of theory choice don't count as truly scientific in the relevant sense. But notice that what is important here isn't whether we call a particular instance of theory choice "scientific" or "metaphysical." It's the claim that if an instance of theory choice involves strong underdetermination, then one cannot justifiably appeal to extra-empirical principles to make a choice between the candidate theories. Surely we don't want to think that scientists are making a mistake when they use gravimetric data to put forward theories of a star's internal structure, or that any of us are making a mistake when

---

[26] On my view the choice between special relativity and a theory that is like special relativity in all respects except that it includes the claim that there is a privileged reference frame is strongly underdetermined. But note that Ladyman claims that special relativity was empirically confirmed by the observation of the Compton Effect (2012, 44), and a full discussion of our disagreement would take us too far afield, so I won't lean too heavily on that example here.

we assert that the universe started with the big bang 13.8 billion years ago, or that blood is pumped throughout my body by my heart, or that humans evolved from primates.

All that by way of arguing that quite a few cases of scientific underdetermination are actually strongly underdetermined. There's also good reason to think that cases of metaphysical underdetermination may well be weak. Most obviously, consider the many historical metaphysical theories that didn't have any testable consequences at the time they were debated, but which were eventually ruled out by scientific data as technology and our concepts evolved. A particularly nice example here is the choice in ancient Greek philosophy over how many elements there were.[27] For the ancient Greeks, these debates probably seemed like they were strongly underdetermined. They had no idea what kind of data would allow them to settle the debate empirically. But of course now we have quite a bit of empirical data that allows us to decisively rule out many of the candidate answers to this question.

Compare that historical case, in which a metaphysical debate turned out to be merely weakly underdetermined, to the debates in contemporary metaphysics about whether there are composite objects. As discussed above, compositional nihilism requires that there be mereological simples—entities that cannot be broken down into further parts. At the moment, fundamental physics seems to leave the existence of such simples as an open question.[28] Could there be empirical data in the future that settled this question? I see no reason to think the answer to this question is no.[29]

Robust Theories as a Potential Disanalogy

Here is a third potential disanalogy. On the face of it, scientific theories look quite different from metaphysical theories. In particular, the latter usually involve some mathematical formalism, while the former often take the form

---

[27] Williamson (2007) talks about this choice, and the analogy with contemporary debates in philosophy, in the last chapter of *The Philosophy of Philosophy*.

[28] My reading is that Ladyman and Ross (2007) take this question to be answered and the answer to be yes, which would of course make this a metaphysical debate that turns out, even on their view, to have been merely weakly underdetermined.

[29] McKenzie (2011) argues that it follows from S-matrix theory that there are no fundamental particles. But here, as is often the case, it is difficult to tease apart the empirical from the extra-empirical aspects of the theory, and thus to determine whether McKenzie's argument, if successful, shows that there is *empirical* data that answers the question of whether there are mereological simples.

of a simple claim like "There are concrete possible worlds" or "It is never the case that two or more things compose a third thing."

Here's how one could use this potential disanalogy to block the argument that we should expect the extra-empirical principles that play a role in scientific theorizing to also have an impact on metaphysical theorizing. Let a *robust theory* be the kind of theory that we usually find in science—a complex set of claims about the world that are captured at least in part in a mathematical formalism. And suppose that the way in which extra-empirical reasoning plays a role in science is via principles that satisfy the following schema:

Extra-empirical principle schema (with robustness). When choosing between two or more robust theories, all of which are empirically adequate, choose the claim that has feature F.

Assume, furthermore, that choices between scientific theories are always between robust theories and that choices between metaphysical theories are never between robust theories. It follows that none of the extra-empirical principles that play a role in scientific theorizing will have any effect on metaphysical theorizing.

Here again, however, I think that it is far from obvious that the robust/non-robust theory distinction maps neatly onto the distinction between science and metaphysics. First and foremost, a more careful understanding of the notion of a robust theory will almost certainly lead to what philosophers of science call the *semantic view*, according to which theories are sets of models, and where models involve formal relations like mathematical relations which can be more or less isomorphic to the relevant features of the world that the theory purports to be about.[30] But there is no obvious reason for thinking that metaphysical theories cannot also be sets of models in the same sense. Consider, for instance, the mereological relations that are under debate when we consider the metaphysical question of whether there are composite objects—just like the dynamical equations of Newton's laws, these mereological relations can be more or less isomorphic to the world.

This point—that metaphysical theorizing involves model building in the same way that scientific theorizing does—is discussed in detail in Paul (2012). Paul writes:

---

[30] See Suppes (1960). French (2020) gives a nice overview of this debate.

> Employing the semantic approach in the service of metaphysics, a metaphysical theory can be understood as a class of models, where the models are composed of logical, modal and other relations relating variables that represent n-adic properties, objects, and other entities. (Paul 2012, 12)

In addition to the example of mereological relations, she includes an example from causal theory:

> Consider a simple counterfactual theory of the causal relation that holds that c is a cause of e if and only if, had c [not] occurred, e would not have occurred. Models for the theory are structures that represent events standing in relations of counterfactual dependence (descriptions of these models are descriptions of these structures). If these structures are isomorphic to causal relations in the actual world, the theory represents actual causal relations and gives an account of the nature of actual causation. (13)

So it is far from obvious that metaphysical theories are, in general, not robust. In addition, I don't think it's plausible that scientific theories *are* always robust. Or at least, insofar as we are interested in extra-empirical reasoning in science we should not restrict our attention only to cases that involve choices between robust theories. Scientists often put forward, dispute, and accept relatively simple claims about what the world is like—they accept, for instance, that some entity exists even though they don't have a complete and formal account of that entity. The first case study that I discuss below (in Chapter 4) involves an examination of several of these kinds of cases, including Faraday's introduction of the electromagnetic field, Pauli's introduction of the neutrino, and contemporary cosmologists' acceptance of dark energy. All of these cases are ones in which scientists were plausibly committed to straightforward claims like "Neutrinos exist" before they had a formal model of the neutrino.

In what follows I will continue to use the term 'theory' in a relatively loose way that encompasses both robust and non-robust theories. Those who have a strong preference for restricting the term 'theory' so that it applies only to robust theories are welcome to do so. When I write things like "When choosing between two scientific theories..." these readers will want to reinterpret this as "When choosing between two scientific theories or *claims*..." What is important for present purposes, in any case, is that the distinction between robust and non-robust theories does not neatly track the distinction between scientific and metaphysical theories, and thus cannot be used to identify a disanalogy between science and metaphysics that would block the expectation that the extra-empirical principles that play a role in the former will also play a role in the latter.

Disanalogies That Undermine Content Naturalism

Finally, when considering potential disanalogies between extra-empirical reasoning in science and extra-empirical reasoning in metaphysics, remember that the discussion of methodological naturalism in this chapter is taking place in a context in which we have also accepted content naturalism. (For the time being, at least. I revisit that assumption in Chapter 8.) What I am interested in, here and throughout, is the version of methodological naturalism that follows from and is held in conjunction with content naturalism. And some potential disanalogies don't just undermine methodological naturalism; they undermine content naturalism as well.

As an example, consider Bueno and Shalkowski's claim that the extra-empirical criteria as deployed in scientific theorizing are merely pragmatic while metaphysical theorizing as usually understood is aimed at the truth (Bueno and Shalkowski 2020, 461).[31] If you agree with this view—that scientific theory choice that is based on theoretical virtues is merely pragmatic, while metaphysical theory choice aims at the truth—that would be an important disanalogy between science and metaphysics that could potentially block any impacts of methodological naturalism. But it would also undermine any reason you might have for being a content naturalist. Why should you care if your favored metaphysical theory conflicts with the content of our best science if what you—qua metaphysician—are after is a true account of what the world is like, while scientists are after an account of what the

---

[31] Note that Bueno and Shalkowski don't just state this claim; they also give an argument for thinking that theoretical virtues are merely pragmatic. They ask, "If empirical considerations are always given the upper hand, what grounds are there for thinking that the virtues [i.e. the extra-empirical principles] are indicators of truth at all? Exactly why can they never aggregate to outweigh the significance of at least some empirical data?" (Bueno and Shalkowski 2020, 459). This is an interesting set of questions, and one to which I don't have a response. But note that it's perfectly compatible with my argument that the theoretical virtues are merely pragmatic when used in science—but given that we are assuming content naturalism, they also need to be merely pragmatic when used in metaphysics. Note also that Schindler (2018 and 2022) has argued that sometimes certain extra-empirical criteria, notably unification, *do* trump empirical accuracy (and that practicing scientists themselves recognize this).

world is like that is (at least in part) chosen because it is easy to use? Here and throughout the book, I am not attempting to argue for methodological naturalism. I am arguing that if you are a content naturalist, then you should also be a methodological naturalist. So potential disanalogies that undermine methodological naturalism while also undermining content naturalism are not a threat to the project.

3.4 Consequences for the Practice of Metaphysics

None of the above concerns, then, is sufficient to undermine the claim that we should expect the extra-empirical principles that play a role in standard scientific methodology to also be relevant to many metaphysical debates. Indeed, at this point it seems that we have no positive reason for thinking that there is *any* such thing as a metaphysical debate that is wholly insulated from scientific considerations. Even if the content of our best scientific theories does not have any consequences for a particular metaphysical debate, the methodology of our best science may well have such consequences.

This attitude has serious implications for the way in which we do metaphysics. First and foremost, it undermines what has become an increasingly standard division between naturalistic and "analytic" or "a priori" metaphysics. According to the methodological naturalist, all metaphysical debates have the potential to be naturalistic. Insofar as there is a division between naturalistic and analytic metaphysics, that division will become clear only after a thorough investigation of scientific methodology. Second, if scientific considerations are potentially relevant to any and all metaphysical debates, via the kind of extra-empirical principles described above, then metaphysicians without a strong background in science and the history and philosophy of science should proceed with caution. Indeed it seems that in order to do well-founded metaphysics one *must* take on substantial commitments with respect to the history and philosophy of science. Or at least, one cannot be a metaphysician who advocates for some metaphysical claims over others unless one has such commitments. (One might, of course, still be able to get away with mapping out possible positions.)

This might sound worrisome to some metaphysicians, especially those without a strong background in science and the philosophy of science. But it is also worth pointing out that the dissolution of the distinction between naturalistic and analytic metaphysics will also go a long way to undermining common concerns about the legitimacy of the field of metaphysics as a whole. Consider, for instance, Ladyman and Ross's contention that for analytic metaphysics, the "criteria of adequacy for metaphysical systems have clearly come apart from anything to do with the truth" (Ladyman and Ross 2007, 13) or Amanda Bryant's (2020) claim that large swaths of contemporary metaphysics are "epistemically inadequate." Perhaps the criteria that metaphysicians in fact currently deploy are problematic in the ways that these authors identify, but given the discussion above, they need not be. There is no reason why, in principle, one cannot have a perfectly naturalistic metaphysical debate about universals or composition or personal identity or the many other paradigm cases of what Ladyman, Ross and Bryant consider to be problematic metaphysics. As long as those debates involve positions that differ with respect to the extra-empirical principles that play a role in scientific theory choice, then we will have reasons—naturalistic reasons—for taking one side in those debates over the others. Or so says the methodological naturalist.

3.5 Two Alternative Ways of Thinking about Extra-Empirical Reasoning

The way that I have presented the material above is, on my view, a natural starting point for thinking about extra-empirical reasoning in scientific theorizing. But extra-empirical reasoning might also play a role in scientific theorizing in other ways. In this section, I will present two of these alternative ways. The key thing to note is that on both of these alternative approaches it is still the case that (a) there is some extra-empirical reasoning in scientific theorizing, and (b) we can expect the relevant kind of extra-empirical reasoning to also affect metaphysical theorizing.

Alternative Approach 1: It's All about the Data

As many philosophers of science have recognized, it is possible for the data that is relevant to the evaluation of a theory to itself be *theory-laden* in various ways. On the one hand, as Paul Feyerabend (1962) noted, the meaning of different observational terms can be different according to different theories; the meaning of the term 'mass', for instance, is different in Newtonian physics than it is in relativistic physics. On the other hand, Kuhn (1962) claimed that what scientists themselves perceive may be different depending on the theory they endorse. A Ptolemaic astronomer will see the sun setting, while a Copernican will see the horizon rising to meet the sun.[32] With respect to the second of these notions, we can distinguish between various ways of presenting (or describing or recording) a piece of data that are more or less theory-laden.

Consider, for instance, the following claim:

S The sun moves across the sky from the east to the west.

If we take S literally as a piece of data, then it follows from the data itself that the sun moves. Compare this with:

S1 The sun appears to move across the sky from the east to the west.

S1 is neutral between a view on which the sun appears to move across the sky because it in fact orbits the Earth and a view on which the sun appears to move because the Earth rotates on its axis. If one were comparing two theories, one of which included the claim that the sun moves around the Earth and one of which included the claim that the Earth rotates, only the former would be empirically adequate with respect to S. But both theories would be empirically adequate with respect to S1.

Throughout the discussion above, I have been assuming that when we are wondering whether a theory is empirically adequate we should always describe the relevant data in the most theory-neutral way possible. Similarly, when wondering whether a particular instance of theory choice is underdetermined by the data, we should always construe the relevant data in a way that is neutral between the competing theories, if possible. Often this will require us to think about the relevant data as being merely a claim about the way that things appear to us, as in S1. Consider, for instance, the choice between H1 and H2:

H1 Blood is pumped throughout my body by the heart.

---

[32] This example is from Reiss and Sprenger (2020), which includes a helpful discussion of theory-ladenness in general.

H2   I don't have a body or a heart. All there is is my brain, floating in a nearly empty region of space...

Our everyday way of talking about the data that is relevant to H1 and H2—which presumably includes claims about observations of the human body—is compatible only with H1. According to H2 there is no such thing as a human body. So on the approach I am advocating, in order to tell whether H1 and H2 are both empirically adequate we need to think about the relevant data as merely my having an experience as of making certain observations of the human body (or as of remembering others telling me about those observations, or what have you). Both theories, then, are empirically adequate. The choice between them is a choice that is underdetermined by the data.

Some philosophers prefer a *thicker* notion of data, according to which it is part of the data that we collect, for instance, that there are human bodies. But note that even these philosophers presumably do not think that *every* piece of data is precisely as it appears to us. For instance, they presumably do not think that it is literally part of the data that the sun moves. Or that it is literally part of the data that the straight stick that I place in water suddenly becomes bent. Instead they think that it is part of the data that the sun *appears to* move and the stick *appears to* bend. So these philosophers need to have some principles that determine which aspects of the way things appear to us are actually part of the data, and which aspects are not. These principles will be extra-empirical. (Perhaps it would make sense to call them *pre-empirical.*)

What this shows is that the way you think about the data we collect in the laboratory—and in particular how theory-laden you think that data is—will not affect the claim that there are extra-empirical principles that play a key role in scientific theorizing. It will affect only where you think those extra-empirical principles come into play. If you have what I have called a thick account of data, then you will think that the extra-empirical principles come into play in determining what the data is. And empirical adequacy will then be a fairly high bar for a theory to cross. If you have a thin account of data, then you will think that empirical adequacy is quite easy to achieve, and you will think that extra-empirical principles come into play in deciding between empirically adequate theories.

It's also worth noting that it isn't obvious how this "thick data" approach to extra-empirical reasoning could account for all instances of extra-empirical reasoning in science. Consider, for instance, the choice between special relativity and the Lorentzian alternative, or between the different geological theories of the Earth's internal structure discussed in section 3.1. On any plausible construal of the data, these cases still involve multiple empirically adequate alternative theories, and thus even once the data is fixed, these cases must involve some further kind of extra-empirical reasoning.

Alternative Approach 2: It's All Just Confirmation Theory

A different way of trying to understand extra-empirical reasoning is as involving instances of confirmation theory. The thought here is that there is an important distinction between a theory being empirically adequate, and that theory being supported by the evidence to a certain degree. Two theories that are both empirically adequate might still be supported by the evidence to a different degree.[33]

One way of spelling out this approach is to argue that standard scientific practice involves the following principle:

> *Bayesian theory choice.* When choosing between two empirically adequate theories, choose the theory that has a greater degree of confirmation as determined by Bayes' theorem.

The first thing I want to emphasize here is that as I have defined the term 'extra-empirical reasoning', Bayesian theory choice itself involves extra-empirical reasoning—it involves reasoning that goes beyond determining whether or not a theory is empirically adequate. Bayesian theory choice is therefore not in and of itself a challenge to methodological naturalism. It's just a different way of thinking about what methodological naturalism will involve—instead of involving the kinds of extra-empirical principles that I am focusing on, it will involve instances of Bayesian theory choice.

There is a challenge in the vicinity, however. This challenge arises if it is the case both that Bayesian theory choice is the *only* kind of extra-empirical reasoning in science and if Bayesian theory choice cannot be effectively deployed to choose between metaphysical theories. If both of these conditions obtain,

---

[33] This is why, in general, I have been avoiding the term 'empirically equivalent'. As some philosophers use this term two theories are empirically equivalent as long as they are able to accurately predict all the same data. As other philosophers use it, two theories are empirically equivalent only if they are supported by the data to the same degree.

then the aspect of scientific methodology that involves extra-empirical reasoning will not have any impact on metaphysical debates. One can (and perhaps should) be a methodological naturalist, but that commitment won't change anything of significance in metaphysical theorizing.

Is it the case both that Bayesian theory choice is the only kind of extra-empirical reasoning in science and that it cannot be effectively deployed when choosing between metaphysical theories? A full discussion of these points is not possible in the space I have here, but here are a few key points to help convince even committed Bayesians that they too should be interested in methodological naturalism and be open to it having significant consequences for metaphysical theorizing.

First and foremost, let's consider the claim that Bayesian theory choice is the only kind of extra-empirical reasoning in science. I think we should be skeptical of this claim for the straightforward reason that many of the paradigm historical cases in which scientists chose between empirically adequate theories are obviously not cases in which those scientists had Bayes' theorem in mind. It follows either that we think these cases were in fact not successful instances of extra-empirical reasoning in science, which strikes me as unacceptably radical, or that we think that at least some instances of extra-empirical reasoning in science do not involve the explicit use of Bayes' theorem. As I discuss further below, it might be that there is an underlying Bayesian justification for the use of more straightforward extra-empirical principle like Occam's Razor or inference to the best explanation. And that the historical cases inherit their justification from Bayes' theorem in this indirect way. But if that is the case, then there is no reason whatsoever for thinking that Bayesian theory choice won't be impactful for metaphysical theorizing—indeed Bayesian theory choice will underwrite the use of the kinds of extra-empirical principles that have been (and will continue to be) the focus of my discussion.

Let's turn now to the claim that the kind of extra-empirical reasoning involved in Bayesian theory choice won't be impactful in metaphysical theorizing. There are a number of reasons to doubt this claim. First and foremost, consider the way in which prior probabilities are assigned in Bayesian theory choice. Suppose H is some hypothesis and E is some evidence. Then Bayes' theorem says that the way to determine the probability of H given E is as follows:

$$P(H|E) = \frac{P(E|H)\, P(H)}{P(E)}$$

Here, P(H) and P(E) are the prior probabilities, and P(E|H) is the likelihood of the evidence given the hypothesis.

As we can see just from this equation, the value of P(H|E) will depend on the prior probability that one assigns to H and to E (see Huemer 2017 for discussion). So Bayesians need to say something about how to assign prior probabilities. Presumably this will involve rules like "Split your credence equally among all available options," or "Assign lower probability to theories that are radically different than the way the world appears," or "Assign higher probability to especially simple theories," and so on.[34] But these rules are extra-empirical principles, and they seem like precisely the kinds of principles that will also impact various metaphysical debates.

In addition, it is worth noting that an important current project in formal epistemology is the attempt to give an underlying Bayesian justification for various extra-empirical principles involving different theoretical virtues. Following van Fraassen's (1989) contention that inference to the best explanation is incompatible with Bayesian theory choice, some philosophers have argued one can give a Bayesian justification for IBE.[35] Others have attempted to identify a Bayesian justification for choosing more unified or simpler theories.[36]

As an illustrative example, consider Huemer's (2009) claim that simpler theories will in general make more specific predictions than complex theories. As a result, the likelihood of a given bit of evidence given a simple hypothesis is going to be higher than the likelihood of the very same evidence according to a more complex hypothesis. As Huemer puts it,

"Since [the simple hypothesis] is compatible with a smaller range of data, it assigns a higher average probability (or probability density) to those possible sets of data that it allows. [A competing complex hypothesis] spreads its probability over a larger range of possibilities, consequently assigning

---

[34] Note that some Bayesians (so-called *subjective Bayesians*) think there are no rules whatsoever governing the way in which we assign prior probabilities, except that they satisfy the axioms of probability theory. Insofar as one is a subjective Bayesian, however, it becomes especially hard to understand any consensus around historical instances of theory choice in science.

[35] Sometimes these kinds of arguments rely on the idea, mentioned above, that inference to the best explanation may inform the assignment of priors. What I am focused on here is the idea that Bayesian theory choice might provide a justification for following IBE in general, not just in the assignment of prior probabilities. See Henderson (2014), which contains a nice overview of this discussion, as well as Okasha (2000), Lipton (2004), Weisberg (2009), and Pettigrew (2021).

[36] See Myrvold (2017) on unification. On simplicity, see Rosenkrantz (1977), Schwarz (1978), and Huemer (2009).

a lower probability (density), on average, to the possibilities that it allows" (Huemer 2009, 221).

Look again at Bayes' theorem as presented above. And suppose we are comparing two competing hypotheses, a simple hypothesis S and a complex hypothesis C. According to Huemer's argument, $P(E|S)$ is going to be higher than $P(E|C)$. Assuming there is no significant discrepancy in priors, this means that $P(S|E)$ will be greater than $P(C|E)$.

What this type of argument shows, insofar as it works, is that there is an underlying Bayesian justification for the use of a certain extra-empirical principle—in this case an extra-empirical principle involving a certain kind of simplicity. And this is all to the good insofar as the methodological naturalist is concerned. Indeed, insofar as one is a Bayesian, this may help clarify exactly what the extra-empirical principles are that are playing a role in scientific theory choice—it might help clarify, for instance, precisely what type of simplicity is relevant insofar as you think that one ought to prefer simpler theories to complex ones. (Note that I say quite a bit more about simplicity in Chapter 7.)

There is, of course, more to say about the relationship between Bayesian theory choice and the kinds of extra-empirical principles that have been the focus of the discussion so far and that I will argue for in detail in the chapters to come. But I take what has been said here to be enough to establish that Bayesians too should be interested in methodological naturalism and expect it to have significant consequences for metaphysical theorizing.

In closing let me emphasize that it may well turn out that the right way to think about extra-empirical reasoning in science will involve elements of both of the alternative strategies discussed in this section alongside the extra-empirical principles that are the focus of my discussion. In any case, the main conclusion of this chapter—that we should expect methodological naturalism to have a significant impact on metaphysical theorizing—still stands, regardless of which of these approaches (or combination of approaches) you favor. In the case studies that follow I will continue to focus on instances of extra-empirical reasoning that fit the initial pattern I described: after the collection of data, various extra-empirical principles are deployed in order to choose between empirically adequate theories. But this is not to rule out the importance of other aspects of extra-empirical reasoning.

3.6 Recap

Let's recap where we are so far.

In Chapter 1, I argued that most metaphysicians are already committed to content naturalism and that if one is committed to content naturalism then one should also be committed to methodological naturalism. This left readers with two options. They could either revise their commitment to content naturalism or also take on a commitment to methodological naturalism. In Chapter 2, I argued that content naturalism was attractive enough that taking on a commitment to methodological naturalism should be the default response to this choice. In this chapter, I have been arguing that if we adopt methodological naturalism we should expect it to have an impact on metaphysical theorizing. The core idea is that standard scientific methodology involves the application of extra-empirical principles, and that we should expect those principles to also impact debates in metaphysics. Indeed, given the kinds of extra-empirical principles that are plausibly at play (principles involving various theoretical virtues), our default assumption should be that no debate in metaphysics is fully insulated from scientific considerations. Even if it seems to have nothing whatsoever to do with the content of our best science, a metaphysical theory might well be disqualified based on an argument involving scientific methodology.

All of that is fairly abstract. In the next three chapters I will go through three instances of methodological naturalism at work in different ways. Before I do so, let me make a few final comments.

The first comment is by way of moderating the reader's expectations. Although I am about to demonstrate some applications of methodological naturalism, at no point in this book will I attempt to give a complete and final accounting of the extra-empirical principles of standard scientific practice in their entirety. The purpose of this book is to begin this work and demonstrate just how surprising some of the results are likely to be.

Along these lines, I also want to emphasize that the core argument of the book, which I have presented in these initial chapters, is independent of the particular results that I discuss in the case studies. I welcome disagreement from other philosophers about the specific extra-empirical principles that I focus on in these case studies and their potential consequences for metaphysical debates. These sorts of disagreement exemplify the kind of work that methodological naturalists should be engaged in.

Third and finally, let me note that once one is explicit about the role of extra-empirical principles in standard scientific practice, it is natural for those of us with realist tendencies to get uneasy. For any given extra-empirical criteria, what guarantee do we have that those criteria are good guides to the truth? Moreover many of the candidate extra-empirical criteria seem anthropocentric in a worrying way—why should it matter whether a theory is elegant, for instance, except insofar as it gives us some particular joy in using it?[37] These principles seem to be quite clearly the right principles if what we are looking for is theories that are useful or psychologically satisfying. But why should we think that they are good guides to the truth?

I think these worries are real, but in the context of the present discussion they can and should be set aside. As the content-methodology link in Chapter 1 shows, insofar as one is a content naturalist, then one should think that *whatever* methodology scientists use in choosing between empirically adequate theories is also a good methodology for choosing between metaphysical theories. And in this chapter, and the ones that immediately follow, we are assuming content naturalism and exploring its consequences. As such, worries about the justification for the extra-empirical principles that play a role in scientific theorizing are—at least for the moment—moot. In Chapter 8, we will return to the question of whether a better response to the content-methodology link would be to give up content naturalism. Readers who are chary of the kinds of extra-empirical principles discussed above (or in the case studies to come) may end up being more inclined toward that option.

---

[37] Indeed, in the late 20th century, the prevalence of underdetermination was used to argue against scientific realism (van Fraassen 1980). The worry was that if cases of underdetermination are endemic in science, and if no choice between empirically adequate theories can be justified, then there is no reason to think that our best scientific theories are literally true. What is at issue, then, is whether we can in fact make justified choices between empirically adequate theories. (See Laudan and Leplin 1991.)

4

Case Study

Pattern Explanation and the Governing Account of Laws

Let's start with a case study that shows how methodological naturalism can affect a metaphysical debate that is clearly adjacent to science. A long-standing debate in the metaphysics of science is regarding the status of laws of nature. According to some philosophers, laws of nature are mere descriptions of what goes on in the world. According to others, laws of nature are something more. They govern, or determine (in some metaphysically robust sense of 'determine'), what happens. On the governing account of laws, laws "*do* something—they govern what goes on in the universe" (Beebee 2000, 580). Laws that govern are "entities that *produce* or *govern* and thereby *explain* the evolution of events" (Loewer 2012, 118); they are "responsible for (i.e., produce, necessitate, etc.) the regularities exhibited in nature" (Hildebrand 2019, 3).

This debate, while continuing to inspire an extensive literature, seems to be mostly deadlocked—especially with respect to standard naturalistic considerations. Nearly everyone involved in the debate is well-informed with respect to the content of our best scientific theories and wishes to respect that content. But the content of our best scientific theories appears to be largely neutral with respect to the choice between a governing and a non-governing account of laws.

The methodology of science, however, is not neutral. In this chapter, I will argue that a particular extra-empirical principle plays an important role in standard scientific practice. And if one were to use this principle to choose between metaphysical theories, one should endorse the governing account of laws. If one is a methodological naturalist, then, one should think that laws govern.

Here is a plan for what follows. In sections 4.1 and 4.2, I show how a certain principle—the pattern-explanation principle—plays a role in standard scientific practice. In section 4.3, I show how the pattern-explanation principle, when deployed in metaphysics, leads to the governing account of laws.

In section 4.4, I discuss some concerns about the argument that stem from the recent literature on explanationism. In section 4.5, I show how this specific way of arguing for the governing account of laws affects the debate between Humeans and non-Humeans about laws of nature. Finally, in section 4.6, I discuss how all this might guide us in a further analysis of the governing relation.

4.1 The Pattern-Explanation Principle

In this section I will argue that a certain principle—I will call it *the pattern-explanation principle*—constrains theory choice in physics. The rough idea behind the pattern-explanation principle is that one of the most serious flaws that a scientific theory can have is to leave a well-established pattern unexplained. Indeed, even if the only way in which one can explain some well-established pattern is to introduce a type of entity that is metaphysically weird or novel, it is worth the cost of introducing such entities.

To be more precise, let's introduce the notion of *explanatory adequacy*. Recall from the earlier chapters that a theory is *empirically* adequate if it accurately predicts the data that we actually observe. (I have often glossed this as: empirically adequate theories are "compatible" with the data.) A theory is *explanatorily* adequate, by contrast, just in case it does not leave robust patterns in the data that we have collected without an explanation. Here, then, is the initial version of the principle:

> *The pattern-explanation principle—initial version.* When choosing between competing empirically adequate theories, if one theory is explanatorily adequate and the others are not, choose the theory that is explanatorily adequate even if that theory involves the introduction of some type of entity that is metaphysically weird or novel.[1]

---

[1] Readers may wonder about the relationship between the pattern-explanation principle and inference to the best explanation. I say more about this in section 4.4. In conversation I sometimes hear the view that non-explanatorily adequate theories are not genuine theories at all. As far as I can tell, understanding explanatory adequacy in this way would not change anything of philosophical significance in what follows—and, if anything, would make the principle even more plausible. This view would, however, make applications of the pattern-explanation principle (at least in this initial version) look more like what Richard Dawid calls "No Alternatives Arguments" (see Dawid 2013 and Dawid et al. 2015). An interesting project for further research would be exploring the connections between the pattern-explanation principle and Dawid's No Alternatives Arguments in more detail.

I have defended versions of the pattern-explanation principle before (Emery 2017b and 2019), and for my own part I take this principle to be a fairly obvious component of scientific methodology. But since, as I will show below, the principle has significant consequences for contemporary metaphysics, a more detailed defense is warranted. In what follows, then, I will argue for the pattern-explanation principle by examining three historical cases of scientific theory choice in which metaphysically weird or novel entities were introduced. A natural reading of each of these cases suggests that the reason why these entities were introduced was that otherwise a well-established pattern in the data would go unexplained. At the very least, then, these examples, taken together, put the burden clearly on those who wish to deny the pattern-explanation principle to articulate an alternative story about what is going on in each of these cases.

Here is the first example. In the early 20th century, experimental physicists observed that energy and momentum appeared to be lost during a certain type of radioactive decay, called *beta decay*. The total energy and momentum of the observed particles before the decay was not equal to the total energy and momentum of the observed particles after the decay. This pattern was surprising—it appeared to be a violation of the conservation of energy and of momentum—but by the late 1920s it was well established in the data.

In 1930, Wolfgang Pauli suggested that the explanation for this apparent loss of energy was that the particles that scientists observed after the decay were not in fact all of the particles that were produced.[2] There was, in addition, a theretofore unobserved particle—the *neutrino*—that was produced by beta decay, and the energy and momentum of the neutrino that was produced was such that once it was included, energy and momentum were conserved.

Pauli's hypothesis was initially controversial—Pauli himself called it a "desperate remedy." Why was this? For all that has been said so far, several factors may have been at play. For one thing, there was no direct experimental evidence for the existence of neutrinos. For another, neutrinos are strange in several ways. They were thought to be massless,[3] to have no charge, and to barely interact with other particles. As Laurie M. Brown, a physicist and historian of physics, writes, when Pauli first proposed the neutrino, "any other elementary constituent [besides the proton and electron] of the atom

---

[2] See Pauli's open letter to the December 1930 group meeting in Tübingen, reprinted in *Physics Today* 31: 9 (1978). In this letter, Pauli referred to the unobserved particle that he postulated as the "neutron." Enrico Fermi later introduced the name "neutrino."

[3] Experiments in the late 1990s showed that neutrinos in fact have non-zero mass.

would have been considered superfluous, and to imagine that another might exist was abhorrent to the prevailing natural philosophy" (Brown 1978, 23).

When Pauli first suggested his hypothesis, there was still an alternative explanation of the apparent energy and momentum loss in beta decay that didn't require the introduction of the neutrino. This alternative hypothesis, which had been proposed by Niels Bohr, was that the conservation of energy and the conservation of momentum were probabilistic laws similar to the second law of thermodynamics.[4] Although these principles were very likely to hold in most scenarios, there was at least some probability of their being violated. Bohr's suggestion was that the way in which these violations occurred was such that we should expect the observed energy loss in beta decay.

However controversial Pauli's proposal was initially, by the mid-1930s, the neutrino had gained widespread acceptance.[5] What had changed in the intervening years? It was still the case that there was no direct experimental evidence for the existence of neutrinos.[6] And it was still the case that neutrinos were weird and surprising in the ways described above. Instead the key development seems to have been that in 1933 there were new experimental results that showed that Bohr's alternative explanation for the apparent energy loss in beta decay was not viable.[7]

That scientists' attitudes toward the neutrino would change dramatically after these new experimental results ruled out Bohr's alternative explanation (even though little else had changed) would, of course, make perfect sense if

---

[4] See the discussion in Brown (1978).

[5] Pauli himself seems to have wavered with respect to how plausible he found his own hypothesis between 1931 and the fall of 1933. His remarks at the Seventh Solvay Conference in October 1933 seem to mark the turning point at which he is fully confident. See Brown (1978), which includes a translation of Pauli's 1933 remarks.

[6] Direct experimental evidence would not be obtained until the Cowen-Reines experiment in 1956.

[7] These experimental results were due to Charles Drummond Ellis and Nevill Mott, who showed, in mid-1933, that the beta-ray spectrum has a sharp upper limit. See the description and citations in Brown (1978).

Another important development that happened around this time is that in 1934 Enrico Fermi published a quantitative theory of beta decay built around the neutrino. (See Wilson 1968, which contains an English translation of Fermi's 1934 paper, which was published in German in *Zeitschrift für Physik*.) In conversation I have sometimes had philosophers of science suggest that it was Fermi's development of this theory, as opposed to the ruling out of Bohr's alternative hypothesis, that made the neutrino acceptable to physicists. My reading is that what Fermi's theory did was show that Pauli's hypothesis could in fact do the explanatory work for which it was designed, and thus the suggestion that Fermi's theory was an important step in the acceptability of the neutrino is not in conflict with the pattern-explanation principle. For what it is worth, there is also an oft-repeated anecdote about Fermi's paper, according to which it was initially rejected by *Nature* because "it contained speculations too remote from reality to be of interest to the reader" (see Pais 1986, 418 and Close 2012, 24). This suggests that Fermi's development of the theory itself was not enough to make the neutrino acceptable.

the pattern-explanation principle was a constraint on theory choice in fundamental physics. Neutrinos may have been strange, and the evidence for them indirect, but once scientists needed them in order to explain the pattern of apparent energy and momentum loss in beta decay, they were accepted.

In this particular case, one might make the claim that the sort of entity being introduced, however strange, was still in some sense a member of a group of entities that was already accepted by physicists—however unusual a particle, the neutrino was still a particle. But other examples show that when faced with a well-established pattern that would otherwise go unexplained, physicists are also willing to introduce entities that are largely or even wholly novel. The physicists introducing these entities may have hypotheses about what they are, but they admit that these hypotheses are tentative and likely to be overturned. What they seem to be sure of is that there is *something* that explains the pattern in question, whatever sort of thing it turns out to be.

Along these lines, consider a second historical example: the electromagnetic field as introduced by Faraday in 1852 and further developed by Thomson and Maxwell in the later half of the 19th century. Previously, physicists observing various kinds of electromagnetic phenomena had thought that such phenomena had to be explained by some kind of action at a distance, similar to the way that, at the time, gravitational phenomena were thought to be explained. But Faraday had experimental evidence that he thought suggested that electromagnetic phenomena were importantly different from gravitational phenomena, and that showed that the former were not apt for explanation by action at a distance.[8] (In particular Faraday was moved by the observation that electromagnetic forces were exerted along curved lines, and by the fact that at least some electromagnetic forces were affected by the medium between the object exerting the force and the object that the force was acting on.) Instead, Faraday suggested, electromagnetic phenomena must be explained by an electromagnetic field.

What was an electromagnetic field? Faraday himself put forward two different hypotheses about how it might be understood. According to one, the space between the object exerting the magnetic force and the object upon which the force was acting was permeated by an ether of contiguous, unobservable particles which transmitted the force from the acting object to the object being acted upon. According to the other, there were physical lines

---

[8] See Faraday (1852), especially pp. 413–417; Maxwell (1861); and Hesse (1961), especially chapter 8.

of force which existed independently of any particles and which connected the acting object to the object being acted upon.[9] Maxwell, meanwhile, suggested that the electromagnetic field should be understood as a fluid filled with vortex tubes, where the arrangement of the tubes corresponded to the direction of the lines of the field and the angular momentum of the tubes corresponded to the intensity of the field.[10]

Both Faraday and Maxwell were clear that their accounts of the electromagnetic field were tentative at best. And on any of these accounts, the electromagnetic field was a novel entity, and one whose metaphysical nature was not clearly understood. To posit such an entity was surely metaphysically costly—these physicists would have avoided it if they could. Nonetheless Faraday and those who followed him were convinced that there had to be something that explained electromagnetic phenomena, and given that it could not be accounted for in terms of any other, previously accepted entities, they were, however reluctantly, willing to introduce something wholly novel. Again this would make sense if the pattern-explanation principle was a part of standard scientific methodology.

Nor is the case of the electromagnetic field a historical anomaly. If anything, the point is even more vividly illustrated by a final, contemporary example. In the late 1990s, observations from the Hubble Telescope showed that the rate at which the universe is expanding is accelerating. According to the NASA Science website, "No one expected this, no one knew how to explain it. But something was causing it." Indeed the site goes on to say:

> Theorists still don't know what the correct explanation is, but they have given the solution a name. It is called dark energy. What is dark energy? More is unknown than is known. We know how much dark energy there is because we know how it affects the universe's expansion. Other than that, it is a complete mystery. (Nasa Science 2023)[11]

---

[9] The discussion in Harman (1982, 78) is especially helpful in understanding these proposals.

[10] Harman (1982, 89). There is some controversy over how serious Maxwell was being when he proposed this account of the electromagnetic field in terms of vortex tubes. He sometimes said explicitly that this account was merely supposed to be illustrative or suggestive. But he was also explicit that the data he had collected required some kind of explanation. See the discussion in Harman, especially p. 92.

[11] See also Carroll (2007, lectures 14–17). Note that I am using the term 'dark energy' in an expansive sense that includes the possibility that dark energy just is the vacuum energy (or Einstein's cosmological constant). This seems to be relatively standard both in early discussion of dark energy (e.g., Turner 2000; N.B.: Turner is often credited with coining the term 'dark energy') and in more recent summary discussions (e.g., Carroll 2007), but note that some prefer to reserve the term 'dark energy' for those hypotheses that would provide a dynamical explanation that is distinct from the vacuum energy hypothesis. On my reading of the literature (supported by the citations above) there is not a

Here again we have the introduction of an entity that is weird—in this case an entity about which scientists know almost nothing—because without that entity there would be no explanation available for a well-established pattern in the data. In this case, physicists admit that they don't have much of an idea at all as to what dark energy is. They have hypotheses, of course, of one sort or the other. But any such hypotheses are tentative at best. What scientists seem to be convinced of is that there is *something* that explains the accelerating rate of expansion of the universe, and they use the name 'dark energy' to pick out that thing, whatever it is. Yet again, we see here an attitude that would make perfect sense if the pattern-explanation principle was a part of standard scientific methodology.

The thing that all of these examples have in common is that they involve the introduction of entities that are or were (at the time at which they were accepted) metaphysically weird or novel (or both). As such, the acceptance of these entities was a serious cost of the theory in which they appeared. Nonetheless, that cost was considered worth paying. Why? A highly plausible answer, especially when these cases are taken together as a group is: because without such entities, well-established patterns in the data would go unexplained, and, when choosing between competing empirically adequate theories, it is apparently more important to avoid leaving well-established patterns without an explanation than it is to avoid the introduction of some type of entity that is metaphysically weird or novel.

These are, of course, only three examples, and there is far more historical and scientific nuance in each case than I have been able to develop here. I am not claiming, therefore, that these examples prove anything decisive. But taken together these examples are at least highly suggestive. The burden is on those who want to reject the pattern-explanation principle to come up with new examples, or a reinterpretation of these examples, that supports their alternative view.[12]

---

consensus regarding the existence of dark energy if the term is being used in this more restrictive, dynamical sense.

[12] One thing that is important to recognize is that all three of the examples above involved physics, as opposed to other scientific contexts (including "higher-level" sciences). I say more about this in Chapter 7.

4.2 Pattern Explanation as Metaphysically Robust Explanation

The three examples above give us good reason to think that the pattern-explanation principle is a part of standard scientific methodology. The reader will notice, however, that I have said nothing so far about the notion of explanation that is at play in the pattern-explanation principle. And given how multi-faceted the notion of explanation is, we need to say at least something more about that notion if the principle is going to have any substance.

Consider, for instance, the following four ways in which we naturally use the word 'explains':

We say that A explains B when A provides us with some understanding of B.

We say that A explains B when A shows how B is part of a broader pattern of phenomena.

We say that A explains B when A causes B.

We say that A explains B when A grounds B.[13]

These ways of using the word 'explains' are fairly heterogeneous, spanning notions that are relatively metaphysically thin and largely subjective, like the notion of *understanding for creatures like us*, to notions that are metaphysically substantive and seemingly objective, like causal relations and grounding relations.

I think it would be a mistake to argue about which of these ways of talking captures the correct notion of explanation. Certainly in the case at hand we need not engage in anything so contentious. Instead we should focus on the question of what notion of explanation is at play in the pattern-explanation principle. Insofar as a well-established pattern gives rise to an explanatory burden, what sort of explanation is required in order to discharge that burden?

In order to answer this question we can look again at the historical examples discussed above. Although these examples don't obviously support a definitive,

---

[13] I do not claim that this list is exhaustive. I take the idea that explanation involves showing how an event fits into a broader pattern to capture the central idea behind a unification account of explanation, though I'm in principle open to there being a notion of explanation as unification that goes beyond pattern subsumption. See the next footnote for more.

singular reading of the notion of explanation at play in the pattern-explanation principle (e.g., it isn't the case that all three examples involve straightforward causal relations between the explanandum and the explanans), they do give us some insight into that notion. Here, for instance, is a fairly obvious point: the key feature of all three of those examples was that the entities that were introduced in order to explain the patterns in question were metaphysically weird or novel or both; as a result, those entities cannot have been said to do much by way of providing us with any further understanding of the patterns in question. Something other than mere understanding must be required in order to discharge the explanatory burden that these patterns create.

More generally, I claim that the historical examples discussed in the previous section give us good reason to think that when we are faced with a well-established pattern in the data, what we require is a theory that provides what I will call a *metaphysically robust explanation*—an explanation in which the explanans identifies the *reason why* the explanandum occurred.[14] Paradigm cases of metaphysically robust explanations are explanations that identify the cause or the ground of the explanans. Understanding, however, is neither necessary nor sufficient for a metaphysically robust explanation—sometimes the reason why something occurs is beyond our understanding, and sometimes our understanding can lead us astray with respect to the reason why something occurs. (I will say more about the second kind of explanation mentioned above—pattern subsumption—in a moment.)

My claim, then, is that the three examples discussed in section 4.1 do more than just support the initial version of the pattern-explanation principle. They also support the following version of that principle:

> *The pattern-explanation principle—final version.* When choosing between competing empirically adequate theories, choose the theory that does not leave well-established patterns without a metaphysically robust explanation, even if that theory involves the introduction of some type of entity that is metaphysically weird or novel.[15]

---

[14] As I understand it, my notion of metaphysically robust explanation is the same as the notion of *determinative explanation* as discussed in Taylor (2018). According to Taylor, a determinative explanation is an explanation that identifies "whatever metaphysically determines the explanation" (2018, 198), where causation and grounding are paradigm cases of metaphysical determination. Note that nothing I say here commits me to explanatory realism as defined by Taylor, which is the view that all explanations are determinative explanations.

[15] It is worth noting that there is quite a bit about the pattern-explanation principle that is as yet under-specified. In particular, I haven't said anything about what precisely counts as a "well-established pattern." As the notion is clear enough for present purposes without further elaboration, I will leave that elaboration to future work.

I find the notion of metaphysically robust explanation to be useful and thus find this way of phrasing the pattern-explanation principle to be illuminating. But I want to emphasize that the role that the metaphysical robustness of an explanation plays in my argument is only the role of a methodological shortcut. The key claim that I am making here is that the notion of explanation at play in the pattern-explanation principle should be determined by the examples that give us reason to endorse that principle in the first place. Suppose that we observe some well-established pattern, and someone tries to say that an explanation of type E is sufficient to explain that pattern. What I have suggested above is that a good way of testing whether an explanation of type E is in fact sufficient is to ask whether explanations of type E are metaphysically robust—whether they identify the reason why the explanandum occurred. But insofar as one finds questions about the metaphysical robustness of an explanation confused or otherwise difficult to adjudicate, one can skip it entirely and instead ask: Would an explanation of type E have been sufficient to explain the observed patterns in the examples discussed in section 4.1? If not, then explanations of type E are not sufficient to explain the pattern in question in the sense of explanation that is at play in the pattern-explanation principle.

Here is an example (one that is relevant to the discussion of Humean accounts of laws of nature in section 4.5). Suppose one observes a bunch of Fs, all of which are G, and suppose one tries to explain that pattern by claiming that *all* Fs are G. This corresponds to a pattern-subsumption account of explanation according to which if A shows how B fits into a broader pattern, then A explains B.[16]

Are pattern-subsumption explanations metaphysically robust? If A shows how B fits into a larger pattern, does A thereby identify the reason why B? I think the answer to this question is pretty clearly no. We can show how an event fits into a broader pattern of events without thereby identifying the reason why that event occurred. But we need not rely on this claim. We can consider instead the question of whether pattern subsumption would

---

[16] The idea that Humean laws might explain by way of pattern subsumption is discussed in Bhogal (ms). Sometimes Humeans claim that laws explain by unifying without giving the kind of detailed account that Bhogal gives (see, e.g., Loewer 1996), which of course leaves open the possibility that these other Humeans have some alternative account of explanation as unification in mind. That is fine. I am not arguing here that Humean laws cannot explain. My argument is just that in order to do so, they need to give an account on which laws provide metaphysically robust explanations in the sense required by the examples in section 4.1. If the Humean can accomplish this by making use of some version of the unificationist account of explanation, that doesn't undermine my argument. (It will mean, however, that the Humean must face the circularity worries described in section 4.5.)

have been sufficient to explain the sorts of examples that gave us reason for endorsing the pattern-explanation principle to begin with.

Consider, for instance, the fact that in all of our observations, the rate of expansion of the universe is accelerating. Here are two ways of trying to explain that pattern. First, one could introduce an entity as strange and poorly understood as dark energy. Second, one could simply claim that the rate of expansion of the universe is *always* accelerating. Surely if the second route had been a viable way of discharging the explanatory burden created by our observations, scientists would have taken it. But they didn't. This indicates that mere pattern subsumption is not sufficient to discharge the explanatory burden created by a well-established pattern.

Note that nothing that I have said here rules out the possibility that there are genuine explanations that are not metaphysically robust. I am happy to agree that explanations that merely facilitate understanding or subsume some phenomena under a broader pattern are genuine explanations. What I am claiming is that insofar as there are non-metaphysically robust explanations, they are not sufficient to discharge the explanatory burden created by a well-established pattern. When one observes such a pattern, one is pushed to identify the reason why the pattern occurs. Indeed the explanatory burden generated by such patterns is so substantial that it warrants the introduction of metaphysically weird or novel entities in order to establish that there is *some* reason why that pattern occurs, even if, all else being equal, we would prefer to keep such entities out of our metaphysics.

Note also that nothing that I have said here rules out the possibility that explanation stops somewhere. Perhaps the most common objection that I hear in response to the pattern-explanation principle and any particular application of it is the claim "But explanations must end somewhere!" But the pattern-explanation principle is compatible with this. The principle simply identifies where they should end—in particular, they should end somewhere that doesn't involve leaving a well-established pattern without an explanation.

4.3 What This Tells Us about Laws of Nature

So the pattern-explanation principle is a part of standard scientific methodology. Assuming, then, that we are methodological naturalists, the same principle ought to constrain theory choice in metaphysics as well. What follows with respect to the metaphysics of laws of nature? I claim that it follows that laws must govern. Here is why.

Suppose we are living in a Newtonian world. It is a law that $f = ma$. In such a world, in every observation that we make, it is always the case that the net force on an object equals the mass times the acceleration. That is a well-established pattern. Here is a question that it is natural to have: What is the *reason why* that pattern occurs? What, in other words, explains that pattern (in a metaphysically robust sense of explanation)? A natural response to this question is to say that the reason why the pattern occurs is that it is a law that $f = ma$. To endorse this response is to endorse the governing account of laws.

Newton's second law as a governing law. The fact that it is a law that $f = ma$ is the reason why $f = ma$ in all observed cases.[17]

According to the governing account of laws, laws are the reason why things happen the way that they do. They aren't mere summaries of events. Instead they explain those events, in a metaphysically robust sense. Let P be any well-established pattern. If it is a law that P, then, according to the governing account of laws, the fact that it is a law that P is the reason why P.[18]

Now, there are many questions that one might have about the governing account of laws. One might wonder, what is a law anyway? How can we be sure that it is the right kind of thing to play this explanatory role? What if in order to play this explanatory role, laws have to be entities of a sort that we would prefer not to allow into our metaphysics? What if in order to play this explanatory role, laws are such that we cannot give any metaphysical analysis of them at all?

These are all good questions. We would like to be able to answer them in a satisfying way. But according to the pattern-explanation principle, regardless of whether and how we end up answering them, none of these questions can give us a good reason for resisting the governing account of laws, at least not until we can come up with alternative explanations of the patterns in the data that the laws are supposed to explain. One cannot, for instance, reject the governing account of laws in favor of the following strategy:

---

[17] It is worth noting that nothing important hinges on the 'governing' label. If one has in mind a different notion of governance, one is welcome to use different terminology. All of the consequences discussed in the next section will still follow.

[18] More specifically, they determine patterns of events. Do they do so directly? Or do they determine patterns of events by determining the individual instances that constitute those patterns? I don't take a stand on this here.

The no-explanation strategy. There is no explanation for the fact that $f = ma$ in all observed cases.

Why not? Because this would violate the pattern-explanation principle.

And note that not just any alternative explanation will suffice. In order to satisfy the pattern-explanation principle, one needs an alternative explanation that is *metaphysically robust*. One cannot, for instance, reject the governing account of laws in favor of:

The pattern-subsumption strategy. The explanation of the fact that $f = ma$ in all observed cases is that $f = ma$ in *all* cases.

As argued in section 4.2, pattern subsumption is not sufficient to satisfy the type of explanation required by the pattern-explanation principle.

It may seem surprising that we can arrive at the conclusion that we should accept the governing account of laws without putting forward any account whatsoever about what laws are. But it follows from the pattern-explanation principle that if the only way to explain the pattern of instances of a law is by appealing to the law itself, then it doesn't actually matter what sort of entities laws are—it doesn't matter how weird or novel they may turn out to be or how little we understand them—we can be sure nonetheless that they exist and that they provide metaphysically robust explanations of patterns of their instances. If they did not, those patterns would go unexplained and the pattern-explanation principle would be violated.

Of course, nothing that has been said so far forecloses the possibility of giving a reductive, or at least an illuminating, metaphysical account of laws. Surely everyone who is party to the debate should think that, all else being equal, such an account is preferable to an account that takes laws to be primitive or otherwise mysterious. The upshot of the argument in this section is merely that *even if* it turns out that we can't give a reductive or illuminating account of laws, we still must accept their existence and we must still remain committed to at least one aspect of the role that they play—that they provide metaphysically robust explanations of patterns of their instances. Even if laws strike us as just as surprising and strange as the neutrino struck Pauli, even if we know as little about laws as Faraday knew about the electromagnetic field or contemporary cosmologists know about dark energy, we still have to accept laws—the kind of laws that can provide metaphysically robust explanations—into our metaphysics. To do otherwise would be to violate the pattern-explanation principle. And that is not something that, as methodological naturalists, we ought to do.

4.4 The Pattern-Explanation Principle, Inference to the Best Explanation, and Explanationism

In the next section, and the one following it, I will say some more about consequences of accepting the governing account of laws as laid out above. Before I do so, however, let me address a couple of concerns that one might have about the argument above.

First and foremost, a very natural question to have about the discussion so far is about the relationship between the pattern-explanation principle and inference to the best explanation. This is especially salient because of recent concerns about the idea that metaphysicians can justify their use of inference to the best explanation as a methodological principle on the grounds that scientists use inference to the best explanation as well. Following Saatsi (2017), let's call the view that scientists use inference to the best explanation when choosing between competing theories *scientific explanationism* and the view that metaphysicians are justified in using inference to the best explanation when choosing between competing theories *metaphysical explanationism*. At least on the face of it, scientific explanationism, combined with methodological naturalism, leads to metaphysical explanationism. But Saatsi and others (I will focus in particular on Amie Thomasson's manuscript "Should Ontology Be Explanatory") think that metaphysical explanationism is a mistake. Does this raise issues for the argument for the governing account of laws as laid out above?

My view is that it does not. I won't be able to go into detail regarding all parts of these arguments, but I will point out two important differences between my argument for the claim that metaphysicians should adhere to the pattern-explanation principle and the metaphysical explanationists' argument that they should be allowed to appeal to IBE because scientists do so as well.

First and foremost, note that there are important differences between the pattern-explanation principle and inference to the best explanation. In inference to the best explanation we often have several viable explanations, and we decide how to choose between them based on a further set of criteria. The pattern-explanation principle, by contrast, focuses on the choice between whether to explain a certain set of data at all, or to leave it unexplained. It may be the case that all candidate explanations have features that, all things considered, we would like to avoid. But because the alternative is to leave a robust pattern in the data unexplained, we accept one of those candidates anyway. Another way of thinking about the pattern-explanation principle, then, is not as an instance of inference to *the best* explanation, but as instead involving inference to the existence of *an* explanation.

Inference to the best explanation (IBE). If E1 and E2 are both candidate explanations for some phenomena, and E1 has features that make it a better explanation than E2, then we should accept E1.

Inference to the existence of an explanation (IEE). If a certain set of data has form F, we ought not leave that data without an explanation, even if all candidate explanations have features that would usually make us judge them to be relatively poor explanations.

So the pattern-explanation principle is distinct from inference to the best explanation. And some of the recent critiques of explanationism clearly target the use of the former in metaphysics without necessarily applying to the latter. Consider, for instance, Saatsi's critique of "the simple picture ... according to which scientists appeal to unification as a theoretical virtue much like metaphysicians do, via inference to the best explanation" (2017, 23). This "simple picture" is not a straw man. It was a key component, for instance, in Armstrong's argument for analyzing laws of nature as universals. (Armstrong wrote about his own argument, "The premiss required here is that . . . in the natural sciences what, before anything else, counts as a good explanation is something that unifies the phenomena" [1996, 235].) But as Saatsi points out, most sophisticated contemporary accounts of scientific explanation, including Woodward's (2003) counterfactual account and Strevens's (2008) kairetic account, raise significant issues for this simple picture. What is important for our purposes, however, is that even if Saatsi's argument here succeeds, it does little to undermine the claim that scientists use IEE in the way that I have suggested here, and in a way that supports the governing account of laws.

Of course, there is still the possibility that other aspects of Saatsi's or Thomasson's critique will extend from IBE to IEE.[19] One aspect of Saatsi's

---

[19] Although some of the metaphysical explanationists that Saatsi and Thomasson criticize (like Armstrong) clearly have IBE in mind, others at least sometimes sound like they are relying only on

argument that may be relevant here is his contention that IBE is actually the source of quite a bit of error across the historical scientific record. I discussed this point in detail in Chapter 2 and won't say anything more about it here, but the reader who is interested in how it impacts my argument is invited to revisit section 2.4. Instead I'll focus on a strand of argument that shows up in Thomasson's paper that seems to apply to IEE just as much to IBE.

Thomasson distinguishes between two different situations in which one posits an entity that has some explanatory impact. On the one hand, positing the relevant entities merely "enables," "enhances," or "simplifies" the explanations that the theory provides. On the other hand, positing the relevant entities genuinely "fuels the explanatory success" of the theory.[20] On Thomasson's view, when scientists posit entities they are doing the latter. But when metaphysicians posit entities they are often doing the former.

Now, on the face of it, this argument looks like it is targeting IBE, not IEE. On the face of it, the introduction of the neutrino, for instance, did not merely enable, enhance, or simplify an existing explanation of beta decay. Before Pauli introduced the neutrino scientists did not have an explanation of the energy lost in beta decay.[21] That is why Pauli was licensed in introducing such a strange entity. But let's set that aside and focus on the idea that the introduction of entities in order to meet an explanatory demand is legitimate only when that introduction meets the further condition of genuinely fueling the explanatory success of the theory. When is that condition met?

Thomasson attributes this condition to Katherine Hawley, who writes:

If a claim H is to be involved in generating a prediction in a way that entitles it to share in the confirmation which successful prediction brings [and so to 'fuel' its success] ... H must satisfy two conditions with respect to the generation of the prediction. First, it must be the case that the theory minus H cannot generate the prediction alone. Second, it must also be the case that

---

IEE. Consider, for instance, Chris Swoyer's explanationist argument for the existence of abstracta, in which he claims, "We often infer that something exists on the grounds that its existence would explain something that would otherwise be puzzling ... Such inferences seem common in science" (Swoyer 2008, 6). This sounds more like an appeal to IEE. (Though note that in other places Swoyer explicitly refers to his methodology as involving IBE.)

[20] Thomasson gets this terminology from Psillos (1999, 110).
[21] More carefully: after experimental results ruled out Bohr's alternative explanation, unless they accepted the neutrino, scientists did not have an explanation of the energy lost in beta decay.

there is no available, sensible alternative to H which could have done the work just as well. (Hawley 2006, 462)

How do these criteria interact with the pattern-explanation principle? It's hard to say, without knowing more about what counts as a successful prediction. But I think it's quite hard to give more content to this criterion in a way that both correctly captures what happened in the historical cases in section 4.1, while also generating the result that including governing laws does not yield successful predictions. (And remember, if the criteria, properly understood, yield the result that the historical cases that I described above were misguided—that Pauli shouldn't have introduced the neutrino, and Faraday shouldn't have introduced the electromagnetic field—then the methodological naturalist should take no interest in those criteria.)

Consider, for instance, the following fact: when you introduce an entity that provides a robust metaphysical explanation for some pattern, you thereby, in general, generate predictions about whether that pattern will continue. If the energy lost in beta decay is due to the fact that the relevant kind of decay produces a neutrino, then we should expect to continue to observe a loss of energy in these cases. Indeed in this case, little was known about the nature of the entity being introduced, other than that neutrinos were the reason why the relevant pattern in the data obtained. So this kind of prediction was, at least at first, the only kind of prediction that was generated.

But if this is the way in which the introduction of the neutrino (or the electromagnetic field or dark energy) generated successful predictions when it was first introduced, then note that the introduction of governing laws generate successful predictions in precisely the same way. If the pattern of instances of $f = ma$ is explained by the fact that it is a law that $f = ma$, then we can expect that pattern to continue.

Now, it's easy to imagine someone replying that this kind of prediction doesn't satisfy Hawley's second condition. For here is a sensible alternative to the hypothesis that it is a law that $f = ma$, which is that it is always the case that $f = ma$. Maybe this counts as a "sensible alternative that does the work just as well," and maybe it does not. But if it does, then notice that there were also sensible alternatives to the electromagnetic field and the neutrino and dark energy that do the work that those entities do just as well—namely those alternatives that said only that the patterns of data that are observed is part of larger patterns and therefore is expected to continue, without saying anything about the reason why those larger patterns obtained.

The situation is of course complicated somewhat by the fact that in the case of the neutrino and the electromagnetic field these entities eventually generated other novel predictions. But it is not at all historically obvious that these entities had generated other novel and successful predictions at the time at which they were accepted by the scientific community. Instead it seems that they were accepted on the basis of filling an important explanatory role. Certainly even at the time that they were introduced, scientists hoped that they would be able to generate novel predictions from these entities, but it does not seem that the acceptance of these entities was premised on any understanding of what form these predictions would take.

4.5 The Governing Account and Humeanism about Laws

In the preceding sections, I have argued that laws must provide metaphysically robust explanations of patterns of their instances. In other words, I have argued for the governing account of laws. This argument did not rely on the idea that the governing account is a conceptual truth.[22] Instead it followed from a straightforward interpretation of standard scientific practice combined with methodological naturalism. For a methodological naturalist, then, the governing account should be the starting point for any metaphysics of laws.

This much, I think, is already substantive. But in this section, I will show how my argument also bears on the familiar debate between Humeans and non-Humeans about laws. In particular, I will argue that it makes it much more difficult to be a Humean about laws of nature than one might previously have thought. This will be especially worrying for Humeans who like to think of themselves as naturalists. For, as I have argued in the previous chapters, content naturalism is a highly plausible form of naturalism, and if one is a content naturalist, then one must also be a methodological naturalist—and thus face the consequences discussed below.

Before getting into the core of this discussion, however, it is worth emphasizing something important about the way that I am understanding the governing account of laws. In conversation, I sometimes encounter the view that the "governing account of laws" is a term that is correctly applied only to either an Armstrong-style analysis of laws in terms of universals

---

[22] A move criticized in Beebee (2000).

(Armstrong 1983) or to primitivist accounts of laws à la Maudlin (2007). On this sort of approach, there is a mutually exclusive distinction between the governing account of laws, Humean accounts of laws, and various *dispositionalist* accounts of laws (like the one found in Bird 2007). It is important to recognize that nothing that I have said so far in defense of the governing account of laws requires that this mutually exclusive tripartite distinction hold. I have argued that laws govern in the following sense: if P is some well-established pattern and it is a law that P, then the fact that it is a law that P is the reason why P. If a dispositionalist or powers-based account of laws is able to satisfy this condition, then that account will qualify as one on which laws govern. Indeed, it is even compatible with my view that there is some version of a Humean account of laws that turns out to satisfy the governing account. All that would be required would be that there be a Humean account according to which its being a law that P is the reason why P (where P is some well-established pattern).

Given what has been said so far, then, there is no reason why a Humean can't endorse the governing account of laws. Nonetheless, it turns out that this will be quite difficult to do.

Why does my argument make it more difficult to be a Humean? Because it gives rise to an especially difficult version of the circularity challenge for Humeanism originally raised by Armstrong (1983) and Maudlin (2007).[23] Versions of the circularity objection have been spelled out in great detail in the recent literature.[24] Here is the version that is made salient by the argument above.

The defining feature of Humean accounts of laws is that laws are in some sense nothing over and above the *Humean mosaic*, where the Humean mosaic is the distribution of categorical (non-nomic) properties throughout spacetime. It is natural to think that it follows from the fact that Humean laws are nothing over and above the mosaic that the following principle is true:

---

[23] Beebee (2000) also claims that the governing account of laws is a key component of the supervenience challenges raised by Carroll (1994), Tooley (1977), and Menzies (1993). I won't discuss those challenges in detail here, but it is worth noting that if Beebee is correct, then this is a second way in which the argument that I have presented for the governing account of laws will make it harder to be a Humean. One can no longer resist the supervenience objections by resisting the governing account of laws that (according to Beebee at least) underlies those objections.

[24] In addition to Armstrong and Maudlin, see Lange (2013), Hicks and van Elswyk (2015), Miller (2015), Marshall (2015), Roski (2018), and Hicks (2021).

> *Mosaic to laws.* The reason why the laws are what they are is because the mosaic is what it is.

In other words, the Humean mosaic provides a metaphysically robust explanation of the laws. (If you're skeptical of the idea that Humeanism should be understood in this way, note that I will say more about this assumption below.)

But now notice that, given the argument in the previous sections, we must also agree that the laws provide a metaphysically robust explanation of at least part of the mosaic—the part that corresponds to the pattern of instances of those laws.

> *Laws to mosaic.* Part of the reason why the mosaic is what it is is because the laws are what they are.

Perhaps there are some parts of the mosaic (the unpatterned parts) that go without explanation or that have explanations that do not involve appeals to the laws. But there are also at least *some* parts of the mosaic that, given the argument in section 4.3, are what they are because the laws are what they are. The mosaic of a Newtonian world, for instance, consists of many, many instances in which $f = ma$. Why is that? As argued above, it must be because it is a law that $f = ma$.

Thus we have an explanatory circle: the laws provide a metaphysically robust explanation of part of the mosaic, and the mosaic provides a metaphysically robust explanation of the laws. And this seems deeply problematic. If A is the reason why B, B cannot be part of the reason why A. At the very least, to accept such a circle is a serious theoretical cost.

What are the prospects for the Humean in responding to the circularity challenge? First, they can try to insist that the circularity is not problematic. I won't say anything more about the plausibility of this move below. If Humeans must take this route, that is surely a surprising and unintuitive cost. Second, they can try to avoid the circle. But notice that given my argument above, the Humean cannot avoid the circle by claiming that laws do not provide metaphysically robust explanations of the mosaic. They must instead claim that laws are not in fact explained by the mosaic. More carefully, given my argument, they must claim that the mosaic is not the reason why the laws are what they are. And while the view that the mosaic is not the reason why the Humean laws are what they are is plausibly compatible with the view that the Humean laws supervene on the mosaic, it is a surprising view nonetheless. If, according to the Humean, the mosaic is not the reason why the laws are what they are, then why *are* the laws what they are? It is unclear how the Humean will answer this question. Third, and finally, the Humean can find some way of avoiding my argument for the governing account of laws. Doing so will require either a surprising reinterpretation of the examples that I gave in section 4.1, or giving up both methodological *and* content naturalism.

One important thing to notice here is that this way of presenting the circularity objection avoids disputes over whether Humeans should frame their account of laws in terms of grounding. The recent trend, especially following Schaffer (2008) and Loewer (2012), has been to understand Humeanism as the view that laws are grounded in the Humean mosaic.[25] As grounding talk started to seem like a promising way of making sense of "nothing over and above" locutions throughout metaphysics, it only made sense to apply it in this case as well. But recently some philosophers, including Miller (2015), have suggested that it may be a mistake to think of Humean laws in this way.[26] These philosophers sometimes suggest that the circularity objection may be avoided simply by returning to an account on which what it is to be a Humean about laws is merely to think that laws supervene on the mosaic. This move may be especially attractive to those who wish to stick close to the views of the most famous proponent of Humeanism, David Lewis, as well as those with Humean inclinations who are skeptical of grounding claims in general.[27]

But what the argument above shows is that we can set aside discussions of Lewis's intentions and of the plausibility of grounding claims in general as well as in this particular case. Regardless of how those discussions turn out, Humeans face a serious challenge to do with explanatory circularity. Either they say that the mosaic is the reason why the laws are what they are, in which case circularity threatens. Or they say that the mosaic is not the reason why

---

[25] Beebee (2000) also includes grounding locutions, although it is unclear whether ultimately she thinks that the Humean is committed to thinking that laws are grounded in the mosaic.

[26] See also Hall (forthcoming) and Kovacs (ms). It may be that a non-trivial proportion of metaphysicians interested in laws never endorsed the shift to grounding-talk to begin with. Consider, for instance, the *Stanford Encyclopedia of Philosophy* article on laws of nature, authored by John Carroll (2016), which exclusively presents the Humean view in terms of supervenience and makes no mention of grounding.

[27] Although Lewis occasionally used language suggesting that the Humean was committed to some kind of reduction, he may have thought that in some cases asymmetric supervenience—such as the asymmetric supervenience of Humean laws on the Humean mosaic—was itself sufficient for reduction. The discussion in Miller (2015), especially footnote 8, is helpful here.

the laws are what they are, in which case they face the question: Why are the laws what they are? Unless they have some way of answering this question, or some way of convincing us that it need not be answered, we ought not be Humeans.[28]

4.6 What Is Governance?

Here is the key upshot of the discussion so far. I have argued that it follows from methodological naturalism that laws govern in the following sense: if P is some well-established pattern and it is a law that P, then the fact that it is a law that P is the reason why P.[29]

The fact that laws provide metaphysically robust explanations in this way is, on my view, the core of the idea that laws govern. But I'm sympathetic to the idea that we should at least attempt to provide a further account of the governance relation, and indeed I think that the argument above suggests several options for such an account. Going through these options helps demonstrate that the kinds of contribution that methodological naturalism can make to metaphysics are not all negative—they don't always involve ruling out otherwise attractive theories. Methodological naturalism can also help shape the development of new metaphysical theories.

Start from the fact that—as established by a careful examination of the historical cases discussed in sections 4.1 and 4.2—the key feature of governance is that the governing relation supports metaphysically robust explanatory relations. One way of putting this is that the governing relation is a *dependence relation*, where a dependence relation is just a relation that supports metaphysically robust explanation. As noted above, two other paradigm examples of dependence relations are causation and grounding. A relatively natural move, then, would be to build an account of governance on these other, already widely accepted dependence relations. There are three ways of doing this.

---

[28] A strategy that I haven't discussed for avoiding the circularity objection is the higher-level explanation approach found in Hicks (2021). In brief, although I think Hicks's strategy might allow him to avoid the circularity objection for particular instances of laws, he still faces the dilemma described above for lawlike regularities.

[29] As noted above, this claim explicitly leaves open whether the governance relation holds directly between the fact that it is a law that P and P, or whether the governance relation instead holds between the fact that it is a law that P and individual instances of P, where the combined individual instances of P are then the reason why P.

The first two ways of building an account of governance on already widely accepted dependence relations are obvious: we could simply say that governance is just a type of causation or we could say that governance is just a type of grounding.

Governance as causation. The fact that it is a law that P is the reason why P in the sense that the fact that it is a law that P causes P.

Governance as grounding. The fact that it is a law that P is the reason why P in the sense that the fact that it is a law that P grounds P.

The obvious advantage of endorsing one of these accounts is that many of us are already committed to causation and grounding and to the idea that causation and grounding support metaphysically robust explanations. So if governance just is a type of causation or if governance just is a type of grounding, then many of us aren't adding anything new to our metaphysics, and the fact that governance supports metaphysically robust explanations isn't especially surprising.

But both of these accounts also have a downside: they will require revising widely held beliefs about what causation or grounding consist in. Consider first governance as causation. Causation is widely held to be a relation that holds between events, but governance is a relation that takes, as one of its relata, a fact about laws. Facts about laws are not events.[30] So if we endorse governance as causation, then we have to give up a widely held belief about causation.[31]

The same will be true of governance as grounding, although this may not be as immediately obvious. To see why, consider the fact that grounding is widely held to be metaphysically necessitating in the sense that if F grounds G, then any metaphysically possible world where F occurs is a world in which G also occurs. But we shouldn't accept any view of governance that requires governance to be metaphysically necessitating in this sense; many laws,

---

[30] See Paul and Hall (2013).
[31] Someone who wanted to endorse Governance as Causation might point out that in principle at least it is easy to translate between facts and events—for every fact there is the event of that fact obtaining. One thing to note, however, is that if there is such a thing as the event corresponding to the fact that it is a law that P, then that event is not spatiotemporally localized, which makes it importantly different from most paradigm examples of events that stand in causal relations. In any case, note that if you think there is no issue here for taking governance to be causation, then that is all to the good as far as my argument is concerned.

including some of our current best candidates for the fundamental dynamical laws, are indeterministic, and the relation between such laws and their instances (or between such laws and patterns of those instances) is not metaphysically necessitating. Indeed it is not even nomologically necessitating.

Suppose you take a bunch of silver atoms and send them through a set of magnets that creates an inhomogeneous magnetic field (a magnetic field that is stronger in one direction than another). The field will deflect some of the silver atoms in one direction—call it *up*—and the rest of the magnets in another direction—call it *down*. Suppose you then take all and only the silver atoms that were deflected up through the first set of magnets and send them through a second set of magnets, which is rotated slightly with respect to the first. The vast majority of the atoms will go up again through the second set of magnets. Call this pattern *P-M*.

According to several of our current best candidate theories of quantum mechanical phenomena, the only available explanation for P-M is the fact that the fundamental laws assign a very high objective probability to each silver atom going up through the second set of magnets (given that it went up through the first set of magnets). Call the laws that assign these objective probabilities *L-M*. According to the pattern-explanation principle, then, the fact that it is a law that L-M is the reason why P-M. But notice that on any standard view about objective probability, there are metaphysically and even nomologically possible worlds in which L-M obtains but P-M does not. These are worlds in which the objective probability of each silver atom going up through the second set of magnets (given that it went up through the first set of magnets) is very high, but in fact many or even all of the silver atoms end up being deflected down through the second set of magnets instead. Such worlds are not very likely, but they are nomologically possible.

What this example shows is that the pattern-explanation principle will require a governing account of both deterministic and indeterministic laws.[32] As such, and given the fact that some of our best candidates for the fundamental dynamical laws are indeterministic, one should allow that the governing relation itself is not necessitating. And insofar as one thinks that governance is grounding, one should therefore think that grounding, contrary to widespread belief, is not necessitating either. Many philosophers,

---

[32] The argument above follows Emery (2019).

especially those steeped in the contemporary literature on grounding, will find the idea that grounding is not even nomologically necessitating to be difficult to accept.[33]

So to say that governance just is causation or just is grounding comes with costs. Are those costs worth paying? I don't want to take a stand on that here.[34] Instead, I want to emphasize that for those unwilling to pay the costs, there is a third way to proceed: to take governance to be a distinct member of the family of dependence relations that also includes causation and grounding. On this view, governance cannot be analyzed in terms of causation or grounding; instead it is a novel type of dependence relation.

This view is especially plausible when one realizes that the key features of governance relations that might in one context seem worrying are also features that it has in common with either causation or grounding. Consider, for instance, the fact that governance relations are not necessitating. This might be a reason for thinking that governance is not grounding, but it can't be a reason for thinking that governance is not a member of the family of dependence relations. After all, we (or most of us, at least) have already accepted a dependence relation that isn't necessitating—causation. It is widely accepted that F can cause G even if F doesn't necessitate G.

Or consider the fact that governance relations don't hold between events. This might be a reason for thinking that governance is not causation, but it can't be a reason for thinking that governance is not a member of the family of dependence relations. After all, many of us have already accepted a dependence relation that doesn't hold between events—grounding. It is widely accepted that the grounding relation need not take events as relata.[35]

Taking governance to be a novel dependence relation has the advantage that we need not revise any widely accepted views about causation or grounding. The cost of this view, obviously, is that it involves introducing a novel dependence relation into our metaphysics. All else being equal, we

---

[33] One reason to be especially adamant about holding the line here is if you endorse the view that causation and grounding are very similar and one of the only important differences between the two is that the latter is necessitating, while the former is not. See Schaffer (2016).

[34] In Emery (2019), I argued for governance as grounding, because I thought that governance as causation was more costly. Today I am more inclined toward the view that governance is a novel dependence relation.

[35] What exactly the grounding relation does take as relata is up for debate. Some philosophers (e.g., Schaffer 2009a) are ecumenicists about this and think that grounding relations can hold between a wide range of relata. Other philosophers (e.g., Rosen 2010 and Audi 2012) insist that grounding relations hold only between facts. I know of no one who thinks that grounding holds only between events.

should avoid introducing novel relations into our metaphysics if we can. That said, it is worth emphasizing that there is an important difference between saying that grounding is a *novel* dependence relation and saying that grounding is a *primitive* dependence relation. Nothing in what I have said here requires that those who take this third option accept that grounding is unanalyzable. The key feature of this approach, rather, is that governance is not analyzed in terms of causation or grounding—that is what makes it novel.

So there are three ways of developing a further account of grounding that builds on already widely accepted dependence relations. I am not here advocating any one of these views over the others, and in principle, at least, I am open to other options. The key feature of governance that follows from my argument is just that governance is a dependence relation in the following sense: it supports metaphysically robust explanations. The discussion in this section is supposed to illustrate that there are several ways of further fleshing out the notion of governance in a way that is compatible with this feature.

Of course, all three of the options I set out above come with costs. But here is a position that is not viable, given the argument of this chapter: one cannot simply refuse to accept a governing account of laws because one does not want to pay these costs. To see why, return to some of the examples presented in section 4.1. Consider, for instance, the introduction of dark energy to explain the accelerating rate of expansion of the universe. Scientists have little idea what dark energy is. So of course they can have no guarantee that the way in which dark energy explains the accelerating rate of expansion of the universe will be cost-free. Perhaps the only way for dark energy to play the relevant explanatory role will require either revising accepted explanatory relations or even introducing a novel kind of explanatory relation.[36] Hopefully that doesn't turn out to be the case, but the fact that it might doesn't prevent scientists from thinking that dark energy exists. Why not? Because they need there to be *something* to explain the accelerating rate of expansion of the universe. Otherwise they would violate the pattern-explanation principle.

---

[36] In conversation, I sometimes have heard the following response to this line of reasoning: "But we at least know *something* about how dark energy explains—it explains in the way that energy in general explains." My view is that given the wide range of possibilities for what dark energy is, the claim that dark energy explains in the way that energy explains is far more complicated to evaluate than it first appears. Moreover, a defender of a governing account of laws can also point out that in a similar way, we know *something* about the way in which laws explain—they do so by providing reasons why, just like other, less controversial dependence relations like causation and grounding do.

The same sort of attitude should be adopted in the case of laws. We need governing laws in order to explain patterns in the data. It may be that the way in which governing laws provide these explanations comes with costs. That is perhaps unfortunate, but it isn't a reason to reject the governing account of laws.

5
Case Study

Mooreanism and Nihilism about Composition

Here is a second case study. Whereas the case study in Chapter 4 illustrated how methodological naturalism would impact a debate that is clearly adjacent to science, this case study illustrates how methodological naturalism can affect debates in metaphysics that have traditionally been thought of as largely insulated from scientific concerns.

Suppose some metaphysical theory accords well with our intuitions. Is that a reason to accept it? Suppose a certain view about the nature of some entity conflicts with common sense. Is that a reason to discard it? Consider the fact that the world appears to contain some thing. Is that a reason to think that thing exists? To answer "yes" to any of these questions is to adopt some version of *Mooreanism about metaphysics*.

The philosopher who thinks that we ought to accept the view that there are objective, determinate criteria for personal identity over time because that view just seems obvious is a Moorean. So too is the philosopher who says that the view that there are a plurality of concrete possible worlds is just too crazy to be believed. When Thomson (1998, 153) rejects the view that objects are identical to their parts because "philosophy should not depart more than it absolutely has to from what we ordinarily think and say," she is showing her Moorean *bona fides*. Similarly for Zimmerman (2008, 211) when he writes, "Are there objective differences between what is past, present and future? . . . Are present events and things somehow more "real" than those wholly in the past or future? I should like to respond "Yes," to both questions. Affirmative answers sound obvious and commonsensical, at least to me."

It is common these days, especially among naturalistically inclined philosophers, to think that Mooreanism in metaphysics is deeply misguided. Indeed the prevalence of Moorean reasoning in metaphysics is often cited as a reason for thinking that the field as a whole is deeply flawed. Consider, for instance, the opening chapter of Ladyman and Ross, where (as mentioned in Chapter 3) the authors claim that the "criteria of adequacy for metaphysical systems have clearly come apart from anything to do with the truth" (2007, 13).[1] Why do Ladyman and Ross think this charge is warranted? Because, they say, much contemporary metaphysics "proceeds by attempts to construct theories that are intuitive, commonsensical, palatable, and philosophically respectable" (13). They take it to be quite obvious, in other words, that Mooreanism is bad practice in metaphysics.

In this chapter, I argue that this way of thinking about Mooreanism is a mistake. Indeed, anyone who is a methodological naturalist ought to endorse at least one version of Mooreanism about metaphysics. This is because, as I will argue, a particular version of Mooreanism—I call it *the principle of minimal divergence*—plays an important though under-appreciated role in standard scientific methodology. It follows that if one is a methodological naturalist, then one ought also to use the principle of minimal divergence in choosing between metaphysical theories.[2]

I then show how Mooreanism has significant consequences for a specific first-order debate in metaphysics—the debate over whether there are composite objects. This debate is often thought to be a paradigm case of a metaphysical debate that is largely insulated from scientific considerations and is often disparaged or avoided by naturalistically inclined metaphysicians as a result. The argument below shows that this attitude is a mistake.

5.1 Minimal Divergence

Mooreanism comes in many varieties. First and foremost, versions of Mooreanism can be differentiated based on the specific sort of consideration that they take to be relevant when evaluating metaphysical theories. Above I suggested that appeals to intuition, to immediate appearances, and to surprisingness are all varieties of Mooreanism. I take it that all of these considerations can at least loosely be thought of as ways of appealing to *common sense*, and thus that Mooreanism can be defined in the following way:

---

[1] See also, for instance, Bryant (2020) on what she calls "free range metaphysics."
[2] In Emery (2017a) I claimed that a specific version of this argument creates problems for interpretations of non-relativistic quantum mechanics according to which the fundamental space that we inhabit has something on the order of 10^{80} dimensions. The goal here is to defend a more general version of this argument and to explore its consequences for debates that are central to contemporary metaphysics (as opposed to philosophy of physics).

Mooreanism about metaphysics. The extent to which a metaphysical theory coheres with some type of common sense is at least some reason to think that theory is true. And the extent to which a metaphysical theory departs from common sense is at least some reason to think that theory is false.

But this definition is only as clear as one's understanding of what counts as common sense, and in what follows I will not attempt to clarify that notion. With respect to this way of differentiating varieties of Mooreanism, my thesis will be quite circumscribed: I will only argue that considerations to do with one particular type of common sense—the way the world appears to be—are relevant when evaluating metaphysical theories. Perhaps other varieties of Mooreanism are viable as well, but I will not take up that question below. Indeed insofar as the reader is skeptical that there is any well-defined group of theses that are appropriately labeled Moorean, she still can—and indeed I think still should—endorse both my argument and the consequences that follow. Nothing important turns on my suggestion that the type of common sense that plays a role in that argument is a member of a well-defined larger group.

Another way of differentiating varieties of Mooreanism is in terms of the strength of the reasons to which the relevant type of common sense gives rise. At one end of the spectrum, a Moorean might think that the relevant type of common sense gives us a reason to believe some theory, but that it is a highly defeasible reason. At the other, a Moorean might think that coherence with the relevant type of common sense is a necessary condition, without which we ought not accept a candidate theory.[3]

With respect to this way of differentiating varieties of Mooreanism, my thesis will be more expansive. I will argue that considerations to do with the way the world appears to be are among the most important extra-empirical considerations that are relevant when evaluating metaphysical theories. Considerations to do with the way the world appears to be do not only hold when all else is equal. Sometimes even when there are substantive reasons in favor of some metaphysical theory, that theory is nonetheless ruled out because it conflicts with the way the world appears to be.

---

[3] Many philosophers whom you might not have thought of as having especially Moorean inclinations endorse the view that common sense is in some sense relevant to theory choice in metaphysics. In *On the Plurality of Worlds*, for instance, Lewis admits a role for common sense, though he also insists that it "has no absolute authority in philosophy" (1986, 134).

In order to understand the particular version of Mooreanism that I will be interested in below, start with the *manifest image*: the way the world appears to be. It will be helpful to think of the manifest image as generating a set of propositions M that accurately represent the way the world appears to be. The necessary and sufficient conditions for membership in M will undoubtedly be controversial, and I will not attempt to defend any such conditions here.[4,5] But as examples of relatively uncontroversial members of M, consider the following:

(1) I exist.
(2) There are such things as tables and chairs.
(3) The space we inhabit has three dimensions.

The particular version of Mooreanism that I am interested in is one that says that an important consideration in whether to adopt a theory is the extent to which it diverges from the manifest image.

> *The principle of minimal divergence.* Insofar as you have two or more candidate theories, all of which are empirically and explanatorily adequate, you ought to choose the theory that diverges least from the manifest image.

There are several technical terms in the principle of minimal divergence, some of which are familiar from the earlier chapters. A candidate theory is *empirically adequate* insofar as it accurately predicts the data that we actually observe.[6] And a candidate theory is *explanatorily adequate* insofar as it does

---

[4] Readers who are worried about the notion of the manifest image as it plays a role in the argument below should be sure to read the first few objections and replies in section 5.3.

[5] Note that in terms of the argument that follows, nothing important turns on whether my use of the term 'manifest image' is the same as that found in, e.g., Sellars (1963). Indeed, nothing important turns on the use of that term at all. All that matters for the argument is that the reader have some sense of the way the world appears to be, and a way of generating a set of propositions that represent the way the world appears to be of which (1) through (3) below are paradigm examples. We can then define divergence from the manifest image below in terms of conflict with that set of propositions.

[6] As mentioned in section 3.4, throughout the book I will be understanding the empirical data as quite thin—as consisting just of a description of our experience that is as theory-neutral as possible. So when I look at a table, for instance, the data is a description of my experience that is neutral between there being a table before me, and there being a bunch of atoms arranged tablewise before me, and my envatted brain being stimulated in such a way as to produce the experience of a table before me—so our data would be something like that we are having an experience as of a solid, brownish rectangular shape before us. On this view the manifest image, which was described above as including propositions like (1) through (3), goes substantially beyond the empirical data. And one way—though certainly not the only way—of further spelling out the notion of the manifest image at play here is that it is the set of propositions that you get when you combine our data (as characterized above) with a commonsense theory of what the world is like. On such a theory, tables are the sorts of

132 NATURALISM BEYOND THE LIMITS OF SCIENCE

not leave robust patterns in the phenomena unexplained. A theory that just consists of a large list of all of the events that actually happen would be highly empirically adequate, but also highly explanatorily inadequate.[7]

What about the notion of *divergence* from the manifest image? In what follows, I will adopt the following definition:

A theory *diverges* from the manifest image insofar as for some m that is a member of M, the theory entails ~m.

There are, plausibly, other ways in which a theory might depart from the manifest image, which I will say nothing about here but which deserve further investigation. For instance, for some n that is not a member of M, a theory might entail n, or for some pattern p that holds throughout M, a theory might entail some set of propositions N such that p does not hold throughout the union of M and N. But I won't say anything about these other sorts of departure from the manifest image here.[8]

These definitions are rough and leave many interesting questions unanswered. (What exactly constitutes an observation? When does some phenomenon count as satisfactorily explained? In cases where all candidate theories diverge somewhat from the manifest image, how exactly should one weigh the extent of one theory's divergence against another?) The hope, however, is that these definitions are sufficiently clear to allow the principle to play the role that it is supposed to play in the arguments below, and that we can therefore leave those sorts of further details, interesting as they are,

---

things that give rise to experiences as of solid, brownish, rectangular shapes before us, so when our data consists of that sort of experience, the manifest image includes the proposition that there is a table before us.

As also mentioned in section 3.4, it is possible to have a thicker notion of data, according to which, when I look at a table, the data itself entails that there is a table before me. On this thicker notion, the data itself rules out, e.g., compositional nihilism or the hypotheses that we are brains-in-a-vat. But note that on this view, one will still need something like the principle of minimal divergence, though it won't play the role described above. Instead it will be a principle that determines, based on our experiences and perhaps in conjunction with other principles, what our empirical data is. It will be a principle that determines, for instance, that when we have an experience of a solid, brownish rectangular shape in front of us, our empirical data is (in part) that there is a table before us instead of our empirical data being that there are some atoms arranged in a certain way before us or that our envatted brains are being stimulated in a certain way.

[7] Note that it is plausible that both empirical and explanatory adequacy come in degrees, but I am going to ignore this complication in what follows.

[8] In Emery (2017a) I discuss the former sort of divergence in detail and defend a version of the principle of minimal divergence in which it plays a role.

unspecified. Indeed I take it that part of what the argument below should do is to motivate interest in working out those further details.

Here, then, is a more detailed version of the argument that will be the focus of what follows:

P1   The principle of minimal divergence is a part of standard scientific methodology.
P2   We should be methodological naturalists.

The conclusion of the argument is that the principle of minimal divergence should constrain theory choice in metaphysics as well. In other words:

Minimal divergence in metaphysics. If the principle of minimal divergence favors metaphysical theory A over competing metaphysical theory B, we ought to adopt metaphysical theory A.

In what follows I will refer to the argument that establishes this conclusion as *the minimal divergence argument for Mooreanism in metaphysics*. Or, for short, the *minimal divergence argument*.

5.2 Mooreanism as a Part of Standard Scientific Practice

As we are assuming methodological naturalism for the purpose of the case studies, the key premise of the minimal divergence argument is P1. My argument for this premise will proceed in two steps.[9] First I will present a group of hypotheses that conflict with our best scientific theories. Then I will argue that the best, and possibly the only, explanation of the fact that all of these hypotheses conflict with our best scientific theories is that the principle of minimal divergence is a commitment of standard scientific practice. I will call the relevant group of hypotheses *radical metaphysical hypotheses*.

Radical metaphysical hypotheses include the following:

---

[9] See Emery (2017a) for a discussion of the similarities and differences between my defense of this premise and related claims made in the debate over quantum ontology, including those found in Monton (2006) and Allori (2013).

Solipsistic idealism. I do not have a physical body or brain. All that exists are my mental states. There is nothing corresponding to the world that I appear to inhabit.

The simulation hypothesis. I do not have a physical body or brain. I am a part of a computer simulation which gives rise to my experiences. The physical world, of which the simulation is part, is not at all the way the world appears to be.

The brain-in-a-vat hypothesis. I do not have a physical body. My brain is being stimulated in a way that gives rise to my experiences. The physical world around me is not at all the way the world appears to be.

The Boltzmann Brain hypothesis. I do not have a physical body. My brain formed in a nearly empty region of space due to an extraordinary series of coincidences. The world around me is not at all the way the world appears to be.

The evil demon hypothesis. I have a physical body and brain, but an evil demon is causing me to have experiences that do not in any straightforward way correspond to the world around me. The world around me is not at all the way the world appears to be.

More specifically, my focus will be on versions of these hypotheses that are further spelled out in such a way as to be empirically and explanatorily adequate.[10]

Readers will of course recognize these sorts of hypotheses as motivating various skeptical concerns in epistemology. (I say more about the relation between my argument and traditional discussions of skepticism in section 5.5.) But for now, the key thing to recognize is that all of these radical metaphysical hypotheses conflict with our best scientific theories. Our best

---

[10] Note that there is a difference between claiming that these hypotheses can be spelled out in such a way as to be explanatorily adequate (i.e., they do not leave robust patterns in the phenomena unexplained) and claiming that they can be spelled out in such a way as to provide better explanations than, e.g., our best scientific hypotheses. The latter view has been questioned by, among others, Vogel (1990) and Huemer (2016). But I need to assume only the former. Note that one way of explaining patterns in the phenomena is to simply posit lawlike connections between them. This is presumably the strategy that the solipsistic idealist would take in order to make her theory explanatorily adequate.

scientific theories say that we have physical bodies and brains, and that our bodies and brains are causally connected in a straightforward way to the world around us. So, if any of the radical metaphysical hypotheses listed above turned out to be true, our best scientific theories would have turned out to be false. And indeed this is not just a feature of our current best scientific theories. Throughout the history of science, our best scientific theories at each time have conflicted with the various versions of these radical metaphysical hypotheses that were spelled out in such a way as to be empirically and explanatorily adequate at that time.[11]

Given that these radical metaphysical hypotheses conflict with our best scientific theories, we ought to ask: Why? Why is it that standard scientific practice systematically dismisses these hypotheses?[12] By stipulation, it is not a matter of empirical or explanatory adequacy, since by stipulation the radical metaphysical hypotheses in question are spelled out in such a way as to be empirically and explanatorily adequate. By what criteria, then, are these hypotheses ruled out?

I claim that the best and perhaps the only plausible answer to this question is that the principle of minimal divergence is a commitment of standard scientific practice.

A defense of this claim starts from the observation that what all of the radical metaphysical hypotheses in question have in common (besides conflicting with our best scientific theories and being empirically and explanatorily adequate) is that they all diverge significantly from the manifest image. It is a central feature of these hypotheses that the world is very different than it appears to be—that many of the propositions in M are, in fact, false. Indeed even given that we have said virtually nothing about how to weigh relative divergence among competing theories, I take it that on any plausible way of spelling out such comparisons, the radical metaphysical hypotheses listed above diverge more from the manifest image than do our best scientific theories. It follows that the radical metaphysical hypotheses would be ruled out by the principle of minimal divergence.

Now note that, in addition, there does not appear to be anything further that unifies these hypotheses. It is not the case, for instance, that all of the

---

[11] Note that it is compatible with the claim that our best scientific hypotheses conflict with the radical metaphysical hypotheses that scientists sometimes take radical metaphysical hypotheses seriously. What they are doing when they take such hypotheses seriously is seriously considering the possibility that our best scientific theories might be false.

[12] Or: Why is it standard scientific practice to systematically ignore these hypotheses? I say more about this second way of thinking about things in the objections and replies section below.

radical metaphysical hypotheses are unnecessarily complicated. Solipsistic idealism is both more qualitatively and more quantitatively simple than our best scientific theories. Nor is it the case that all of the radical metaphysical hypotheses listed above are especially unlikely. On standard ways of assigning probability in statistical mechanics, the Boltzmann Brain scenario can be spelled out in such a way that it is *more* likely than my experiences being the result of an embodied brain in a region of spacetime that corresponds in any straightforward way to my experiences.[13] Nor is it the case that all of the radical metaphysical hypotheses are less explanatorily powerful than our best scientific theories. Consider the simulation hypothesis. Such a hypothesis has the potential to explain not only the robust patterns currently explained by science, but also those phenomena that our best scientific theories take to be genuine coincidences—such coincidences could be given a straightforward causal explanation in terms of the simulation.[14]

Here is the upshot of the discussion so far: the only *unified* explanation of why the radical metaphysical hypotheses conflict with our best scientific theories is an explanation that appeals to the principle of minimal divergence.[15]

Might there be an alternative, non-unified explanation of why the radical metaphysical hypotheses conflict with our best scientific theories—an explanation that goes through the list of such hypotheses one by one identifying something that disqualifies each of them? We would have to see exactly how such an explanation goes in order to evaluate it fully, but here are a few important reasons for thinking that this way of proceeding is unpromising at best.

First, notice that the list above can be expanded in various ways. The radical metaphysical hypotheses listed above are merely exemplars of a more

---

[13] Suppose, for instance, that the Boltzmann Brain is the result of a random fluctuation that occurs in a universe that spends most of its history very close to thermal equilibrium.

[14] A similar point is that the simulation hypothesis (and similar radical metaphysical hypotheses) might be able to give better explanations for the correlations observed in so-called EPR experiments than any of our best theories of non-relativistic quantum mechanics (Emery 2022). A important follow-up question here is: Does the simulation give rise to further explananda? It depends on how the hypothesis is spelled out. But insofar as one thinks that the simulation is carried out in a world that is similar in kind to ours (as in Bostrom 2003), then it need not do so.

[15] In conversation I sometimes have people claim that we can rule out the radical metaphysical hypotheses in a unified way because they are, in general, less scientifically fruitful than our best scientific theories. Obviously, much depends on what you mean by "scientifically fruitful," but at the very least note that if you accept, e.g., the simulation hypothesis, that is no reason to give up on scientific inquiry. It's just that you should understand further scientific inquiry as telling us how the simulation is programmed.

general category. Any non-unified explanation will need to deal not only with that list, but also with the threat of novel radical metaphysical hypotheses which might be designed expressly to avoid the issues identified with each of the existing hypotheses. The constraints on such hypotheses, after all, are quite limited—any hypothesis which is explanatorily or empirically adequate, which conflicts with our best scientific theories, and which diverges more from the manifest image than those theories, will do.

Second, notice that, as suggested above, the obvious weaknesses of many radical metaphysical hypotheses turn out to be strengths of other hypotheses on the list. One might think, for instance, that the problem with the evil demon hypothesis is that it is unnecessarily complicated relative to our best scientific theories. But note that relative to solipsistic idealism, many of our best scientific theories themselves appear to be unnecessarily complicated.

Third, notice that, in general, we take unified explanations to be better than non-unified explanations, and that in this case there may be a special reason for doing so. In this case, a unified explanation makes it easier to understand the widespread agreement among scientists on the inadequacy of the radical metaphysical hypotheses, even though they receive little or no explicit training when it comes to extra-empirical theory choice.[16]

Let me make one final point about the general strategy of trying to rule out the radical metaphysical hypotheses using some other extra-empirical criteria (whether unified or not) besides the principle of minimal divergence. Notice that we don't just find these radical metaphysical hypotheses all things considered worse than our best scientific theories. We think that they are obviously bad, nor do we seem amenable to being talked out of our views regarding these hypotheses. Our degree of commitment regarding our best science being superior to these hypotheses is significant. But in general when we choose between theories on the basis of extra-empirical criteria like simplicity or explanatory power or what have you, we are not committed to the theory that we choose to any especially strong degree. All things considered, for instance, we don't think that someone who adopts the Lorentzian

---

[16] Note that what I mean by there being "widespread agreement among scientists on the inadequacy of the radical metaphysical hypotheses" is just that there is widespread agreement among scientists in endorsing theories that conflict with the radical metaphysical hypotheses.

Note also that this is not to suggest that people cannot internalize fairly complicated rules without explicit instruction in such rules—a good counterexample to such a suggestion would be grammatical rules. But generally speaking, cases in which we are successful in such internalization involve exposure to an enormous amount of data. It is not at all clear that scientists in training are exposed to an enormous amount of data regarding extra-empirical scientific theory choice.

alternative to special relativity is correct, but we also don't think that person is wrong in quite such an obvious way as someone would be wrong if they genuinely endorsed the brain-in-a-vat hypothesis. This suggests that there is something else besides the familiar extra-empirical criteria like simplicity or explanatory power that is playing a role in these cases. My claim is that the relevant "something else" is the principle of minimal divergence.[17]

Taken together, these considerations suggest that at the very least, the default view ought to be that the principle of minimal divergence is a commitment of standard scientific practice. It is up to those who want to reject premise 1 not only to come up with a plausible alternative explanation for the fact that the radical metaphysical hypotheses conflict with our best scientific theories but to argue that that explanation is *better* than the unified explanation provided by the principle of minimal divergence. Until they do so, we ought to accept the first premise of the minimal divergence argument.

And note that these considerations also suggest that the principle of minimal divergence is not just one among many extra-empirical considerations of roughly equal weight. After all, most of the other familiar extra-empirical considerations that are purported to play a role in standard scientific practice are exemplified by one or another of the radical metaphysical hypotheses. (Solipsism is simple, for instance, and the Boltzmann Brain hypothesis is more likely than alternatives.) If the principle of minimal divergence did not trump those other extra-empirical considerations, then it would not in fact rule out those radical metaphysical hypotheses, and we would be back to the question that motivated the discussion above: Why are our best scientific theories incompatible with those hypotheses?

5.3 Objections and Replies

The previous two sections presented my defense of the first premise of the minimal divergence argument for Mooreanism in metaphysics. The second premise is methodological naturalism. Taken together these premises establish the following claim:

---

[17] My thanks here to Chris Meacham, who made this point in the course of comments at the 2021 New England Metaphysics Workshop, that defended my paper "Against Radical Quantum Ontologies" (Emery 2017a).

Minimal divergence in metaphysics. If the principle of minimal divergence favors metaphysical theory A over competing metaphysical theory B, we ought to adopt metaphysical theory A.

In the next section I will show how this conclusion impacts a specific debate in first-order metaphysics. But first let me consider some objections and replies to the argument as presented above.

Objection 1: Many of our scientific theories diverge radically from the manifest image. Therefore, the principle of minimal divergence is not in fact a part of standard scientific methodology.

Reply: The principle of *minimal* divergence is not the same as the principle of *no* divergence.

The principle of no divergence. Insofar as you have two or more candidate theories, you ought to choose the theory that diverges least from the manifest image.

The principle of no divergence says that we must always choose the theory that diverges least from the manifest image. The principle of minimal divergence says that we should sometimes choose theories that diverge significantly from the manifest image—as long as that divergence is required in order to establish empirical or explanatory adequacy. So it is entirely compatible with minimal divergence that the surface of the earth is curved, for instance, or that apparently solid objects are made up of mostly empty space—one just needs to maintain that there are no empirically and explanatorily adequate rivals to these theories.

Objection 2: The way the world appears to be is sensitive to variation between individuals and cultures. But something that is so sensitive cannot play a role in either scientific or metaphysical theory choice.

Reply: The reader who is worried about this objection should take note of my response to what I call "nuanced nihilism" in section 5.5, but as a quick initial response let me note that I am open to the idea that there are many questions about the way the world appears to be that have no definitive answer. (Examples: "Is the dress blue and black or white and gold?" "Is the ski run scary?") That is no impediment to my argument. We can simply say that in such cases the minimal divergence norm has no bearing on which theory we ought to accept.

What is important for my argument is that there are also cases in which there is a definitive answer to questions about the way the world appears to be. It is in those cases that the principle of minimal divergence applies. As an example of the latter sort of case, consider the fact that the world appears to contain three spatial dimensions. There is (I assume!) little or no cultural or individual disagreement about that fact. So insofar as a theory says that the world contains far more than three spatial dimensions, that theory diverges from the way the world appears to be. And insofar as there is an alternative, empirically and explanatorily adequate theory that does not diverge as significantly, we ought to accept that alternative theory instead.

Someone might protest, "Sure, there is not in fact any cultural or individual disagreement about whether the world contains three spatial dimensions. But there could be!" But I think we should take care here. Certainly there could be creatures in a world just like ours who *say* that the world appears to contain far more than three dimensions. But could there be creatures in a world just like ours for whom the world *appears* to contain far more than three dimensions? Without first deciding what our world is like, I don't think that we have any evidence in support of this claim.

Objection 3: There are examples from the history of science that violate the principle of minimal divergence. Therefore, the principle of minimal divergence does not constrain theory choice in science.

Reply: A full reply to such examples will have to proceed on a case-by-case basis. But let me work through a particular example with which I am often presented in conversation, in order to illustrate the various philosophical moves that are available in response to objections like this.

To this purpose, consider the shift from the Ptolemaic to the heliocentric models as discussed in Chapter 3. Let's grant that the sun and stars appear to revolve around the Earth. So the heliocentric model diverges substantially from the manifest image. Plausibly it diverges more than Ptolemaic astronomy. How, then, did it come to gain widespread acceptance among physicists when it did? And isn't the fact that it did gain such acceptance a clear counterexample to the claim that the principle of minimal divergence is a commitment of standard scientific practice?

When I discussed this example in Chapter 3 I noted that although the choice between Ptolemaic and heliocentric models is often framed as a choice of a straightforwardly simpler theory over a more complex one, the details of the historical case show that this is not plausible. Here is an alternative suggestion: this choice was instead based on a certain kind of explanatory deficiency in the Ptolemaic models. In particular, especially after Galileo's early observations with the telescope became widely known, there was a great deal of data that suggested, *contra* Aristotelean physics, that the other bodies in the solar system were quite similar to Earth. Galileo's observation of supernovae showed that the distant heavens were not unchanging, for instance. His observations of the moons of Jupiter showed that other planets had satellites just as Earth did. His observations of the surface of the moon showed that it had geological features similar to those found on Earth. And he also was able to observe that the Earth reflected light just as other bodies in the solar system did. There was a pattern in this data that would be explained only by the heliocentric model, according to which Earth was just another planet. Perhaps, then, we can make the case that the Ptolemaic model was not in fact explanatorily adequate.[18] If so, then the choice of the heliocentric model over the Ptolemaic model is not a counterexample to the principle of minimal divergence.[19]

This looks like it is enough to resolve the objection—once one pays close enough attention to issues of empirical and explanatory adequacy, one sees that we do not in fact have a counterexample to the principle of minimal divergence here at all. But an additional point is also worth stressing. Suppose that in the end we could not find any reasonable explanation for the fact that Copernican astronomy gained widespread acceptance when it did that is compatible with the principle of minimal divergence. Should that convince us that P1 in the minimal divergence argument is false? I think the answer to this question is clearly "no"—for the challenge posed by the radical metaphysical hypotheses remains. There must be some explanation for the fact that scientific theory choice rules out those hypotheses. If P1 is false, then what is it?

In light of this challenge, we should be open to there being particular cases in which the principle of minimal divergence is violated—even if the principle

---

[18] Norton makes a similar claim, though while focusing on a different type of explanatory deficiency. He writes, "Our moving vantage point gives the illusion of further circular motions by the planets. Since these illusory motions resulted from a single origin, the motion of our vantage point, the illusory motions are highly correlated. Crudely put, the planets appear to wobble in synchrony because we view them from a wobbling platform. With this insight, Copernicans could then identify certain correlated motions within the Ptolemaic system as being just these projections. The projections could be separated from the true motions of the planets themselves. This gave the Copernicans a powerful advantage, for they could explain the coordination among these motions as necessities of a heliocentric system, whereas Ptolemaic astronomers could only ascribe them to arbitrary coincidences within the geocentric system" (2021, 156). See also the discussion in Sober (2015, 12–22).

[19] As I said when I discussed this case in Chapter 3, I think there is a lot of historical nuance here, so I don't want to put too much weight on the account I am proposing. My point is just that this certainly isn't a clear-cut case of the violation of the principle of minimal divergence.

of minimal divergence is a commitment of standard scientific methodology. These particular cases are cases in which an instance of scientific theory choice itself did not conform to standard scientific practice. (Surely a principle can be a part of standard scientific methodology without being correctly employed in every instance of scientific theory choice.) For my own part, I have yet to be convinced that there are clear cases in the history of science in which the principle of minimal divergence is violated.[20] But it is important to keep in mind that, even if there are, that does not straightforwardly undermine premise 1.

Objection 4: Throughout section 5.4 I made it sound as though scientific practice involves the active, explicit rejection or dismissal of the radical metaphysical hypotheses. But scientists don't actively consider and reject these hypotheses. They just ignore them entirely.

Reply: Whether it is true that scientists 'simply ignore' (as opposed to 'explicitly reject') the radical metaphysical hypotheses is going to depend both on how one spells out that distinction and on the particular case at hand. But in any case nothing important turns on this. It may be that scientists do not explicitly rule out the radical metaphysical hypotheses but instead simply ignore them or never entertain them to begin with. If so, then the key question under consideration in section 5.4 will be: Why is it standard scientific practice to systematically ignore, or systematically fail to entertain, the radical metaphysical hypotheses? But the options for answering that question and my argument for the principle of minimal divergence will remain unchanged. (It is of course possible that there is no principled reason for scientists ignoring this group of hypotheses, but I take it that no one who is at all naturalistically inclined should respond in this way.)

Objection 5: The argument in section 5.3 turns on the assumption that the radical metaphysical hypotheses are false. But those hypotheses have long been used to motivate various skeptical arguments. And those skeptical arguments are taken seriously by philosophers. So the argument in section 5.3 turns on an unfair assumption.

---

[20] The other most common examples that I am presented with in conversation are (a) the choice of configuration space realist views in quantum ontology over so-called primitive ontology views and (b) the choice of special relativity theory over the view that there is a privileged reference frame but it is empirically impossible to determine which it is. With respect to (a) note that configuration space realism is hardly the consensus view among philosophers or physicists. Indeed in Emery (2017a) I argue that the principle of minimal divergence provides an important reason for thinking that we should reject configuration space realism. With respect to (b), I am less certain, though one possibility is to try to appeal to the kinds of considerations found in Hofweber and Lange (2017) as a reason for thinking that theories that include a privileged reference frame are not in fact explanatorily adequate.

Reply: The minimal divergence argument does not rely on the assumption that the radical metaphysical hypotheses are false. Instead it relies on the claim that the radical metaphysical hypotheses listed in section 5.3 conflict with our best scientific theories—a claim that I provided some argument for by pointing to aspects of the latter that are false according to the latter. Insofar as any of the radical metaphysical hypotheses turned out to be true, our best scientific theories would have turned out to be false.

Does the claim that the radical metaphysical hypotheses conflict with our best scientific theories undermine traditional skeptical arguments? It depends on the details of those arguments, and I do not have space to go into the substantial literature on this topic here. But consider the following three claims:

(1) It is possible that we are brains in a vat.
(2) It is compatible with all of the empirical evidence that we have collected that we are brains in a vat.
(3) We are not justified in thinking that we aren't brains in a vat.

It follows from my claim that the radical metaphysical hypotheses conflict with our best scientific theories, that anyone who asserts (1) is committed to (1*), anyone who asserts (2) is committed to (2*), and anyone who asserts (3) is committed to (3*):

(1*) It is possible that our best scientific theories are false.
(2*) It is compatible with all of the empirical evidence that we have collected that our best scientific theories are false.
(3*) We are not justified in thinking that our best scientific theories are true.

Of these three claims, the first two are entirely plausible. It is of course possible that our best scientific theories are false. And our best scientific theories are in general underdetermined by the empirical evidence we have collected. We arrive at those theories by deploying various extra-empirical criteria alongside that empirical evidence.

However, (3*) is not plausible. Or at least, (3*) is not at all plausible insofar as one is a content naturalist. Insofar as one is a content naturalist, one should think that we are justified in thinking that our best scientific theories are true (or approximately true, or whatever epistemic standard is relevant). Perhaps there is a certain sort of dialectical context—the context in which epistemologists are operating when they consider various skeptical scenarios—in which it is appropriate to accept (3*), but this is surely not a context in which the content naturalist should operate. If it were, there would be no reason to have our metaphysical theories constrained by the content of our scientific theories. So insofar as epistemologists take seriously (3*), or some argument that leads them to (3*), we ought not—as content naturalists—follow their lead.

Here is the upshot: insofar as skeptical arguments merely involve commitment to (1) or (2), the claim that the radical metaphysical hypotheses conflict with standard science does not threaten them. Insofar as skeptical arguments involve commitment to (3), then those who take such arguments seriously must either reject a sort of naturalism that is commonly thought to be an important part of philosophical inquiry into what the world is like or insist that they are operating in a specific kind of dialectical context in which that sort of naturalism can be set aside—perhaps because they are trying to find a justification for that sort of naturalism.

5.4 Minimal Divergence and Nihilism about Composite Objects

Let's turn now to a discussion of the implications that the conclusion of the minimal divergence argument has for a particular debate in first-order metaphysics. Consider *nihilism about composite objects*—the view that there are no objects that have proper parts.[21] According to the nihilist, there are no tables or school buses or sidewalks. There are only simples—fundamental particles or the like—arranged table-wise or school bus–wise or sidewalk-wise.[22]

---

[21] Note that nihilism, as it is described here, is importantly different from the view that there are composite objects but those objects are not fundamental. Defenses of nihilism include Dorr (2005) and Sider (2013). Discussions of the composition debate in general include van Inwagen (1990), Merricks (2001), Bennett (2009), van Cleve (2008), and Korman (2015).

[22] Note that I am assuming, for the nihilist's sake, that we can understand our best scientific theories as being neutral between saying that there are brains and saying that there are atoms arranged brain-wise. If this is false, then there is an even more straightforward argument against nihilism, one that turns not on a conflict between nihilism and standard scientific practice but on a conflict between nihilism and the content of our best scientific theories. One might ask why we aren't willing to give the radical metaphysical hypotheses in section 5.3 the same treatment. Why not say that our best scientific theories are neutral between us having bodies and between us having the experience of having bodies that is caused by a simulation? I don't have a lot to say here except that it seems like a far more substantial stretch of the content of the best scientific theories to claim that that content is compatible with the radical metaphysical hypotheses than it is to claim that that content is compatible with nihilism.

The debate over whether or not we ought to be nihilists is often supposed to be a paradigm case of a metaphysical debate that is largely independent of scientific considerations.[23] But this attitude, I will argue, is a mistake. Considerations from scientific practice, if not from the content of scientific theories, do in fact bear on this debate. The conclusion of the minimal divergence argument suggests that we should not be nihilists.[24]

More carefully, I will argue that the conclusion of the minimal divergence argument suggests that we should not be nihilists but also that the reason why it suggests as much depends on what sort of nihilism one adopts. In particular it depends on whether the nihilist is willing to allow that the world appears (mistakenly, on her view) to contain tables and chairs and school buses and other everyday composite objects, or if she instead insists that the way the world appears to be is neutral between there being tables and school buses and there merely being simples arranged like tables and school buses. Let us call the version of nihilism that says that the world does appear to contain tables and the like—despite the fact that, on her view, those appearances are seriously misleading—*radical nihilism*. And let us call the version of nihilism that says that in fact the way the world appears to be is neutral between there being everyday composite objects and there merely being simples arranged like such objects *nuanced nihilism*. According to nuanced nihilism, the way the world appears to be is "theory-laden" in the sense that the way the world appears will depend on the theory that we implicitly or explicitly endorse. It is only because we aren't nihilists that we think the world appears to contain tables and chairs. Were we to fully internalize the nihilist position, we would not see school buses, only atoms arranged school bus–wise.

The Minimal Divergence Argument against Radical Nihilism

The argument above applies to radical nihilism in a relatively straightforward way. As a first step, notice that radical nihilism diverges significantly from the manifest image. For many propositions that are part of the

---

[23] See, for instance, Ladyman (2012, 39).
[24] Does it also suggest that we should not be universalists about composition (that we should not think that any two or more things compose a third thing)? Maybe. But it is difficult to say whether universalism *conflicts* with the manifest image, or if it merely *goes beyond* the manifest image in the sense described in section 5.2. If it is the latter, a version of the principle of minimal divergence that tells against universalism may be slightly different from the one under consideration here.

manifest image—that there is a desk before me, that there is a school bus on the road outside my window, and so on—radical nihilism contradicts these propositions.

That is only a first step, however. In order for the principle of minimal divergence to have any bearing on radical nihilism we need also to establish that there is an empirically and explanatorily equivalent alternative theory that diverges less from the manifest image. The most obvious candidate for such a theory would be some sort of *conservatism* about composition. According to conservatism, what we think of as ordinary composite objects, like chairs and school buses, do in fact exist, but surprising composites of ordinary objects and their parts, like an object that is composed out of the chair I am sitting on and the school bus passing by outside my window, do not. (Conservatism is distinct, therefore, from both nihilism, which says that no composite objects exist, and *universalism*, which says that for any two or more objects those objects compose a further object.)[25]

But—and this is important—not just any sort of conservatism will do. Consider, for instance, *brute* conservatism: the view that those composite objects that appear to exist (like chairs and school buses) in fact exist, and those composite objects that appear not to exist (like chair-buses) do not in fact exist *and there is no further reason why some composite objects exist and some do not*.[26] Brute conservatism clearly diverges less from the manifest image than nihilism. But it is not explanatorily adequate. To put forward such a view is to leave an important pattern unexplained—some groups of objects compose further objects and some do not, and there is no further reason why the former do and the latter do not.

The kind of alternative that the principle of minimal divergence will most obviously favor over nihilism, then, will be a theory that is both *conservative*—in the sense that it says that ordinary composite objects do in fact exist—and *principled*—in the sense that it provides some explanation for why some composite objects exist and some do not. Are there viable ways of constructing a *principled conservativist* theory of composition? I can neither fully survey the options for such a theory nor adequately defend any of those options here, but let me say a bit about two types of objections to such

---

[25] Again, I will not say anything here about how the principle of minimal divergence bears on universalism. This is a more complicated question than it first appears. See footnote 24 above. For a discussion of how some sort of Mooreanism might actually favor universalism over conservatism, see Fairchild and Hawthorne (2018).

[26] See Markosian (1998). (Thought note that this is no longer Markosian's view of composition. See Markosian (2014).)

theories and how those objections are affected by the minimal divergence argument.[27]

The first group of objections to principled conservatism are objections by counterexample. Consider the view that some things compose a further thing if and only if the things are dynamically integrated—they all tend to move together. Call this view *dynamical conservatism*. Dynamical conservatism coheres nicely with quite a bit of the manifest image. It says there are chairs and school buses but no chair-buses. But it may also yield some surprising results. Consider the complaint that dynamical conservatism will count a newborn calf and its mother as composing a further object—a *cowf*—since they tend to move together.[28]

Is dynamical conservatism really committed to the existence of cowfs? Insofar as it is, does that mean that dynamical conservatism contradicts the manifest image in the way that is relevant to the principle of minimal divergence? Both of these are difficult questions to answer with any precision. But happily, we can set both questions aside. For the key thing to notice here is that even if the answer to both questions is yes, that does not mean that the principle of minimal divergence rules out dynamical conservatism. The principle of minimal divergence, remember, does not say that we ought not accept any theory that diverges from the manifest image. It says that of two (empirically and explanatorily adequate) candidate theories, we ought to accept the one that diverges least. And even if dynamical conservatism diverges somewhat from the manifest image in positing cowfs, it hardly diverges as much as nihilism does. For *every* case in which there appears to be a composite object, nihilism says that there is no such thing.

The point here is just that looking for an empirically and explanatorily adequate alternative that diverges less from the manifest image than nihilism does is not the same thing as looking for a theory of composition that perfectly tracks which composite objects appear to exist and which do not. It is plausible that there are candidate theories—perhaps dynamical conservatism is one—that accomplish the former task even though they do not accomplish the latter.

The other group of objections to principled conservative theories of composition are what we might call objections by philosophical principle.

---

[27] Defenses of particular versions of principled conservatism about composition include Carmichael (2015) and Korman (2015).

[28] This objection is inspired by Markosian (1998, 226). Obviously whether or not dynamical conservatism is so committed depends on how you understand the phrase "tend to move together."

Philosophers have argued that any principled conservative theory will face worries about vagueness, for instance, or arbitrariness or overdetermination. If these sorts of considerations can be said to trump considerations to do with the principle of minimal divergence, then perhaps we ought to be nihilists after all. Of course, these arguments are contentious.[29] I don't have space to go into the details of each of these arguments here, but let me make two points about how they will be affected by the minimal divergence argument.

First, once the minimal divergence argument is on the table, one must be careful to make sure that similar objections by philosophical principle do not support any of the radical metaphysical hypotheses listed in section 5.3 over our best scientific theories—if they did so, a modified version of the principle of minimal divergence that respected such arguments would no longer explain why standard scientific practice consistently chooses theories that conflict with those hypotheses.

Consider, for instance, the view put forward in Sider (2013). Sider notes that a potential objection to nihilism is that we have perceptual evidence for composite objects, but even if such evidence provides some initial justification for the view that there are composite objects, that initial justification "vanishes" once further evidence is collected (2013, 20–23). This, he argues, is how perceptual evidence works with respect to conflicting scientific evidence: it appears to us that tables are solid, for instance, and that provides some initial justification for the view that tables are solid, but as soon as we collect the scientific evidence that supports atomic theory, that initial justification is not just outweighed; it no longer counts for anything at all. The same goes, he contends, for the evidence that supports nihilism—once we recognize that further evidence, the perceptual evidence that supports the view that ordinary composite objects exist is no longer relevant.

In response to this argument note first that the principle of minimal divergence is wholly compatible with the view that evidence that calls into question a theory's empirical or explanatory adequacy makes perceptual evidence irrelevant. As such the principle of minimal divergence itself can explain the apparent irrelevance of perceptual evidence to, e.g., the question of whether a table is solid, once the evidence for atomic theory is recognized.[30]

What about the further evidence that Sider thinks (a) supports nihilism and (b) is also capable of making perceptual evidence irrelevant? Sider's own

---

[29] For a survey of and detailed discussions of these sorts of objections, see Korman (2015). See Rettler (2018) for a strategy for dismissing them wholesale.

[30] It is also sufficient to capture the other three examples that Sider (2013) discusses on pages 22–23.

argument for nihilism is based on the *ideological parsimony* of that view—where a theory is ideologically parsimonious to the extent that it does not rely on undefined notions. Since nihilism does not rely on the notion of a *part*, and alternative approaches to the debate over composition do, nihilism is more ideologically parsimonious than its rivals. So Sider's thought is that when some candidate theory T is more ideological parsimonious than its rivals, that is sufficient to make any perceptual evidence in favor of T's rivals irrelevant.

But once the minimal divergence argument is on the table, this claim is problematic. For some of the radical metaphysical hypotheses themselves are more ideologically parsimonious than our best scientific theories (most obviously solipsistic idealism and the Boltzmann Brain hypothesis, though others, like the brain-in-a-vat or evil demon hypotheses, can also be constructed so as to be ideologically parsimonious).[31] So if Sider is correct that ideological parsimony makes perceptual evidence irrelevant, the principle of minimal divergence would not provide a satisfactory explanation of the fact that our best scientific theories conflict with the radical metaphysical hypotheses. And, as discussed, in section 5.3, we have no good alternative explanation of the fact that our best scientific theories do so conflict. So we ought not accept Sider's objection to principled conservatism. Until we have some plausible alternative on the table, we cannot simply jettison the principle of minimal divergence, or reinterpret it in such a way that it no longer does the work for which it was designed, no matter how tempted we might be to do so in defense of our favored philosophical views.

Here is a second, more general point about how the minimal divergence argument should change the dialectic around these sorts of arguments against conservatism. Previously one might have thought that all that various versions of principled conservatism had going for them was that they cohered nicely with the manifest image, and assumed that such coherence, if it was a consideration at all, counted for little. So as soon as it is pointed out that in order to maintain principled conservatism one must find a way of avoiding these various objections by philosophical principle, and that that avoidance comes with at least some cost, one ought to retreat happily to nihilism. But the minimal divergence argument above shows that this way of

---

[31] Just as an example, suppose that the world is actually Newtonian, but our envatted brains are being stimulated with data that suggests all the complexity of post-Newtonian physics. Surely this theory is more ideologically parsimonious than our best scientific theories.

thinking about the potential costs and benefits of principled conservatism is mistaken. It is a significant and serious count against a theory to diverge more than empirically and explanatorily adequate rivals from the manifest image. Such divergence trumps other sorts of extra-empirical criteria that play a central role in scientific theory choice. Perhaps at the end of the day we will be forced to accept such divergence in order to maintain highly important philosophical principles. But the bar is set very high for anyone who wants to argue this much. Principled conservatism ought to be the default position[32] not just in the sense that it is familiar from ordinary language and thought, but in the sense that there are weighty considerations from standard scientific practice that pull in its favor.

The Minimal Divergence Argument against Nuanced Nihilism

So much for radical nihilism. What about nuanced nihilism? The conclusion of the minimal divergence argument also suggests that we ought not be nuanced nihilists, but for somewhat different reasons. After all, nuanced nihilism does not diverge substantially from the manifest image. According to the nuanced nihilist, the way the world appears to be is neutral between her theory and her competitor's—the way the world appears to be is neutral between it containing tables and school buses and it containing particles arranged table-wise and particles arranged school bus–wise. Because few of us are nihilists, we talk and act in a way that suggests that the world appears to contain tables and chairs and school buses, but this is just a result of the fact (according to the nuanced nihilist) that the way the world appears to be is influenced by the theory we have implicitly or explicitly adopted.

But once the minimal divergence argument is on the table, it would be a serious mistake for the nihilist to insist on this kind of neutral interpretation of the way the world appears to be. For if we take appearances to be neutral in this way, we undermine the extent to which minimal divergence can provide a good explanation for the fact that our best scientific theories conflict with the radical metaphysical hypotheses. If we were allowed to play the nuanced

---

[32] At least insofar as it is being compared with nihilism. Again, I make no commitments here regarding how the argument extends to universalism.

card, so to speak, then we would no longer have an explanation for why the radical metaphysical hypotheses conflict with our best scientific theories.

Here is why. Above, I assumed that we should take it as uncontroversial that all of the radical metaphysical hypotheses listed diverge significantly from the manifest image. But if the nuanced nihilist is allowed to claim that her theory does not in fact conflict with the way the world appears to be, then surely she should presumably *also* be willing to allow that the radical metaphysical hypotheses do not conflict with the way the world appears to be. The world does not in fact appear to contain school buses; instead it appears to be such that either it contains school buses or it contains atoms arranged school bus–wise *or* it contains a simulation of a school bus. And the principle of minimal divergence would no longer provide any explanation at all for the fact that our best scientific theories conflict with the radical metaphysical hypotheses.

So the argument above also gives us reason not to be nuanced nihilists. If we were to allow appearances to be theory-laden in the way that the nuanced nihilist does we would have to give up the first premise of the minimal divergence argument. And we shouldn't give up the first premise; it was the best and perhaps only explanation for the fact that our best scientific theories are incompatible with the radical metaphysical hypotheses.[33]

5.5 Recap

I have presented and defended the minimal divergence argument for Mooreanism in metaphysics and shown how that argument impacts a particular first-order debate in metaphysics—the debate over whether there are composite objects. The goal has thus been to convince the reader not only that the argument is sound, but also that it is impactful. Much work is left to be done in making the principle of minimal divergence precise and in investigating whether and how the minimal divergence argument impacts other metaphysical debates. But in the meantime, naturalistically inclined philosophers—and methodological naturalists in particular—should not be so quick to disparage metaphysics in general on the grounds that it involves appeals to Moorean principles. For at least one type of Mooreanism plays

---

[33] Note that this is not a story about what exactly is wrong with the nuanced nihilist's story; instead it is an argument that something must be wrong with it.

an important role in standard scientific methodology as well. Nor should they be so quick to disparage particular first-order debates in metaphysics as pointless because the content of our best scientific theories is silent with respect to those debates. For the methodological naturalist, standard scientific practice may still have important consequences for those debates via the extra-empirical principles that play an important role in that practice, like the principle of minimal divergence.

6
Case Study
Excess Structure

Let's turn now to a third case study. In this case study, I'm going to demonstrate a more complicated way in which methodological naturalism can yield interesting results. Instead of arguing for one particular metaphysical view, I'm going to demonstrate how methodological naturalism can have consequences for the combinations of views that we accept.

The focus of this chapter will be on the relationship between debates about *temporal ontology* (debates about whether the past and future exist in addition to the present) and debates about *modal ontology* (debates about whether merely possible worlds exist in addition to the actual world). It has often been observed that there are interesting structural similarities between these debates. The metaphysician of modality faces the choice between *actualism*, which is the view that only the actual world exists, and *possibilism*, which is the view that in addition to the actual world, merely possible worlds also exist. Similarly the metaphysician of time faces the choice between *presentism*, which is the view that only the present moment exists, and *eternalism*, which is the view that in addition to the present, the past and future exist as well. On the face of it, it seems plausible that those who are initially drawn to actualism will also be drawn to presentism, and that those who are initially drawn to possibilism will be drawn to eternalism. The former combination of views will be attractive to those who have a preference for a certain kind of simplicity—a Quinean taste for desert landscapes, perhaps—while the latter combination will be attractive to those who are happy to have an expansive ontology that straightforwardly provides truthmakers for the wide range of claims that we make about the world.

In practice, however, there are very few presentists, while actualism remains a highly popular account of modal metaphysics. Why is this the case? For two reasons. First, as mentioned in Chapter 1, there is a conflict between presentism and a straightforward account of the content of the theory of special relativity. Since most metaphysicians are content naturalists, and few metaphysicians are willing to take a revisionary position regarding the content of special relativity, this means that few metaphysicians are willing to be presentists.[1] Second, there is no similar conflict between actualism and the content of special relativity. It looks, therefore, as though there is a serious objection to presentism that leaves actualism unscathed.

In this chapter, I argue that this last claim is a mistake. Yes, it is true that there is a conflict between presentism and special relativity such that content naturalists should not accept presentism. And yes, it is true that there is no conflict between actualism and the content of special relativity. But it does not follow that there is an objection to presentism that leaves actualism unscathed. This is because, as I argued earlier in this book, one should be a content naturalist only if one is also a methodological naturalist. So if one is willing to give up presentism on content naturalist grounds, due to a conflict with special relativity, one should also be willing to take the methodology that produced special relativity on board as a guide to theory choice in metaphysics quite generally. And while there is no conflict between the content of special relativity and actualism, there is a methodological principle that plays a key role in the acceptance of special relativity over its rivals, and that principle bears on actualism as well. Indeed, as I will argue, if one rejects presentism due to the conflict with special relativity, one should also reject actualism.

Here is a plan for this chapter. In section 6.1, I present the relativity objection to presentism and show how this objection turns on the claim that there is no *privileged reference frame*. In section 6.2, I show how one could level an analogous objection against actualism as long as one is willing to claim that there is no *privileged modal perspective* (more on what that is below). In section 6.3, I argue that the methodological principle that underwrites the claim that there is no privileged reference frame also supports the claim that there is no privileged modal perspective. In section 6.4, I put all of this together to argue that if one rejects presentism due to the conflict with special relativity, one should also reject actualism.

A couple of quick comments about the intended scope of the argument before we begin.

---

[1] For discussions of the objection to presentism from special relativity, see, for instance, Putnam (1967), Callender (2000), Savitt (2000), Sider (2001), Saunders (2002), Balashov and Janssen (2003). Defenders of presentism in light of the relativity objection include Hinchliff (2000), Craig (2000), Markosian (2004), and Bourne (2006). See also helpful discussion in Hawley (2009).

First, in what follows I focus on *radical actualism*, the view that only actually existing things exist, and on *radical presentism*, the view that only presently existing things exist. But the argument I present will apply straightforwardly to *ersatz actualism*, the view that only actually existing things are concrete (but there are non-concrete mere possibilia) and *ersatz presentism*, the view that only presently existing things are concrete (but there are non-concrete past or future entities).[2] Insofar as a version of the relativity objection to presentism gives us reason not to be ersatz presentists, a version of the relativity-inspired objection to actualism gives us reason not to be ersatz actualists either.[3] When relevant, I will point out slight differences between these different versions of the argument in the footnotes.

Second, it is worth emphasizing up front that I will present the relativity objection as an objection from special relativity, and will say nothing about whether and to what extent that objection extends to general relativity or quantum gravity.[4] This is in keeping with the majority of the literature.

6.1 How the Lack of a Privileged Reference Frame Creates Difficulty for Presentism

According to the relativity objection to presentism, there is an unavoidable conflict between presentism and relativity theory. In this section, I am going

---

[2] Other views in the vicinity include proxy actualism, according to which mere possibilia do not exist, but there are non-concrete entities that play the role that mere possibilia would play if they had existed; and proxy presentism, according to which wholly past and future entities do not exist, but there are non-concrete entities that play the role that past and future entities would play if they had existed. I discuss these distinctions, and how they bear on the relativity objection to presentism, in Emery (2017c and 2021).

[3] So my argument will support one of the key claims that Zimmerman (2008) makes in his defense of A-theories of time (theories of time that say, in part, that there is something metaphysically distinctive about the present time). Zimmerman claims that the relativity objection has the following form: "Physics does not imply that one out of some class of things has a special status; so, for a person who has learned the relevant physics, there is no reason to believe that one of them is special." But he goes on, "[P]hysics alone will not tell us whether [concrete possible worlds] exist—at least, I can see no argument from statements in the language of physics, describing the contents of our universe and its laws, to the conclusion that merely possible worlds are not universes much like ours but merely spatially and temporally disconnected from us. Nevertheless, I believe that I remain fully justified in maintaining my conviction that this universe is special—that it is radically unlike the merely possible ones, if there are any such things. This belief is something that I quite reasonably take for granted; and the fact that it finds no support from physics is quite irrelevant" (Zimmerman, 2008, 219-220). As the reader will see below, both of these claims require more detailed treatment than Zimmerman is able to give them in the piece in question, but that more detailed treatment clearly supports Zimmerman's conclusion.

[4] See Savitt (2000), Norton (2000), Monton (2006), and Wüthrich (2010 and 2011) for discussion.

to present my favored way of thinking about that conflict, but it is worth emphasizing that different philosophers spell out this conflict in different ways.[5] The key point to note is that everyone agrees that the conflict between presentism and relativity turns on the claim that there is no privileged reference frame. (I'll say a lot more about what that claim means below.) And it is the claim that there is no privileged reference frame that plays a key role in my argument. So, even if you prefer a different way of thinking about the conflict between presentism and special relativity, everything that I say below should extend to your way of thinking.

The Relativity Objection to Presentism

As noted in Chapter 1, one of the key commitments of relativity theory is the following principle:

The conventionality of simultaneity. There are pairs of events such that there is no fact of the matter as to whether those events happen at the same time.[6]

---

[5] The way of presenting the relativity objection that I focus on follows Markosian (2004) and Hawley (2009). Others focus on the claim that presentism is in some sense *directly* incompatible with the relativity of simultaneity. (See, e.g., Tooley 2012, Saunders 2002, and Balashov and Janssen 2003.) Closely related versions of the objection involve claims about the direct incompatibility of the structure of Minkowski spacetime and the spatiotemporal structure needed by the presentist, as in Sider (2001) or Skow (2015). Again, what will be important for my argument below is that all of these objections involve a commitment to the conventionality of simultaneity. That goes also for Putnam (1967) (although the way in which the conventionality of simultaneity features in Putnam's argument is more complicated).

[6] Two points about the way that I am using the locution 'there is no fact of the matter as to p.' First, there being no fact of the matter as to p is wholly compatible with there being lots of facts regarding p *relative to some salient kind of restriction or qualification*. For instance, as I am using the locution, there being no fact of the matter as to whether Mika is to the left of Sabryna is entirely compatible with it being the case that Mika is to the left of Sabryna *when you look at them from my perspective*—what is important is just that there is no non-perspective-relative fact as to whether Mika is to the left of Sabryna. In the case at issue here, there is no fact of the matter, for any two spacelike separated events, whether those events happen at the same time. This is wholly compatible with there being facts about whether those events happen at the same time *for some observer* and indeed with there being facts about whether those events happen at the same time *in some reference frame*, whether or not that frame is "occupied" (i.e., whether or not that frame is one that is natural for some existing observer to use. What is important is just that there is no non-observer-relative, or non-reference-frame-relative fact as to whether those events happen at the same time. Second, as I am using the locution 'there is no fact of the matter as to whether p,' it follows from it being indeterminate whether p that there is no fact of the matter as to p and it also follows from it making no sense to ask whether p that there is no fact of the matter as to p. So, for instance, those who think that what relativity teaches us is that it doesn't make sense to ask whether two spacelike events happen at the same time in some non-reference-frame-relative sense should still accept the conventionality of simultaneity as defined above.

Physicists call such pairs of events *spacelike separated*, so another way to state the conventionality of simultaneity is that for any two spacelike separated events, there is no fact of the matter as to whether those events happen at the same time.[7]

In what follows, I will have quite a bit to say about the conventionality of simultaneity and why scientists endorse it (some of which was foreshadowed in Chapter 1). For the moment, however, I want to focus on the way in which the conventionality of simultaneity, once accepted, gives rise to an objection to presentism. With that goal in mind, note that the conventionality of simultaneity leads straightforwardly to the following principle:

The conventionality of presentness. There is at least one entity such that there is no fact of the matter as to whether that entity presently exists.

Consider, for instance, some event that is happening now—say, your experience of reading these words. (Those who are already used to a relativistic way of thinking about things may insist that there is no such event—for each event, there is no fact of the matter as to whether it is happening now. But if that is your view, I take it that you are already committed to the relativity of presentness.) And consider some muon, MU, in the upper atmosphere. Let MU be such that the decay of MU is spacelike separated from your experience of reading these words. (Since there are lots of muons and they are relatively short-lived, there almost certainly is such a muon.) MU presently exists if and only if MU decays after your experience of reading these words. (Since muons are fundamental particles, it is especially implausible to think that MU survives decay in any sense.) But according to the conventionality of simultaneity, there is no fact of the matter as to whether MU decays after your experience of reading these words. So there is no fact of the matter as to whether MU presently exists.

But now the challenge to the presentist is clear. It follows from the conventionality of simultaneity that there is no fact of the matter as to whether MU presently exists. And according to the presentist, for any entity, that entity exists if and only if it presently exists. So, according to the presentist, there

---

[7] For more details on how the conventionality of simultaneity arises in special and general relativity, see Geroch (1981) and Mermin (2009). One key point is that everything I say here and throughout follows even if you think of relativity theory as a theory about the geometrical structure of spacetime. For instance, if you think of special relativity as the claim that the structure of spacetime is the structure of Minkowski spacetime, then there is no fact of the matter as to the temporal distance between two spacetime points. The conventionality of simultaneity follows.

is no fact of the matter as to whether MU exists. But that is absurd. For any muon, either that muon exists or it doesn't.

In what follows it will help to be able to refer to the premises of this argument clearly, so let's set them out as so:

P1   If presentism is true, then for any entity, that entity exists if and only if it presently exists.

P2   There is at least one entity such that there is no fact of the matter as to whether that entity presently exists.

P3   If presentism is true, then there is at least one entity such that there is no fact of the matter as to whether that entity exists.

P4   It is not the case that there is some entity such that there is no fact of the matter as to whether that entity exists.[8]

C   Presentism is not true.[9]

Presentists are committed to P1.[10] P4 is highly plausible—in Chapter 1 I called this claim *determinate existence* and noted that almost no one disputes it. And P3 follows straightforwardly from P1 and P2.[11] So it seems that the only real way for a presentist to resist the argument is by resisting P2. But P2, remember, is just the conventionality of presentness, which, as we said above, follows straightforwardly from the conventionality of simultaneity. And on

---

[8] If you are inclined to think that there is ontic vagueness in the world, you may find P4, in the general form it takes here, implausible. In that case, you should replace each instance of the word 'entity' in this argument with 'muon'. Even those who think that there is ontic vagueness presumably don't think that the existence of a fundamental particle like a muon can be vague in the sense relevant here. A similar part applies, *mutatis mutandis*, to the relativity objection to actualism presented in the next section.

[9] The version of this argument that targets ersatz presentism can be generated just by replacing each instance of 'exists' with the words 'is concrete.' The reader will note that this leaves P2 unchanged. So insofar as the presentist wishes to reject P2, it makes no difference whether she is a radical or an ersatz presentist.

[10] Some might try to respond to this objection by replacing P1 with a principle of the form: For any thing, that thing exists if and only if it exists at R, where R is a region of spacetime that is such that (a) according to relativity theory there is a fact of the matter as to whether a point is within R, and (b) the shift to this new principle can plausibly be construed as a revision, as opposed to a rejection, of presentism. (Both Hinchliff 2000 and Sider 2001 contain overviews of these sorts of attempts.) But these sorts of moves won't end up being relevant here, since there is no analogous way of responding to the relativity-inspired objection to actualism that I will present in section 6.3—that is, there is no obvious way of avoiding that objection by rejecting premise A1. (And remember, my claim is only that if you accept the relativity objection to presentism, then you ought to accept the relativity-inspired objection to actualism. I make no claim as to whether you should in fact accept the relativity objection to presentism.)

[11] I am assuming the following is a valid inference: from *X if and only if Y* and *there is no fact of the matter as to whether Y* conclude *there is no fact of the matter as to whether X*.

any standard way of thinking about the content of special relativity, the conventionality of simultaneity is a part of that content.

It follows, then, that content naturalists should not be presentists.

The Importance of No Privileged Reference Frame

Let's look a bit closer, though, at the conventionality of simultaneity, and the reason why we accepted a theory that had this claim as a part of its content in the first place.

Why do scientists endorse the conventionality of simultaneity? Part of the answer is that scientists have empirical results that show that there are pairs of events that are such that, according to some reference frames, those events happen at the same time, and according to other reference frames, those events happen at different times. But on their own, those empirical results—I'll call them the Michelson-Morley results—are not enough to establish the conventionality of simultaneity.[12] Those results must be combined with the claim that there is no fact of the matter as to which reference frame is correct. As I put it in Chapter 1, the conventionality of simultaneity follows from the following two principles:

The relativity of simultaneity. There are pairs of events such that in some inertial reference frames those events happen at the same time and in some inertial reference frames they do not.

No privileged reference frame (NPRF). If two or more inertial reference frames disagree about some feature of the world, then there is no fact of the matter with respect to that feature.

Notice that insofar as there is some privileged reference frame—insofar, that is, as there is some non-merely-reference-frame-relative fact about which reference frame is correct—that would in turn determine some fact of the matter as to which pairs of spacelike separated events happen at the same

---

[12] The Michelson-Morley experiment was the most famous experiment involved, but hardly the only one. What it showed, as I say below, is that the speed of light is independent of the speed of the source. It's actually somewhat controversial whether Einstein himself was motivated by these empirical results (he refers to them in his 1905 paper, but only parenthetically) or if he was solely motivated by the thought that Maxwell's laws should hold in every inertial reference frame. See Mermin (2009) for discussion.

time. So insofar as there is a privileged reference frame, the conventionality of simultaneity is false. If you deny NPRF, you must deny P2. And if you accept P2, you must also accept NPRF.

Although this point will be familiar to many, it is worth going through it in detail, since when we get to the argument below it will be crucial to be clear on what a reference frame is and what it means to claim that there is no privileged reference frame.

Start with the notion of a reference frame. A reference frame is just a certain kind of coordinate system—a coordinate system that assigns spatial and temporal coordinates in such a way that it determines the temporal and spatial distance between any two events. Consider, for instance, the natural way in which I would describe the motion of the various objects that I observed while standing on the train platform this morning: the station platform was stationary while the northbound train traveled past at a constant, high velocity. In describing the motions of the platform and the train in this way I am making use of a coordinate system in which the various parts of the platform occupy the same regions of space at successive moments of time. That reference frame—the platform frame—is a particularly natural one for me to use because it is one in which I am stationary. But I also could have described the situation using the northbound frame—the frame in which the train was stationary and the platform itself was moving south at a constant, high velocity.

The first thing to note about reference frames is that the laws of physics hold in more than one of them. Here, for instance, is a result familiar since Galileo. Let RF1 and RF2 be references frames such that the only difference between RF1 and RF2 is that every object that is traveling at velocity v at time t in RF1 is traveling at v + c at t in RF2 (where c is some constant). It will follow that the laws that accurately predict and explain experiments performed in RF1 will also accurately predict and explain experiments performed in RF2.[13] Galileo argued for this by thinking about experiments performed in the hold of a smoothly sailing ship that was traveling at a constant velocity— the results of those experiments, he argued, would be accurately predicted and explained by the very same laws that accurately predict and explain the results of experiments performed on land. But the same point will be familiar to anyone who has woken up on a train and had to look out the window in

---

[13] This is often called the *relativity principle*. And the way physicists often put it is that the relativity principle shows that the laws are invariant with respect to changes in uniform velocity.

order to determine whether the train was stopped at a station or traveling at a constant speed in one direction or another.

The second thing to note about reference frames is that the laws of physics do not hold in *all* of them. Suppose that as I stood on the platform this morning there was also a southbound train pulling into the station. In the platform frame the southbound train was decelerating. In the southbound frame, it was stationary and the platform was decelerating instead. But there was no force acting on the platform that would cause this deceleration. Nor did the force that was acting on the southbound train—the pressure applied by its brakes—result in a corresponding change in the motion of that train in keeping with the relevant laws. Instead, the train remained stationary. So the laws do not hold in the southbound frame.[14]

Let's call a reference frame in which the laws of physics hold a *nomological reference frame*.[15] What Galileo showed was that, with respect to the laws of classical physics, nomological reference frames will at least sometimes disagree about the velocity of objects upon which no force is acting. The platform frame and the northbound frame, for instance, will disagree about whether the northbound train is moving. In the platform frame it is, but in the northbound frame it is not.

Return now to the Michelson-Morley results, which played such an important role in establishing the relativity of simultaneity. What these results showed is that the speed of light is the same regardless of the velocity of the source from which that light is emitted. It follows that nomological reference frames will also at least sometimes disagree about whether certain pairs of events happen at the same time.[16] The argument is familiar from physics texts. Suppose that as the northbound train described above passes through the station, Alice, who is sitting in the middle of one of the cars, turns on a light bulb. Let FRONT be the event of the light from Alice's bulb reaching the front wall of the train car and BACK be the event of the light from Alice's bulb reaching the back wall. In the northbound frame, FRONT and BACK happen at the same time. (After all, the walls of the train car are stationary and are equally distant from the bulb, and the bulb itself is stationary, so the speed at which the light emitted from the front of the bulb is traveling toward

---

[14] As this example shows, the laws are not invariant with respect to acceleration.

[15] In Chapter 1, I used the term *inertial reference frames*. Nomological reference frame are, in principle, a more general category. Given the actual laws of physics, inertial reference frames are nomological reference frames.

[16] This fact can also be characterized as a fact about a further way in which the laws are invariant—they are *Lorentz invariant*.

the front wall is the same as the speed at which the light emitted from the back of the bulb is traveling toward the back wall.)

Now consider the same situation described using the platform frame. It follows from the Michelson-Morley results that in the platform frame, the velocity of the light traveling toward the front of the car and the velocity of the light traveling toward the back of the car are the same as they were in the northbound frame. But in the platform frame, the walls of the train car are no longer stationary. The front wall of the car is moving away from the light emitted from Alice's bulb, and the back wall of the car is moving toward it. So the light has a shorter distance to travel to reach the back of the train car. So, in the platform frame, BACK will occur before FRONT.

There are two important lessons to be drawn from this discussion, both of which will be relevant to the argument below. The first is the one that I emphasized above: on their own, all that the Michelson-Morley results establish is that there are pairs of events—like BACK and FRONT—such that according to some reference frames, those events happen at the same time, and according to other reference frames, those events happen at different times. It is only if, in addition, you accept NPRF that you can establish the further claim that for such pairs of events there is no fact of the matter as to whether those events happen at the same time. Anyone who endorses the conventionality of simultaneity, therefore, must have some reason for accepting NPRF.

The second important lesson is that whatever scientists' reasons for accepting NPRF, they do not also support the claim that all reference frames are on a par. Consider, for instance, the situation before the Michelson-Morley results were observed. At that time, no physicists endorsed the conventionality of simultaneity. But it was still the case that at that time there was a reference frame—the northbound frame, as described above—in which BACK and FRONT were simultaneous, and a reference frame—the platform frame, as described above—in which BACK occurs before FRONT. Why didn't that disagreement lead to physicists accepting the conventionality of simultaneity even before the Michelson-Morley results were observed? Because before the Michelson-Morley results were observed, physicists thought that the platform frame was not a nomological reference frame. They thought it involved violations of the laws of physics. So the fact that the platform frame disagreed with some nomological reference frame was irrelevant.

So NPRF—the claim that there is no privileged reference frame, which is required in order to establish the conventionality of simultaneity—is not the claim that insofar as there are disagreements between any two reference frames, there is no fact of the matter as to which reference frame is correct. Rather, NRPF is the following claim:

No privileged reference frame (NPRF). Insofar as there are disagreements between nomological reference frames, there is no fact of the matter as to which of those reference frames is correct.

As we will see below, this gives us an important starting point in investigating what would be a good reason for thinking that NPRF is true.

6.2 The Relativity-Inspired Objection to Actualism

Consider a view that I will call *modal relativism*. The modal relativist believes that there is no fact of the matter as to which entities are actual. From the perspective of this world, all and only entities that exist in this world are actual. From the perspective of a possible world in which purple cows exist, purple cows are actual. Depending on one's situation, some modal perspectives will be more natural to use than others. But crucially, according to the modal relativist, there is no fact of the matter as to which modal perspective is correct. There is no privileged *modal perspective*.[17]

Most possibilists are modal relativists. But possibilism and modal relativism can come apart. One could be a possibilist and say that there is a fact of the matter as to which entities are actual.[18] Can one also be an actualist and

---

[17] Recall from footnote 6 above that there being no fact of the matter as to which entities are actual is wholly compatible with there being facts of the matter about which entities are actual *relative to some salient qualification or restriction*. In this case the salient restriction is a restriction to some modal perspective or other, so there being no fact of the matter as to which entities are actual is wholly compatible with there being facts about which entities are actual *relative to some modal perspective*. The key claim to which the modal relativist is committed is the claim that there are no facts about what is actual that do not merely hold relative to some modal perspective or other. In terms familiar from Lewis (1986, 93), the modal relativist denies that there are any facts about what is *absolutely actual*, or *actual simpliciter*. Lewis assumes that actualists require a notion of absolute actuality, and thus that actualists should not be modal relativists. In what follows I spell out a more detailed argument for that conclusion. Those philosophers who think that the notion of absolute actuality or actuality simpliciter just doesn't make sense will automatically be modal relativists and will therefore, insofar as they want to be actualists, automatically face the objection below. (As will become clear momentarily, though, this doesn't mean that they automatically cannot be actualists; they just need to reject what I will call A4.)

[18] The obvious example of a possibilist who is also a modal relativist is Lewis (1986). For a defense of possibilism without modal relativism, see Bricker (2006 and 2008).

endorse modal relativism? Maybe. But anyone who takes this position faces a serious challenge.

The source of the challenge is the fact that modal relativism leads straightforwardly to:

> *The conventionality of actuality.* There is at least one entity such that there is no fact of the matter as to whether that entity actually exists.

Think, for instance, of some particular purple cow, COW. Does COW actually exist? According to the modal perspective that is natural for us to use, she does not. According to the modal perspective that is natural for COW to use, she does. And according to modal relativism, no modal perspective is privileged. So, according to modal relativism, there is no fact of the matter as to whether COW actually exists.[19]

But now the challenge to the actualist is clear. It follows from modal relativism that there is no fact of the matter as to whether some particular purple cow actually exists. And according to the actualist, for any entity, that entity exists if and only if it actually exists. So, according to the actualist, there is no fact of the matter as to whether the relevant purple cow exists. But that is absurd. For any purple cow, either that cow exists or it doesn't![20]

As above, it will help to make the premises of this argument explicit:

A1 If actualism is true, then for any entity, that entity exists if and only if it actually exists.

A2 There is at least one entity such that there is no fact of the matter as to whether that entity actually exists.

A3 If actualism is true, then there is at least one entity such that there is no fact of the matter as to whether that entity exists.

A4 It is not the case there is some entity such that there is no fact of the matter as to whether that entity exists.

---

[19] As with the argument from the conventionality of simultaneity to the conventionality of presentness, there are ways of resisting the argument in this paragraph, but none of them is very plausible. For instance, you could avoid the argument by claiming that every entity that exists necessarily exists. (And those who think that every entity necessarily exists tend also to think that every entity always exists, which will also allow for an analogous way of avoiding the argument from the conventionality of simultaneity to the conventionality of presentness. See Williamson 2002.)

[20] Versions of ersatz actualism that are compatible with modal relativism face a similar worry, but it is a worry about concreteness, as opposed to existence.

C   Actualism is not true.[21]

Actualists are committed to A1. A4 is highly plausible. (It's just another instance of determinate existence.) And A3 follows straightforwardly from A1 and A2. So it seems that the only real way for an actualist to resist the argument is by resisting A2.

Here's where there appears to be an important disanalogy between the modal case and the temporal case. Presentists were in a great deal of trouble here because P2 followed from the content of special relativity. But there is no scientific theory, analogous to special relativity, that supports A2.

Once one has accepted the connection between content naturalism and methodological naturalism, however, this disanalogy turns out not to be all that important after all. This is because—as I will argue in the next section—one should adopt the claim that there is no privileged reference frame only if one is committed to a certain methodological principle. And that methodological principle will also support the claim that there is no privileged modal perspective. To accept the claim that there is no privileged modal perspective, remember, is just to be a modal relativist, and modal relativism, as noted above, leads straightforwardly to A2.

So even though the content of special relativity is silent with respect to actualism, the methodology that produced special relativity creates just as much trouble for actualism as it did for presentism. And insofar as one respects the content of special relativity, one should also accept the methodology that produced that content. It follows that unless you have some antecedent reason for being an actualist without also being a presentist, you shouldn't reject presentism because of the conflict with special relativity unless you also reject actualism as well.

6.3 Privileged Reference Frames and Privileged Modal Perspectives

Let's recap. A reference frame is a coordinate system—a way of assigning spatiotemporal coordinates to events. To claim that there is no privileged

---

[21] The version of this argument that targets ersatz actualism can be generated just by replacing each instance of 'exists' with the words 'is concrete.' The reader will note that this leaves A2 unchanged. So insofar as the actualist wishes to reject A2 it makes no difference whether she is a radical actualist or an ersatz presentist.

reference frame (in the sense relevant to the conventionality of simultaneity) is to claim that there is a group of reference frames—the nomological reference frames—within which, insofar as there are disagreements between those reference frames, there is no fact of the matter as to which reference frame is correct. We are calling this claim NPRF.

Turn now to the question of why we should accept NPRF. Why do scientists accept this claim? I submit that it is because the following principle is a part of standard scientific methodology:

The excess structure principle. When choosing between empirically adequate theories, do not choose a theory that posits excess structure.

Of course, the excess structure principle is not going to be especially substantive unless one says something more about what counts as "excess structure." Here, I think, the restriction to nomological reference frames discussed at the end of section 6.1 gives us a natural starting point. What seems to have been important to scientists in adopting the conventionality of simultaneity is that there are disagreements about simultaneity within the group of nomological reference frames. Disagreements between any old pair of reference frames don't matter. But disagreements between nomological reference frames do.

This suggests that the main motivation for NPRF is something like the combination of the excess structure principle with the following:

The law-neutrality principle. Suppose that you have more than one way of describing what there is and the accepted laws of physics hold according to all of them. A theory that privileges one of those ways of describing what these is over the others—that says that one such description is correct while the others are incorrect—is a theory that posits excess structure.[22]

According to this way of thinking, the reason for accepting NPRF is that there is a group of reference frames with respect to which the laws are entirely neutral. The laws themselves give you no reason for thinking one reference

---

[22] As an example of someone who defends this way of understanding the excess structure principle, consider North, who writes, "Physics adheres to the methodological principle that the symmetries in the laws match the symmetries in the structure of the world. This is a principle informed by Ockham's razor; though it is not just that, other things being equal, it is best to go with the ontologically minimal theory. It is not that, other things being equal, we should go with the fewest entities, but that we should go with the least structure" (North 2009, 64).

frame is privileged, and to think that one reference frame is privileged, therefore, is to posit excess structure.

But insofar as the excess structure principle, understood in this way, gives us reason to accept NPRF, it also gives us reason to think that there is no privileged modal perspective. A modal perspective, after all, can also be thought of as a kind of coordinate system—it is a way of assigning modal coordinates to events. (What is it to assign a modal coordinate to an event? At the least, it is to label the event as either actual or possible. Perhaps in addition modal coordinates should be thought of as specifying accessibility relations or closeness relations, but I'll leave that open here.) Moreover the laws are neutral with respect to a range of nomological modal perspectives—those corresponding to the nomologically possible worlds—in precisely the same way that they are neutral with respect to the nomological reference frames. The laws themselves give you no reason for thinking that one modal perspective is privileged in precisely the same way that they give you no reason for thinking that one reference frame is privileged.[23] And the claim that one modal perspective is privileged will go beyond the laws in precisely the same way as would the claim that there is a privileged reference frame.

Insofar as the excess structure principle gives us reason to accept NPRF, then, it also gives us reason to accept:

No privileged modal perspective (NPMP). Insofar as there are disagreements between nomological modal perspectives, there is no fact of the matter as to which of those modal perspectives is correct.

Before going on, let me take a moment to say something about how the law-neutrality principle relates to another way of understanding excess structure. In my experience, the reason that physicists most often bring up in conversation for resisting a privileged reference frame is that a privileged

---

[23] The fact that laws are neutral with respect to a range of modal perspectives in this way is not supposed to be a surprising observation—it follows straightforwardly, for instance, from the fact that the laws do not specify the exact initial conditions. So whereas the feature of laws that makes it the case that they are neutral between a range of what we now know to be nomological reference frames was not at all obvious and was something that we had to discover in the early 20th century, the feature of laws that makes it the case that they are neutral between a range of modal perspectives is something that should be pretty obvious. Why, then, is the relativity-inspired objection to actualism so under-appreciated? Presumably due to the fact that the principle that motivates NPRF is rarely made explicit and thought through in the context of theory choice in general (as opposed to in a context where only theories of spacetime are relevant).

reference frame is undetectable.[24] This suggests that they endorse the following principle:

The undetectable features principle. Insofar as a theory says that there are undetectable features of the world, that theory posits excess structure.[25]

But it is worth being careful here. First, notice that physicists often posit entities that are such that they are not straightforwardly detectable, given the technological capabilities of the time. (Think, for instance, of the introduction of the neutrino as discussed in Chapter 4.) So mere undetectability doesn't seem to be all that important. What does seem to be important, if we look at the particular case in hand, though, is a certain kind of *in principle* undetectability.

Consider the sense in which a privileged reference frame would be undetectable. Insofar as two nomological reference frames disagree as to whether p, there is no experiment that we can perform that will tell us which of those reference frames is correct. Of course the results of one and the same experiment might be different in different nomological reference frames. But the results in each frame will be what the laws say they should be. Let's suppose that in the platform frame the northbound train is traveling at a speed of 20 m/s. Then in the platform frame, the northbound train will be 100 meters farther north after 5 seconds. In the northbound frame, however, it will be in precisely the same place after 5 seconds. These results are different, and depending on your situation it may be more natural for you to use one of them rather than another. But—and this is the crucial part—according to the laws, each of these results is equally good. Each result is precisely what the laws say we should expect the results to be in that reference frame.

What this suggests is that insofar as undetectability matters it is in principle undetectability.

---

[24] It's harder to find them explicitly in print, but here's Feynman: "Whether or not one can define absolute velocity is the same as the problem of whether or not one can detect in an experiment, without looking outside, whether he is moving" (Feynman et al. 1963, 16-2).

[25] This way of understanding excess structure is defended, for instance, by Dasgupta, who writes, "What is wrong, epistemically speaking, with favoring a Newtonian view of space [on which there are facts about absolute velocity] over a Galilean one? . . . We have reason to think that [features of the world that vary between reference frames] are not real because (i) they are undetectable, and (ii) there is a more basic Occamist norm advising us to dispense with undetectable structure" (Dasgupta 2016, 841–842).

The in-principle undetectable features principle. Insofar as a theory says that there are in principle undetectable features of the world, that theory posits excess structure.

And note that the notion of in principle undetectability here involves a certain kind of law-neutrality. The reason why a privileged reference frame is in principle undetectable in the relevant sense is that the accepted laws of physics hold in all reference frames.

This suggests to me that there isn't actually that much difference between saying that excess structure is determined by law-neutrality or by undetectability. But note that even if you disagree with me, and think there is a substantive difference here, we will still end up with the same result. For a privileged modal perspective is also undetectable in the way that a privileged reference frame is. Insofar as two nomological modal perspectives disagree as to whether p, there is no experiment that we can perform that will tell us which of those perspectives is correct. Of course the results of one and the same experiment may be different from different nomological modal perspectives. In a world where the northbound train is even with the platform at t and is traveling at 20 m/s, the northbound train will be 100 meters beyond the platform 5 seconds after t. In a world in which the northbound train is 10 meters past the platform at t and is traveling at 20 m/s, the train will be 110 meters beyond the platform 5 seconds after t. These results are different, but—and this is the crucial part—according to the laws, each of these results is equally good. Each result is precisely what the laws say we should expect the results to be from that modal perspective.

In what follows I am going to assume that understanding excess structure in terms of law-neutrality and understanding excess structure in terms of in-principle undetectability amount to the same thing, and focus my discussion on the latter. But even if you disagree, note that a privileged modal perspective is going to count as undetectable in the same way that a privileged reference frame does, and therefore that it will still be the case that your reasons for endorsing NPRF will also give you reasons to endorse NPMP.

Of course, if you have some antecedent reason to think that actualism is more plausible than presentism, then you might use that reason to motivate adopting NPRF without also adopting NPMP. Take, for instance, the following point which I sometimes encounter in conversation:

> Here's a reason for insisting that there is a privileged modal perspective. I'm an actualist. Therefore, I think that only one possible world exists. So obviously I think there is a privileged modal perspective. It's the modal perspective that says that the one possible world that exists is the actual world!

That might be a perfectly fine reason to reject NPMP. But unless you have some antecedent reason for thinking actualism is more plausible than presentism, if you make the little speech above, then you should be just as happy to make the following speech as well:

> I'm a presentist. I think that only one time exists. So obviously I think there is a privileged reference frame. It's the reference frame that says that every event that exists is simultaneous with every other event that exists.

And in so doing, reject NPRF.

Similar considerations will arise with respect to someone who argues as follows:

> I don't think that the unnecessary structure principle carries no weight. Nor do I think that it is inviolable. Instead I think that violating the relevant principle comes at a cost, but sometimes it is worth paying that cost. Specifically, since I think there are some significant philosophical benefits of being an actualist, I think it is worth violating the relevant principle in order to accept a privileged modal perspective. But there are no similarly significant philosophical benefits of being a presentist that make it worth violating the relevant principle in order to adopt a privileged reference frame.

Before this line of reasoning will be convincing, we need to hear what the relevant philosophical benefits of actualism are (and make sure the presentist can't make analogous claims). But in any case, those who take this line explicitly claim to have some antecedent reason for being an actualist without also being a presentist. And the claim I have argued for in this section is only that unless you have some antecedent reason for being an actualist without also being a presentist, any good reason for accepting NPRF is going to also be a good reason for accepting NPMP.

Here is a related point. Many philosophers (and physicists) insist that we absolutely must accept something like the excess structure principle on the grounds that such a principle also plays a crucial role in eliminating other sorts of seemingly superfluous spatiotemporal structure—like absolute velocity or absolute direction.[26] But notice that this is not, in itself, an objection to my argument. What my argument establishes is that unless you have some antecedent reason for being an actualist without also being a presentist, any good reason for accepting NPRF is going to also be a good reason for accepting NPMP. This is perfectly compatible with thinking that there is good reason for accepting NPRF. If you have good reason for accepting NPRF and good reason for rejecting NPMP (and those reasons don't amount to antecedent reasons for thinking that actualism is more plausible than presentism), that would amount to an objection. But the considerations presented above suggest that such reasons are not readily available, if they exist at all. At the very least the burden is on anyone who thinks they have such reasons to present and defend them.

6.4 Objections and Replies

Let's turn now to consider some possible objections to the argument above.

Spacetime-Specific Principles

The first objection that I will consider involves some alternative principles that would motivate NPRF without motivating NPMP. I claimed in section 6.3 that no such principle is plausible. But principles that treat a privileged reference frame and a privileged modal perspective differently are actually quite easy to come by. Consider:

> *The excess structure principle—spacetime-specific version.* One ought not endorse a theory that posits excess spatiotemporal structure (but other kinds of excess structure are fine).

---

[26] In response to the question of whether the elimination of a privileged reference frame requires some kind of verificationism, Saunders, for instance, writes, "[I]f it is verificationism that is needed, to do away with an absolute 'up' in the face of rotational symmetry, then it is a form of it that is perfectly defensible, that we should all of us embrace: the form of it which eliminates an absolute state of rest in the face of the relativity principle" (2002, 290; Saunders attributes this point to Stein 1991).

Someone who endorses the spacetime-specific version of the excess structure principle but does not endorse the general version presented in section 6.3 can give a reason for accepting P2 that is not also a reason for accepting A2. But that is because such a person is *building in* an important difference between spatiotemporal structure on the one hand and modal structure on the other. They haven't provided a reason for thinking there is such a difference.[27] And the obvious question that faces someone who takes that route is: Why? Why endorse the spacetime version of the unnecessary structure principle without endorsing the general version? It will not do for them to answer "Because I think that our metaphysics of space and time is constrained by the laws of physics but our metaphysics of modality is not." For that just pushes the question back a step. Why should we think that our metaphysics of space and time is constrained by the laws of physics but our metaphysics of modality is not? Nor will it do to just point to the fact that philosophical discussions often focus on the spatiotemporal versions of the relevant principle.[28] A wholly plausible explanation for that fact is that the arguments that those philosophers are engaged in are arguments specifically about the correct spacetime structure. That they put forward something like the spacetime-specific version of the excess structure principle doesn't mean they wouldn't (or shouldn't) accept the general version of that principle if pressed.

In conversation I sometimes hear philosophers who are attracted by this line of reasoning claim that the reason why our metaphysics is constrained by the laws of physics but our metaphysics of modality is not is because the laws of physics are about past and future times but they aren't about other possible worlds. But I see no antecedent reason—no reason that comes prior to wanting to defend one's being an actualist without also being a presentist—for holding this view. The laws convey information about how systems evolve over time. But they also convey information about how systems would evolve if things had been different. Perhaps there is some specific sense of aboutness that is at play here. But until the relevant sense of aboutness is spelled out in detail, there is no reason to think that it will yield the result that the laws are

---

[27] I am open to the thought that this is—or at least might be—somewhat different from having an antecedent reason for thinking that actualism is more plausible than presentism, which is why I consider it a genuine objection.

[28] Consider, along these lines, Earman (1989) and discussions it has inspired. Belot, for instance, writes, "Why was it (in hindsight, in one sense) a mistake for Newton to postulate absolute space? Because he thereby postulated more spacetime structure than was required for his dynamics" (Belot 2013, 328).

about time but aren't about modality in a sense that would justify endorsing the spacetime-specific version of the excess structure principle but not the more general version.[29]

Arguments from the Content of Experience

Another way of objecting to my argument would be to try to point to some important difference between the modal content of experience on the one hand and the temporal content on the other. Such a difference could, at least in theory, be used to argue for a privileged modal perspective without also arguing for a privileged reference frame. Here is an example:

> My experience gives me good reason to think that some particular object—that very tree, for instance—actually exists. So my experience gives me good reason to think that there is a privileged modal perspective. The privileged modal perspective is the one that says that the modal content of my experience is accurate—that says, for instance, that that very tree exists.[30]

The first thing to note about this objection is that it relies on a substantive claim about transworld identity—that the objects that are available to us via perception do not exist according to other modal perspectives. I won't say anything about whether this is plausible or not, but at any rate, it is by no means obvious.[31]

The second thing to note is that the objection, as it stands, is incomplete. If we are allowed to appeal to that sort of argument as the reason for believing that there is a privileged modal perspective, then we should be willing to appeal to an analogous argument as providing good reason to think that there is a privileged reference frame. The analogous argument goes:

---

[29] Nor should one be tempted by the thought that merely possible worlds are just not the sort of thing that physics is designed to address because they are isolated from us in some important way (causally or spatiotemporally). Physicists have shown themselves quite willing to take seriously multiverse theories, where the other universes being posited are similarly isolated from us.

[30] A version of this objection that concerns ersatz actualism will focus on the fact that my experience gives me good reason to think that some particular object—that very tree, for instance—is concrete. (And not just concrete from my perspective—concrete full stop.) My response to this objection will mirror what I say in the main text. The key question is why we shouldn't be able to make a similar claim about the temporal content of our experience.

[31] Theories of transworld identity that are modeled on endurantist theories of perception, for instance, will disagree. See the discussion, for instance, in McDaniel (2004).

My experience gives me reason to think that some particular pair of events—my typing a particular sequence of words, and the branch tapping against the window of my office, for instance—are happening simultaneously. So my experience gives me good reason to think that there is a privileged reference frame. It is the one that says that the temporal content of my experience is accurate—that says, for instance, that my typing is simultaneous with the tree branch's tapping.

In the present context it is not enough to gesture to the modal content of experience; one must gesture to some difference between the modal content of experience, on the one hand, and the temporal content, on the other. With respect to the specific objection here, one needs to identify some way in which the modal content of experience might fix a privileged modal perspective which is not also a way in which the temporal content of experience might be used to fix a privileged reference frame. At the very least, this will require quite a bit of further argument.[32]

And it is also worth noting that if there is an objection along these lines it does not seem to be anything to do with relativity theory. Insofar as the temporal content of our experience fails to fix a privileged reference frame, presumably this is because it fails to fix a unique present moment. But then relativity theory becomes irrelevant. The objection is that our experience—according to this line of reasoning—is sufficient to fix a unique modal perspective, but it isn't sufficient to fix a unique temporal perspective, where a temporal perspective is a specification of which time is present. But this is just as much of a problem for the presentist in a pre-relativistic spacetime. So if there is a reason for being an actualist without also being a presentist here, it is not a reason to do with relativity theory.

A similar point applies to the observation that we are plausibly already committed to the temporal content of our experience being misleading in a certain sense. It seems to me, when I am looking through my telescope, that

---

[32] This is especially true once one recognizes that there is no particular reason why the presentist cannot allow that the present is not a single instantaneous instant, but a slightly extended temporal interval. (Obviously the extent to which the relevant interval is extended will need to be fairly minimal, if this sort of position is going to be plausibly considered to be a version of presentism.) Given the present context it is probably worth emphasizing that shifting from an instantaneous to an extended present does not involve adding any additional spatiotemporal structure. An extended temporal interval can be defined using an instant and what is called the *spacetime interval*—a way of measuring spatiotemporal distance in relativistic spacetime. An extended temporal interval EI, for instance, can be defined as all of the spacetime points in temporal instant I, and all of the points within spacetime interval S from a point within I.

the supernova is happening at the same time as various events that are happening nearby. But even if we insist that there is a privileged reference frame, this will not be correct, since the light that travels from the supernova has taken a very long time to reach me.

This observation might provide an opening for the actualist who does not also want to be a presentist, but notice that if it does, it is nothing to do with relativity theory. The key point, presumably, is that the motivation for presentism is undermined by the fact that the temporal content of our experience is misleading in a certain way. But that is something that we could have concluded as soon as we learned that our senses function by way of stimuli—like light—that take time to travel various distances. So if there is a reason for being an actualist without also being a presentist here, it is not a reason to do with relativity theory.

Arbitrariness and Error Theory

Here's a different line of objection. One way that reference frames and modal perspectives differ is that I can remember having occupied different reference frames—that is, I can remember times when it was natural for me to use reference frame R1 to describe my experience, and times when it was natural for me to use reference frame R2 to describe my experience, where R1 and R2 are distinct. (This isn't difficult—all I need to do is to recall the hour I spent on the train this morning.) So if I think there is a privileged reference frame, then I have to think that, with respect to which events are simultaneous with which, either (a) my experience while I was on the train this morning was misleading, or (b) my experience now is misleading, or (c) both experiences were misleading. Any choice between the first two options seems arbitrary. And the third choice involves a worrisome sort of error theory, especially for the presentist, who thinks that insofar as the temporal content of my experience is misleading, my experience is likely to end up being misleading with respect to what exists.

But this disanalogy between reference frames and modal perspectives is not a genuine disanalogy. Or at least there's no reason for taking it to be a genuine disanalogy unless you have antecedent reason to treat time differently from modality. After all, although I don't remember having occupied a different modal perspective than the one I occupy now, I could have occupied a different modal perspective. So if I think there is a privileged modal perspective, I have to think that, with respect to what entities are actual, either (a) my current experience in the actual world is misleading, or (b) my experience in which, say, I have an older brother would have been misleading, or (c) both experiences are misleading. Why think that a choice between these three options is any less troubling than the supposed trilemma that faced the presentist above?

A related objection, does somewhat better, however. This related objection turns on the fact that different people will occupy different reference frames at the same time. Consider a situation in which I am standing on the platform, and in which Alice is traveling past me at a constant velocity on the northbound train. Since Alice is traveling past me at a constant velocity, it is natural for her to use a different reference frame to describe her experiences. That means that if there is a privileged reference frame, either my experience is in some sense misleading with respect to which pairs of events are simultaneous, or Alice's is, or both. But it seems arbitrary to think that my experience is any better a guide to the privileged reference frame than Alice's, or vice versa. And it seems worrisome, especially for the presentist, to adopt the sort of wholesale error theory that comes with thinking we are both wrong.

This point needs to be spelled out carefully if the disanalogy being suggested is going to be substantive. After all, consider Bob. Let's assume Bob does not actually exist, but he does exist in a nearby possible world—one in which the train traveling past me is going at a slightly slower speed.[33] Since Bob is in a different possible world, it is natural for him to use a different modal perspective to describe his experiences. That means that if there is a privileged modal perspective, either my experience is in some sense misleading with respect to what actually exists, or Bob's is, or both. Why isn't it just as arbitrary to think that my experience is a better a guide to the privileged modal perspective than Bob's, or vice versa? Why is it any less worrisome for the actualist to adopt the sort of wholesale error theory that comes with thinking that both of our experiences are misleading in this respect?

There is a difference, however, between Alice and Bob. Whereas the presentist thinks that Alice exists (since she presently exists), the actualist does not think that Bob exists (since he does not actually exist). This gives the

---

[33] We could of course construct a case in which Bob exists in a nearby possible world in which the train is going at a slightly slower speed, and in the actual world. But that case can be handled in the same way in which I handled the case where I could have occupied a different modal perspective. The Bob case as described in the main body of the text raises somewhat different concerns and gives the advocate of this kind of arbitrariness objection a new opening, which is discussed below.

advocate of the sort of arbitrariness objection I have been considering here a new opening. She could claim that the problem with a privileged reference frame is that the presentist has to make an arbitrary choice between which of two (or more) existing persons' experiences are a better guide to what the privileged reference frame is or attribute a systematic error to existing people. The actualist need not make any such choice.

Does this disanalogy help the advocate of the arbitrariness objection? If it does, it isn't clear that it does to any great extent. Anyone wishing to take this line of reasoning will need to tell us why existing people are so important. They need to explain, in other words, why violating the first principle (as the presentist must do) is problematic, while violating the second principle (as the actualist must do) is not.

The no arbitrary privilege principle (existing person version). Insofar as we systematically disagree with other existing people about some feature of the world, we should think that there isn't a fact of the matter as to that feature.

The no arbitrary privilege principle (more general version). Insofar as we systematically disagree with some group of other people about some feature of the world (where that group contains all and only people who satisfy certain specific conditions C, whether or not those people exist), we should think that there isn't a fact of the matter as to that feature.

This question gives rise to a series of interesting further questions about why we think it is important to avoid attributing systematic error to other people. I don't have anything complete to say about this issue here. But the most obvious reason for thinking that it is a mistake to attribute systematic error to other people is that there is something epistemically self-undermining about such a maneuver. If other people have similar rational and perceptual capacities to our own, and we think that they are systematically mistaken about certain kinds of facts, then that should make us question whether we ourselves might not be mistaken in the same way. And insofar as we are considering the possibility that we ourselves might be mistaken, this surely undermines the evidence we had for thinking that others are mistaken to begin with.

But if this is the reason for thinking that violating the no arbitrary privilege principle is problematic, then what is relevant is whether the people in question have the same rational and perceptual capacities as us—it doesn't matter whether those people exist. If you accept the existing persons version of the no arbitrary privilege principle, you should also accept the general version. In which case there is no disanalogy here on which to base an objection to presentism that does not also tell against actualism.[34]

A Privileged Reference Frame as Scientifically Revisionary

Here is a final objection, one that I often hear in conversation. One difference between a privileged reference frame and a privileged modal perspective is that a privileged reference frame involves being scientifically revisionary in a fairly straightforward sense. To insist on a privileged reference frame is to give up the conventionality of simultaneity and thus relativity theory. Adopting a privileged modal perspective doesn't require being scientifically revisionary in this sense. There is no scientific theory that says that there is no privileged modal perspective.

In the context of the arguments presented in this book, this objection does not make sense. The objection is pointing out that presentism conflicts with the content of a scientific theory, but actualism does not. But as argued in Chapter 1, we should be content naturalists only if we are methodological naturalists as well. With respect to the debate at hand: we should care about conflicts with the content of special relativity only if we take ourselves to be constrained by the methodology that produced special relativity, e.g., the law-neutrality principle. And if we take ourselves to be constrained by the law-neutrality principle, we ought not be actualists. (At least not unless we have some antecedent reason for being an actualist without also being a presentist.)

---

[34] It is also worth noting that this proposed objection, like the one immediately above, turns on contentious claims about the temporal content of experience. In particular, the argument above assumes that our temporal experience is fine-grained enough that for some existing person, either her experience is misleading with respect to the privileged reference frame or mine is. But for all that has been said so far, as long as the difference in velocity between Alice and me is relatively small, her experience could have the very same temporal content as mine. Especially once you acknowledge the possibility of an extended present, as described in the previous footnote. The laws of nature, of course, tell us that were Alice to accelerate to a speed close to the speed of light, her experience would be very different from mine regarding which entities exist and which events are simultaneous. But remember that in order to maintain a genuine disanalogy between the temporal and the modal cases here, we have to restrict our attention to existing people and their actual experience. It's also possible that an existing person could have experiences that suggested a different privileged modal perspective (e.g., if they were hallucinating and their hallucination in fact corresponded to a way that things could be).

So while this objection might appear initially to have some force, this is only because many metaphysicians fail to recognize the important connection between content naturalism and methodological naturalism.

6.5 Recap

This chapter has focused on the question of whether the relativity objection to presentism might be enough on its own to license us to treat actualism and presentism differently, despite their initial similarities. I have argued that it is not. Given the connection between content naturalism and methodological naturalism, unless they have some antecedent reason for being an actualist without also being a presentist, those who endorse the relativity objection to presentism should also endorse the relativity-inspired objection to actualism that I spelled out above. If there is a reason to be an actualist without also being a presentist, it must go beyond the relativity objection to presentism.

Where does all of this leave those philosophers who want to be actualists but not also presentists? It depends on the prospects for providing some justification for their position that goes beyond the relativity objection to presentism. Unless and until we are able to clearly articulate and defend some such justification, anyone who is an actualist should be a presentist as well.

Here again, then, we see that methodological naturalism can have substantive and surprising consequences for familiar metaphysical debates, including debates, like the debate over modal ontology, that may have initially seemed largely independent of naturalistic concerns.

7
Context Dependence in Scientific Methodology

Here's where we are so far. I have argued that if one is a content naturalist then one should also be a methodological naturalist. This is a conditional claim. One can respond by either accepting both content naturalism and methodological naturalism, or by rejecting content naturalism. I have argued that the default position should be the former. I have then argued that methodological naturalism will be impactful with respect to metaphysical debates—first, in general terms, in Chapter 3, and then in detail in the three case studies in Chapters 4, 5, and 6.

Throughout this discussion I have been making an important assumption. I have assumed that there is such a thing as standard scientific methodology—a methodology for arriving at scientific theories that holds across scientific contexts. This chapter revisits that assumption.

Why is it important to take seriously the idea that at least some aspects of scientific methodology may be context-dependent? Because this idea has the potential to give rise to a serious concern for methodological naturalism. According to methodological naturalism, metaphysicians should, whenever possible, use the same methodology that scientists use. But suppose there is no one thing—standard scientific practice. Instead there are a range of distinct scientific methodologies that arise across different scientific contexts. And suppose that these distinct methodologies give rise to conflicting results when applied to some metaphysical debate. Which methodology, then, should the methodological naturalist follow?

Let's call the worry just outlined the *competing methodologies challenge*. I myself am not convinced that there are in fact any proposals in the literature that establish that the competing methodologies challenge is realized. There are certainly existing proposals on which significant aspects of scientific methodology are context-dependent—two especially notable examples being Elliott Sober's (1990, 2009, 2015) account of simplicity and John Norton's (2021) recent work on his theory of material induction. But, as will become clear, context dependence *alone* does not get us all the way to the competing methodologies challenge. Some kinds of context dependence don't give rise to any issue for the methodological naturalist at all.

At the same time, I also recognize that the competing methodologies challenge has the potential to be a serious concern. As the project that I have endorsed in the preceding chapters—the project of clearly identifying the extra-empirical aspects of scientific reasoning and the ways that those aspects apply to metaphysical debates—develops further, it may turn out that the kind of context dependence that would create difficulties for the methodological naturalist will in fact be realized. And it is therefore worth discussing the kinds of responses available to the methodological naturalist if this issue does arise. These responses, as we will see, help further illuminate the methodological naturalist's project and the ways it can be developed in future work.

Here, then, is how I will proceed. First, in section 7.1, I will work through a specific proposal about context-dependent scientific methodology—Sober's account of simplicity—and why I don't think that account creates an issue for the methodological naturalist. Then, in section 7.2, I will turn to a further, and at present entirely hypothetical, way in which scientific methodology could turn out to be context-dependent, which would in fact give rise to the competing methodologies challenge. In section 7.3, I will discuss the various ways in which the methodological naturalist could respond to this challenge. In section 7.4, I show how these responses on behalf of the methodological naturalist can generalize to other potential types of context dependence that might give rise to competing methodologies, and sum up what the discussion has taught us about how context dependence might impact methodological naturalism.

Before I begin all this, however, let me say something about a different sort of worry that might be inspired by the thought that scientific methodology is context-dependent. This is the worry that if scientific methodology is context-dependent then that methodology just simply won't apply to metaphysical debates. To take an extra-empirical principle that applies in a particular scientific context and apply it to a metaphysical debate is to apply that principle outside of the context in which it legitimately applies. According to this line of reasoning, it may be that we endorse methodological naturalism, but methodological naturalism won't turn out to have any interesting results, for none of the methodology of science in fact legitimately applies to metaphysical debates.

Let's call this kind of concern the *no-applicability challenge*. We have seen versions of the no-applicability challenge before, in Chapter 3. (See, for instance, the discussion of empirical vetting, strong underdetermination, and robustness in section 3.3.) The question here is whether the idea that the extra-empirical aspects of scientific methodology are highly context-dependent inspires a novel version of the challenge. This is a line of thought that I have occasionally heard voiced by those who are familiar with Norton's (2021) recent book *Material Induction*. In his chapter on theoretical virtues, for instance, Norton claims that the project of trying to identify what I have been calling extra-empirical principles[1] that apply throughout science is a mistake; all such principles are context-dependent. He writes that "some such principles work more-or-less well in some domains. But any such principle will always have a limited scope, and eventually we shall pass beyond its domain of applicability to examples where it fails" (Norton, 2021, 159).[2] Some readers may take this thought—that any particular aspect of extra-empirical reasoning always has a limited domain—to inspire a novel version of the no-applicability challenge.

There are several things to say in response to this line of thinking. First and foremost, the claim that all extra-empirical principles are limited in scope is an issue for the methodological naturalist only if the scope of limitations consistently line up with the distinction between scientific debates on the one hand and metaphysical debates on the other. And I see no reason for thinking that this is the case, especially following the discussion in Chapter 3. That discussion, I take it, showed that there is no straightforward distinction between scientific and metaphysical debates that could consistently block the applicability of the methodology of the former to the latter. What seems far more plausible to me, insofar as one wishes to endorse Norton's view as described in the quote above, would be to spell out the account in such a way that extra-empirical principles have limited domains of applicability but that those domains include a subset of scientific debates *as well as* nearby metaphysical debates. One might think, for instance, that there is an important distinction between the extra-empirical principles used in fundamental physics, on the one hand, and in cognitive science, on the other,

---

[1] Norton (2021) takes the kinds of principles I focus on to be members of a larger group of what he calls *principles of inductive inference*, which includes the principles licensing enumerative induction in various contexts.

[2] Kincaid (2013) points to the idea that scientific methodology is highly local as one of the key difficulties facing a methodological naturalist who wants to generate substantive results in traditional metaphysical debates. See also Humphreys (2013).

but wherein the extra-empirical principles used in fundamental physics can be successfully applied to metaphysical questions about the nature of time and space, while the extra-empirical principles used in cognitive science can be successfully applied to metaphysical questions about the mind and brain. Of course, this kind of context dependence might well give rise to the competing methodologies challenge; that will be discussed in detail below. My point here is just that if the way in which scientific methodology is context-dependent cuts across the border between scientific and metaphysical debates, then there's no reason stemming from context dependence to worry about the no-applicability challenge.

Second, note that in order for Norton's style of context dependence to give rise to a serious version of the no-applicability challenge, it needs to apply to *all* extra-empirical principles. Let us suppose for a moment that the two examples that Norton writes about in detail in *Material Induction*—simplicity and inference to the best explanation—turn out to be context-dependent in such a way that they don't legitimately apply to any metaphysical debates.[3] The methodological naturalist need not be especially worried about this outcome. Methodological naturalism can still be impactful; its impacts will just come via other routes besides simplicity and inference to the best explanation. They might instead come primarily via the three extra-empirical principles identified in Chapters 4–6, for instance, or via other principles as yet undiscussed.[4] This result would be surprising, since many metaphysicians appeal to considerations of simplicity and to inference to the best explanation when defending their views. But it is a surprise that should be welcome from the methodological naturalist's perspective—it shows that her view ought to inspire quite a bit of new and exciting work in metaphysics.

For these reasons, I'm going to set aside any further discussion of the extent to which context dependence in scientific methodology might inspire the no-applicability challenge. Instead, the focus in what follows will be on

---

[3] There's reason to be cautious here, though, given that Norton himself claims that his account of simplicity closely corresponds to Sober's account (see Norton 2021, 174), and Sober explicitly discusses the ways in which his account yields results for some metaphysical debates (see chapter 5 of Sober 2015 and also Sober 2022).

[4] One interesting bit of nuance: Norton does appear to endorse at least one universal principle that counts as extra-empirical in my sense—but he says this is compatible with material induction because the principle in question is a "meta-inductive principle." The principle in question is "We should not infer to more than that for which we have good evidence" (2021, 186) and Norton thinks this principle underlies straightforward appeals to quantitative simplicity.

the competing methodologies challenge and the ways in which the methodological naturalist can respond to this challenge.[5]

7.1 Context Dependence as Background Dependence

Let's turn now to Sober's account of simplicity, as an example of an existing proposal for one way in which scientific methodology is context-dependent.

Appeals to simplicity have an august scientific pedigree. In Book 3 of the *Principia*, for instance, Newton put forward several "Rules of Reasoning in Natural Philosophy," the first of which was "We are to admit no more causes of natural things than such as are both true and sufficient to explain their appearances" (Newton 1999, 794). Obviously there are going to be a number of different ways of spelling out Newton's claim. On one such way, Newton is claiming that standard scientific practice involves a commitment to the following extra-empirical principle:

Newtonian parsimony. When choosing between empirically adequate theories, choose the one that posits the fewest number of causes.

There are certainly cases in which Newtonian parsimony seems to be an important part of standard scientific practice. To take one well-known example, consider Le Verrier's postulation of Neptune.[6] During the first half of the 19th century, astronomers observed that the orbit of Uranus differed from what was predicted given current physics and the known bodies in the solar system. As a result, Le Verrier posited the existence of a further planet, beyond Uranus's orbit—which was later observed and which we now know as Neptune. Of course, Le Verrier could have posited the existence of multiple further planets (indeed that possibility was apparently recognized at the

---

[5] Note that the same line of response will apply to those who try to build a no-applicability challenge on the thought that when we appeal to an extra-empirical principle what is really doing the epistemic work is some empirical background assumption. (See, e.g., the discussion of simplicity in Norton 2021 or the discussion of inference to the best explanation in Day and Kincaid 1994.) This is an issue for the methodological naturalist only if (a) *all* successful appeals to extra-empirical principles take this form and (b) the way in which empirical background assumptions play a role cannot be extended to cases in metaphysics. See Chapters 4–6 for reasons to doubt (a) and Sober's application of his own analysis of simplicity to cases in metaphysics (as discussed below) for reasons to doubt (b).

[6] This case is discussed as an example of quantitative parsimony (which involves minimizing the number of things) in Jansson and Tallant (2017). Note that I'm making no claim here about whether Newtonian parsimony is a *fundamental* extra-empirical principle. It may be that Newtonian parsimony derives its justification from some other principle—like a principle of quantitative parsimony.

time).⁷ But he didn't. Why not? Here is a straightforward way of answering that question: because choosing a theory on which the deviations in Uranus's orbit were caused by multiple objects instead of a theory on which they were caused by a single object would have violated Newtonian parsimony.

Or consider again Pauli's hypothesis that the missing momentum and energy in beta decay was the result of a theretofore unobserved neutrino also being emitted as a part of the decay process (as discussed in Chapter 4). Here is an alternative hypothesis that Pauli might have considered: instead of a single unobserved particle being emitted to account for the missing energy and momentum, two unobserved particles might have been emitted, each accounting for half of the missing energy and momentum.⁸ Alternatively, of course, there might have been three unobserved particles, each accounting for a third of the missing energy and momentum, and so on. You get the idea. Pauli didn't take any of these alternative hypotheses seriously (if he considered them at all). Why not? According to one natural way of thinking about it, the issue was that the alternative hypotheses posited more causes than were necessary in order to explain the data. In other words, they violated Newtonian parsimony.

These examples make it seem as though appeals to Newtonian parsimony are straightforward in scientific practice. Sober's account, however, calls this into question. Here is a representative quote from one of Sober's early papers on this topic:

> [W]hen [simplicity] counts, it counts because it reflects something more fundamental . . . When a scientist uses the idea, it has meaning only because it is embedded in a very specific context of inquiry. Only because of a set of background assumptions does parsimony connect with plausibility in a particular research problem. What makes parsimony reasonable in one context therefore may have nothing in common with why it matters in another. The philosopher's mistake is to think that there is a single global principle that spans diverse scientific subject matters. (Sober 1990, 140)

In this quote, Sober is expressing a commitment to the following three claims:

---

⁷ See the discussion in Gould (1850, 11ff.) and Hanson (1962).
⁸ This example is discussed in Nolan (1997, 333).

Simplicity as a proxy. When scientists appeal to simplicity, simplicity is really a proxy for some more fundamental[9] feature of the hypothesis in question.

Simplicity as plural. There is more than one more fundamental feature for which simplicity is a proxy.

Simplicity requires background assumptions. Appeals to simplicity (regardless of what they are a proxy for) involve substantive background assumptions that are specific to the context.

How should a methodological naturalist think about an account of simplicity that is committed to these three ideas? First, note, that simplicity as a proxy for some other features of the relevant hypotheses raises no concerns whatsoever for methodological naturalism. At most, it makes methodological naturalism more interesting and potentially impactful, since we will need to both figure out what feature (or features) simplicity is a proxy for and then examine appeals to simplicity in the metaphysics literature in order to determine whether they are tracking the same feature(s). In cases where they are not, there is no reason for the methodological naturalist to care about simplicity.

What about the fact that simplicity is plural? In principle, this might give rise to a concern about competing methodologies, but it is not a new concern. If more than one of the fundamental features for which simplicity is a proxy can arise in a single context, then the methodological naturalist will of course face questions about how these features weigh against each other. And in principle it could turn out that how these features weigh against each other is different in different contexts. But this is not a new issue for the methodological naturalist—it will arise for any methodological naturalist who thinks that more than one theoretical virtue plays a role in extra-empirical reasoning in science. Again this just seems to give rise to more interesting work for the methodological naturalist: in addition to determining which features of a theory are relevant in extra-empirical scientific reasoning, the methodological naturalist needs to determine how they weigh against one another.

---

[9] I'm following Sober in using the term 'fundamental' here, but I don't think anything much hangs on this, and to the extent that it raises more questions than it resolves, I suspect that the reader can substitute 'other' for 'more fundamental' without any significant change to the philosophical content.

What about the claim that appeals to simplicity involve substantive background assumptions? It is this aspect of Sober's account that gives rise to a distinctive kind of context dependence. But will this kind of context dependence in turn give rise to competing methodologies in a way that is problematic for the metaphysician? I don't think so. To see why, it will help to work through one of the specific ways in which simplicity plays a role in scientific theorizing, according to Sober.

Sober develops two detailed accounts of the kinds of consideration for which simplicity is a proxy.[10] Some scientific appeals to simplicity, on this view, fit the *likelihood paradigm*, according to which we favor the simpler hypothesis because the evidence that we have confers a higher likelihood on that hypothesis. Others fit the *model selection paradigm*, according to which (roughly) we favor the simpler hypothesis because such hypotheses have a higher expected predictive accuracy. I'm going to focus here on the former.

Here is how Sober develops the likelihood paradigm. Consider, for instance, the question of whether chimpanzees and humans have a common ancestry (CA) or evolved separately and independently (SA). Evolutionary biologists claim that similarities between the two species, e.g., that chimpanzees and humans both have tailbones, support CA over SA. One way to describe this inference is in terms of Newtonian parsimony. Both CA and SA are compatible with the data, but the common ancestry hypothesis requires fewer causes. What is really going on, according to Sober, however, is more nuanced.[11] What is really going on is that evolutionary biologists accept the law of likelihood:

The law of likelihood. Observation O favors H1 over H2 if and only if $Pr(O|H1) > Pr(O|H2)$.

And furthermore they think that the following inequality holds:

---

[10] Sober also discusses a third parsimony paradigm in passing in Sober (2015) and in more detail in Sober (2022). And he explicitly acknowledges that these two paradigms may not be exhaustive. "Maybe," he writes, "there is more to scientific parsimony than is dreamt of in my philosophy" (Sober 2015, 246).

[11] It can be a little difficult to tease apart the extent to which Sober's account is an account of how simplicity appeals *in fact* work in science or of how they *should* work. For instance, he writes, "In this paper, I describe the justifications that attach to two types of parsimony argument in science" (Sober 2009, 117), which makes the project sound descriptive. But then later writes that he is identifying "contexts" in which "scientific parsimony arguments are justified" (119), which sounds more prescriptive. In any case, I'm going to gloss over the difference in my discussion since it isn't important to the methodological naturalist.

Pr (chimpanzees and humans both have tailbones|CA) > Pr (chimpanzees and humans both have tails|SA)

It is at this point that background assumptions come in. As Sober writes, "This likelihood inequality is not a consequence of the axioms of probability. Rather, it requires substantive assumptions about the evolutionary processes at work in lineages" (2009, 120). Sober goes on to describe these assumptions in detail (see the appendix in Sober 2009 and the seven assumptions on pp. 107ff. in Sober 2015). I'm not going to go into the exact nature of all of these assumptions here, but just to give the reader a sense, consider what Sober calls the *assumption of positive correlation* (Assumption 3 in Sober 2015):

Assumption of positive correlation. Suppose that groups X and Y both have trait T and let S be a state of the postulated common cause. If S raises the probability of members of X having T, then it also raises the probability of members of Y having T.

If X and Y refer to species, like humans and chimpanzees, and T refers to a trait like having a tailbone, and S refers to a state of the postulated common ancestor of these species, then the assumption of positive correlation seems entirely reasonable. If a state of a postulated common ancestor of humans and chimpanzees raises the probability of humans having a tailbone, then it also raises the probability of chimpanzees having a tailbone.

But, as Sober points out, the assumption is not at all reasonable in other contexts. Suppose X refers to people who tend to be unhappy when they work for a boss who is strict, Y refers to people who tend to be happy when they work for a boss who is strict, T refers to being unhappy, and S refers to being a boss who is strict.[12] In this case, even though S raises the probability of members of X having T, it *lowers* the probability of members of Y having T. So the assumption of positive correlation is violated in this case. Indeed in this case it seems that a similarity in the relevant trait is not evidence for a common cause explanation, even if in some sense that explanation would involve fewer causes.

So far, so good. Sober's account of simplicity as a proxy for likelihood is context-dependent in the sense that it relies on background assumptions,

[12] Sober discusses this example in Sober (2015, 117).

and these background assumptions at least sometimes hold in some contexts but not others.

How should the methodological naturalist think about all of this? Certainly, she should not go about applying the assumption of positive correlation in general throughout metaphysical debates—as Sober's discussion has shown, that assumption applies only in some contexts. But that doesn't mean that there are no general conclusions that we can draw from Sober's discussion. Indeed, one natural way for the methodological naturalist to interpret Sober's discussion is as providing support for the following extra-empirical principle:

Background-sensitive likelihood. When choosing between hypotheses about X, choose the hypothesis that the law of likelihood favors, given the background knowledge that you have about X.[13]

And, crucially, notice that there is no reason for thinking that someone who endorses this background-sensitive likelihood principle will end up with competing methodological principles. Which background knowledge plays a role in the background-sensitive likelihood principle just described will depend on the context that you are working with. So the background knowledge that plays a role in applications of this principle in some debates may well be different from the background knowledge that plays a role in applications of this principle in other debates. But that is no impediment to methodological naturalism.[14] In particular, it doesn't give rise to the competing methodologies challenge.

What all of this shows is that just because an account of simplicity in scientific methodology is context-dependent, it doesn't follow that it automatically gives rise to the competing methodologies challenge. In particular, one way for a methodology to be context-sensitive is for it to be *background-sensitive*,

---

[13] Sober himself would not approve of this principle since he says that considerations of simplicity don't allow us to choose a hypothesis; "rather, we compare two or more hypotheses and see which are better than which others in some relevant sense of better" (Sober 2015, 147).

[14] Of course, we will need a story about how we arrive at the background knowledge relevant to X, where X is some metaphysical debate. But this could happen in several ways—it might be produced by some bit of scientific reasoning (other than the background-sensitive likelihood principle) or it might be the result of some supplemental metaphysical methodology. (Remember, methodological naturalism says that whenever possible, metaphysicians should use the same methodology that scientists use, but it leaves open the possibility of metaphysicians employing a supplemental methodology when the methodology of science leaves metaphysical debates open.)

where a methodology is background-sensitive if it includes principles that satisfy the following schema:

Background-sensitive principle schema. When choosing between hypotheses about X, all of which are compatible with the data, choose the hypothesis that has feature F, given the background knowledge that is relevant to hypotheses about X.

There's no reason to think that extra-empirical principles that fit the background-sensitive principle schema will give rise to any sort of competing methodologies challenge.

Before moving on, it is worth noting that Sober himself says that thinking about appeals to simplicity in terms of likelihood does "not discriminate between hypotheses that are empirically equivalent in the sense of making the same predictions for all possible data" (2015, 147), and one might worry that this reinvigorates the no-applicability worry mentioned above, for many philosophers take it to be obvious that competing metaphysical debates are empirically equivalent. But in fact quite a lot here depends on what one takes to be data, and in any case Sober is understanding that term loosely enough that his account of simplicity does in fact generate results for at least some metaphysical debates.[15]

To take one example, Sober considers the way in which atheists sometimes invoke simplicity in defense of their claim that God does not exist. In particular, he is interested in versions of the argument from evil that have the following form: the existence of evil in the world is evidence against the existence of an *all-PKG God* (a God that is all powerful, all knowing, and all good). One might be tempted to present this argument as involving an appeal to simplicity: the simplest explanation of the fact that there is so much evil in the world is that no all-PKG God exists. But Sober argues that, as with the arguments concerning common ancestry above, this apparent appeal to simplicity can be better understood as an appeal to the background-sensitive likelihood principle. The advocate of this version of the argument from evil is claiming that, given our relevant background assumptions:

$Pr(O|N) > Pr(O|\text{not-}N)$

---

[15] See the last chapter of Sober (2015) for a full discussion of applying his parsimony paradigms to metaphysical debates.

Where N is the claim that there is no all-PKG God and O is the observation that there are events that after very careful considerations we take to be horrendously bad, all things considered (Sober 2015, 248). Crucially, O involves us considering the possibility that there are non-obvious good-making features of the events in question that might outweigh the obvious bad-making features, but ultimately concluding that there are no such non-obvious good-making features.

What are the relevant background assumptions that support the above inequality? Glossing over quite a bit of interesting detail (which the reader can find on pages 247–251 of Sober 2015), the two key assumptions that Sober thinks factor in here are (a) that if there are events that are in fact all things considered evil, then an all-PKG God does not exist[16] and (b) that in cases where in fact there are no events that are all things considered evil, the fact that we make observation O does not itself raise the probability of an all-PKG God existing. As Sober puts it, "If an event isn't bad, all things considered, our failing to grasp this fact isn't evidence for the existence of an all-PKG God" (250).

Here, then, we have an example where, by Sober's own lights, the very same "parsimony paradigm" that played a role in scientific theorizing also plays a role in philosophical theorizing. The background assumptions that are relevant in the philosophical case are different from the background assumptions that are relevant in the scientific case, but in each case the background assumptions are appropriate to the context at hand and therefore underwrite a legitimate conclusion. Does it follow that methodological naturalists should not believe in the existence of an all-PKG God? Maybe. But they have some further work to do first. This is because even if Sober is correct that considerations involving (background-sensitive) likelihood are a part of extra-empirical reasoning in scientific methodology, it is implausible that these considerations *exhaust* extra-empirical reasoning in the way suggested by the simple background-sensitive likelihood principle described above. So before coming to a conclusion in this case, the methodological naturalist needs to think about how background-sensitive likelihood interacts with other principles of extra-empirical reasoning. But as I've noted before, it has never been part of the goal of the discussion here to show that

---

[16] The reason Sober thinks it is fair to make this assumption is that theists tend to respond to the problem of evil by trying to identify non-obvious good-making features of the events in question that might outweigh the bad-making features of those events. This suggests that they too agree that if there are all-things-considered evil events, that is a genuine problem for an all-PKG God.

adopting methodological naturalism will be easy or straightforward or that it won't involve quite a bit of further work. Indeed, my view is that naturalistically inclined metaphysicians have all sorts of interesting and substantive work ahead.

7.2 Level Dependence and Competing Methodologies

Let's turn now to a discussion of the ways in which a context-dependent scientific methodology might in fact give rise to serious issues for methodological naturalists. In particular, I'm going to focus on the possibility that scientific methodology might turn out to be level-dependent.[17]

Let's start with the following relatively familiar (though by no means uncontroversial)[18] picture of science: science is organized into distinct levels, with physics at the lowest level. Higher-level sciences include, most obviously, chemistry and then biology. Other expansions of the list plausibly include psychology, geology, neuroscience, and economics. We might also want to make more fine-grained distinctions within the sciences—for instance, within physics, we might distinguish between statistical mechanics as a theory of the micro-physical, and thermodynamics as a theory of the macro-physical.

The idea that the sciences can be organized into levels usually comes hand in hand with a thesis about fundamentality—theories at lower levels are more fundamental than theories at higher levels—where fundamentality is related in some way to dependence—less fundamental theories depend in some way

---

[17] One might think that the argument for the content-methodology link shows that conflicting methodologies across scientific levels are not possible. After all, there is an argument exactly parallel to the argument for the content-methodology link that suggests that if you are a physical content naturalist (i.e., you think we should not accept higher-level scientific theories that conflict with the content of our best theories of physics) then you should also be a methodological physicalist (i.e., you think that scientists working on higher-level theories should, whenever possible, use the same methodology that physicists use).

If this argument works, then the methodological naturalist need not concern herself with the possibility of level dependence giving rise to the competing methodologies challenge. But note that other kinds of context dependence may still give rise to the challenge. And also, the argument above is open to doubt in two ways that weren't an issue for the original argument for the content-methodology link. First, note that although content physicalism seems plausible to me, it does not seem as straightforwardly secure as content naturalism (consider, for instance, the kinds of concerns raised about the status of fundamental physics in Monton 2011). And second, it seems to me that one might be able to make a plausible case for an alternative methodology for the higher-level sciences along the lines discussed in section 1.3 because of the widespread success of these theories. Thanks to Harjit Bhogal for encouraging me to think more about this.

[18] See, for instance, the criticisms in Rueger and McGivern (2010) and Potochnik (2021).

on more fundamental theories. But we don't need to make any substantive claims of this sort here. Remember, I'm not going to argue that there is any significant aspect of scientific methodology that is in fact level-dependent in a way that gives rise to the competing methodologies challenge. I'm not myself convinced that there is! Instead, I'm using this example to illustrate the ways in which the methodological naturalist can respond if it turned out that there was a problematic kind of level dependence here. At the end of this chapter, I will discuss how what we have learned about level dependence extends to other kinds of context dependence.

In order to have a concrete proposal to hand, let's continue to focus on the way in which simplicity plays a role in scientific theorizing.[19] Consider again the Newtonian parsimony principle described at the beginning of the chapter. Notice that the examples that I gave of cases in which that principle seemed to straightforwardly apply—Le Verrier's postulation of Neptune and Pauli's introduction of the neutrino—came from physics. Sober's analysis of simplicity, which involved replacing Newtonian parsimony with considerations to do with likelihood or model selection, by contrast, focused on the use of simplicity reasoning in biology. Now there's no reason, given what has been said so far, to think that Newtonian parsimony and Sober's analysis will conflict. For one, it might be possible to analyze every successful appeal to Newtonian parsimony in physics in terms of Sober's analysis. Or it may be that cases in which there have been successful appeals to Newtonian parsimony in physics involve some additional parsimony paradigm, beyond the two on which Sober focuses. But let's assume, for the purposes of exploring the competing methodologies challenge, that neither of these is the case. Let's assume—and again these are big and entirely hypothetical assumptions—that Newtonian parsimony is a part of standard practice in physics regardless of whether either of Sober's parsimony paradigms applies. And let's assume

---

[19] At first glance it might seem to be obvious that scientific methodology is level-dependent. Walk into a biology lab and compare what the biologists are doing to the activities you see in a physics lab. But just because biologists and physicists collect empirical data in different ways doesn't meant that they are following distinct methodologies—or at least not in a sense of 'distinct' that would give rise to the competing methodologies challenge. Biologists and physicists are interested in different entities, and one set of methods may well be better suited to the collection of empirical data regarding biological entities while another set is best suited to the collection of empirical data regarding microphysical entities. So biologists will specialize in the latter and physicists will specialize in the former. But there's no need to think that these methodologies compete. If smashing beams of particles together at very high speed at the Large Hadron Collider yielded data that was relevant to debates about biology, then presumably biologists would pay attention. It isn't, in other words, that they think physical methodology yields the wrong results for biological investigation. It's that physical methodology is silent on biological questions. And so they don't pay any attention to it.

that it is part of standard practice in biology to care about parsimony only in cases where one of Sober's paradigms applies. On this proposal, parsimony is level-dependent in the sense that the way in which parsimony matters varies in an important sense from level to level.

Here is another, even more dramatic proposal for a way in which the role of simplicity in scientific methodology might be level-dependent: it is sometimes suggested that while a preference for simpler theories is a part of scientific methodology in physics, it is not (or should not) play any role whatsoever in at least some higher-level sciences. Consider, for instance, the following passage from John Dupré's "The Lure of the Simplistic":

> Human behavior is in one sense biological, but it is also fundamentally social. It is culturally diverse. On occasion it is economic, religious, domestic, competitive or cooperative, and so on. It is, in short, exceedingly complex. Any grand unifying theory of human nature can be confidently predicted to distort many or most of these complexities. It seems to me that here we should not even aspire to approach the topic with a unified tool-kit. Indeed, the more diverse and varied the contents of our tool-kit, the better chance we have of coming to grips with the really interesting problems about human behavior. (2002, S292–S293)

Dupré's point in the paper in which this passage appears is far more nuanced than I can do justice to here. But here's one way of reading the above quote: Dupré thinks that parsimony quite generally is not (and should not) be a part of standard scientific practice in sciences that take human behavior as a target to be explained—sciences like psychology, economics, and so on. Not only is there no reason to adopt a theory that minimizes the number of causes that explain a particular phenomena; doing so may well impede our ability to do good science at these levels. Perhaps when choosing between physical theories, it makes sense to follow Newtonian parsimony. But when choosing between psychological theories, it might actually make sense to endorse the following principle instead:

> *Anti-parsimony.* When choosing between empirically adequate theories, choose the theory that posits more causes.[20]

---

[20] Again, I don't mean to claim that Dupré is in fact committed to anti-parsimony, just that the quote above might be used as a justification for this sort of principle.

This suggests a second way in which scientific methodology could be level-dependent. Scientific methodology could be such that a feature of theories that is desirable at one level is also a count against theories at other levels.

If either of these kinds of level dependence turned out to actually be the case, it would create a serious challenge for the methodological naturalist. For suppose she is faced with a metaphysical debate which involves two theories, one of which posits more causes than the other. Which theory should she endorse?

Here is a particular case to consider: the debate over whether mental states are causally efficacious. Let *mental causation* refer to the view that at least sometimes, my mental states at t1 directly cause my mental states at t2. On an alternative view, which we can call *epiphenomenalism*, the only causally efficacious states are the brain states on which my mental states supervene. My brain state at t1 causes my brain state at t2. My mental state at t1 doesn't cause anything; it simply supervenes on my brain state at that time. And my mental state at t2 is not caused by my mental state at t1; it is caused by my brain state at t1, via my brain state at t2, on which my mental state at t2 supervenes.

Now consider the various approaches to simplicity reasoning discussed above and how they apply to this case. At least on the face of it, if we endorse Newtonian parsimony, then it seems that epiphenomenalism is preferable to mental causation. For mental causation posits two causes for my mental states at t2—my mental state at t1 as well as my brain state at t1 (via my brain state at t2)—while epiphenomenalism requires only one cause. According to Sober, however, neither likelihood nor model-selection considerations favor epiphenomenalism over mental causation.[21] So insofar as one endorses a Sober-style analysis, simplicity considerations do not favor epiphenomenalism over mental causation. And insofar as one takes seriously the anti-parsimony principle described above, one perhaps even has reasons stemming from scientific methodology for choosing mental causation over epiphenomenalism.

Here, then, we have a genuine, though at present entirely hypothetical, instance of the competing methodologies challenge. A methodological naturalist should, whenever possible, use the methodology of science to decide which theory to adopt. So she should use the methodology of science to

---

[21] Note that Sober only explicitly considers model selection considerations, presumably because he thinks that the likelihood paradigm is such an obviously bad fit for this case. See the discussion on pages 260–264 of Sober (2015).

decide whether to endorse mental causation or epiphenomenalism. But the methodology of *which* science? On the line of reasoning we have been developing above it may turn out that the methodology of physical science favors epiphenomenalism over mental causation, while the methodology of biology is neutral between the two, and the methodology of psychology might even favor mental causation over epiphenomenalism.

7.3 Ways of Responding to Level Dependence

How should methodological naturalists proceed if scientific methodology turns out to be level-dependent in the way described above? There are three options. They can adopt a restricted version of methodological naturalism, they can endorse a multi-level metaphysics, or they can adopt quietism about cases where conflicts arise.

Restricted Naturalism

The first option for the methodological naturalist is to accept just one of the conflicting methodologies and use that to guide metaphysical theorizing. Insofar as you take this option, however, you should also be a content naturalist about only that level of science for which you also endorse methodological naturalism.

Consider the following three views:

Physical methodological naturalism. Metaphysicians should, whenever possible, use the same methodology that physicists use.

Biological methodological naturalism. Metaphysicians should, whenever possible, use the same methodology that biologists use.

Psychological methodological naturalism. Metaphysicians should, whenever possible, use the same methodology that psychologists use.

The hypothetical situation under consideration is a situation in which physical methodological naturalism, biological methodological naturalism, and psychological methodological naturalism yield conflicting results when applied to a particular metaphysical debate. One way of responding to this situation is to accept just one of physical or biological or psychological methodological naturalism.

At this point, the idea that physics is in some sense more fundamental than the other sciences may again seem relevant. For one might think that insofar as competing methodologies require us to focus on a single context about which to be a naturalist, the fundamentality of physics gives us a reason for endorsing physical methodological naturalism instead of the alternatives.

The key thing to note is that, given the content-methodology link, insofar as one rejects biological methodological naturalism, one should also reject biological *content* naturalism, and insofar as one rejects psychological methodological naturalism, one should also reject psychological *content* naturalism. In other words, if the only methodological naturalism that one is willing to endorse is physical methodological naturalism, then the only version of content naturalism that one should be willing to endorse is physical content naturalism.

> *Physical content naturalism.* We should not accept metaphysical theories that conflict with the content of our best physical theories.
>
> *Biological content naturalism.* We should not accept metaphysical theories that conflict with the content of our best biological theories.
>
> *Psychological content naturalism.* We should not accept metaphysical theories that conflict with the content of our best psychological theories.

How plausible is this way of responding to the competing methodologies challenge? It is true that, when stating their content naturalist commitments, some philosophers seem mainly focused on the commitment to avoid conflicts with physics. There are a couple of potential reasons for this. The first is the thought that physics is in some sense superior to the higher-level sciences, perhaps in the sense that it is more complete or more objective. (It is easier, for instance, to see how our social or political values might influence theorizing in non-fundamental sciences than it is to see how they would influence theorizing in fundamental science.) This is the kind of motivation that seems to be behind the following quote from Tim Maudlin:

> Metaphysics, insofar as it is concerned with the natural world, can do no better than to reflect on physics. Physical theories provide us with the best handle we have on what there is, and the philosopher's proper task is the interpretation and elucidation of those theories. (2007, 1)

And this view is given further defense in Ladyman and Ross's explication of and argument for their Primacy of Physics Constraint, which states that insofar as there is any conflict between physical theories and higher-level scientific theories, the former ought to be taken to be decisive (2007, 38–45).

But note that even if one takes physics to be in some sense superior to the other sciences, one can still think that metaphysicians ought to respect the content of *all* scientific theories. Thinking physics is superior to the higher-level sciences does not require one to reject, e.g., biological or psychological content naturalism.

On the other hand, one might think that there are reasons stemming from *metaphysics* for endorsing physical content naturalism instead of biological or psychological content naturalism. Suppose, for instance, that you endorse the view that the proper target of metaphysics is not what the world is like in general, but rather what the world is like at the fundamental level. This is a relatively popular view. Sider, for instance, claims that "[m]etaphysics, at bottom, is about the fundamental structure of reality" (2011, 1).[22]

Ultimately, I am fairly suspicious of the idea that metaphysics is exclusively or even primarily about what is fundamental. As Elizabeth Barnes has written, this view would "rule out some of the most interesting and innovative work in contemporary metaphysics as being 'really metaphysics'. Attempts to get to grips with social kinds and social structures—with the social world that shapes our daily lives—are a fascinating part of metaphysical inquiry. They are important questions in metaphysics that go beyond—and perhaps have nothing to do with—the fundamental" (2014, 14).

In addition to this point, consider the fact that many interesting examples of content naturalism involve appeals to non-fundamental science. Consider, for instance, the racialism example in Chapter 1. Or Emma Tobin's (2010) work arguing that standard views about the determinate-determinable relation conflict with our theories of chemistry and should therefore be revised. Or the argument that evolutionary biology requires objective probabilities in worlds where the laws are deterministic and that therefore our metaphysics

---

[22] Similar sentiments are expressed in Fine (2001) and Schaffer (2009a).

of objective probabilities should be compatible with deterministic laws (Sober 2010). Finally, think back to the straightforward argument given in Chapter 2 for taking content naturalism to be the default view. That argument turned on two facts: the fact that science has been so successful, and the fact that there doesn't seem to be any clear distinction between the questions of science and the questions of metaphysics. Both of these points apply equally well to higher-level scientific theories as they do to physics.

All of this suggests, at least to me, that the default view ought not to be to accept *only* physical content naturalism and physical methodological naturalism. Indeed the considerations above suggest to me that we, as metaphysicians, should avoid conflict with the content of *any* scientific theory, and that we should therefore respect, wherever possible, the methodology of *any* scientific context. But how can we do this if the methodologies conflict?

Multi-Level Metaphysics

Here is a second way that the methodological naturalist can respond to the competing methodologies challenge described above: adopt a multi-level metaphysics.

To see how this works, start by observing that for many of the paradigm metaphysical debates about non-fundamental entities, the *only* aspects of science that seem to be relevant are aspects of a particular non-fundamental science. Consider, for instance, the debate over the metaphysics of race that was discussed in Chapter 1. Our best biological theories are certainly relevant to whether racialism is true. But—and this is the interesting part—our best chemical theories and our best physical theories seem irrelevant. Perhaps, then, the metaphysician working on philosophy of race need not take into account our best chemistry or our best physics. Instead she needs to focus only on our best biology.

A similar line might also seem attractive in the hypothetical case described above, in which physical, biological, and psychological methodology gave competing results with respect to the debate about mental causation. One might try to argue, for instance, that of the three scientific contexts under consideration, psychology is especially relevant to questions about what causes various mental states. So perhaps one should really care only about conflicts with psychology—and the methodology of psychology—when addressing this particular metaphysical debate.

This way of thinking about the debates over the metaphysics of race and mental causation suggests that metaphysicians might not need to choose between physical or biological or psychological content naturalism, as defined above. Instead they can endorse:

Level-relative content naturalism. If a metaphysical debate is about a particular level of reality, we ought not put forward theories regarding that debate that conflict with our best scientific theories regarding that level of reality.

And, in turn, they should endorse a corresponding version of methodological naturalism:

Level-relative methodological naturalism. If a metaphysical debate is about a particular level of reality, metaphysicians should, whenever possible, use the same methodology that scientists use when investigating that level of reality.

Level-relative content naturalism suggests a view of metaphysics on which there are distinct fields of metaphysics, corresponding to the levels of science. Let's call this view *multi-level metaphysics*:

Multi-level metaphysics. In addition to fundamental metaphysics (which is focused on theories about what the world is like at the physical level) there are various other subfields of metaphysics that are about what the world is like at other scientific levels.[23]

One can then further spell out one's favored version of multi-level metaphysics by importing one's favored view about the relationship between the different scientific levels as a view about the relationship between the different metaphysical levels. For instance, if one has a view on which the higher

---

[23] This sort of multi-level view of metaphysics has been occasionally mentioned in the literature. Vetter (2018), for instance, follows Busse (2009) in distinguishing *fundamentalist metaphysics* (which is concerned with the fundamental) from *archeological metaphysics* (which is concerned with the non-fundamental). Or consider the claim found in Bihan and Barton that "as long as there is no reduction all the way down of all special science to fundamental physics, we must build applied ontologies of special sciences that stand independently of ontologies of fundamental physics, if we want to use them for practical purposes" (2021, 28).

scientific levels somehow reduce to physics, then one should adopt a corresponding view on which the higher metaphysical levels similarly reduce to fundamental metaphysics. Or if one has a view on which the higher scientific levels are strongly emergent with respect to physics, then one should adopt a corresponding view on which the higher metaphysical levels are also strongly emergent with respect to fundamental metaphysics.

Of course not all metaphysical debates seem level-specific in the way that the debate over the metaphysics of race, for instance, does. Consider, for instance, the debate about the nature of laws. Laws of nature arise at all levels of science. So what kind of content naturalism should the multi-level metaphysician respect when it comes to theorizing about laws? Here I think it is very tempting to say that the metaphysician should follow the results of her theorizing where they lead. Instead of pre-judging whether there is really just one type of thing—laws of nature—that arises at multiple levels, she should see what happens when she applies level-relative content and methodological naturalism at each of the relevant levels. If she ends up with multiple distinct accounts of laws, then that shows that in fact there isn't one single kind of law—there are multiple different kinds, each arising at a different level. There are physical laws and chemical laws and biological laws and each of these kinds of laws is distinct metaphysically.[24]

I will report that in conversation, at least, I have encountered a wide range of responses to the idea of multi-level metaphysics. Some philosophers take this to be a highly revisionary proposal. Others find it entirely obvious and indeed think that metaphysics already involves this kind of multi-level approach. The kinds of examples that the latter group sometimes point to include cases where one and the same concept is given importantly different analyses at different levels. Perhaps this happens with respect to the concept of an individual, which is understood in a different way in biology than it is in physics, or with the concept of causal explanation, which is standardly taken to encompass mechanistic explanations in higher-level sciences but is (perhaps) taken to require simpler causal structure in fundamental science. Or perhaps a multi-level metaphysics is already present in our understanding of laws, when we insist that fundamental laws need to be exceptionless but allow higher-level laws to hold *ceteris paribus*.[25]

---

[24] For what it is worth, though, I find this maneuver hard to countenance when it comes to other concepts, including time, space, and modality. Temporal, spatial, and modal talk occurs at all scientific levels, but I find it quite hard to wrap my mind around the idea that physical time or physical modality might be something different from biological time or biological modality.

[25] Another example: some philosophers (including me—see Emery 2015) think fundamental chances are incompatible with deterministic laws, but non-fundamental chances are not.

One thing that these examples demonstrate is that a multi-level metaphysics view, if explicitly adopted, would have the advantage of allowing us to avoid debates over whether, e.g., ceteris paribus laws are *really* laws or whether the concept of individuals as realized in physics is the *real* concept of individuals. On the other hand, of course, one might think that to avoid these kinds of debates is to give up on important work that metaphysicians are supposed to be engaged in. I won't take a stand on that question here. My point is only that the multi-level metaphysics approach is available to the methodological naturalist who finds herself facing the competing methodologies challenge as a result of the level dependence of scientific methodology.

Quietism

Here is a third and final option available to the methodological naturalist should it turn out that scientific methodology is level-dependent: she can simply claim that in cases where the methodologies of different levels yield conflicting results, scientific methodology as a whole is thereby inconclusive. There just is no conclusion to be drawn on the basis of scientific methodology in that case. If it turns out, for instance, that Newtonian parsimony is a key part of standard scientific practice in physics, but not in biology or psychology, and that Newtonian parsimony would favor epiphenomenalism over mental causation, then it turns out that the methodology of science just does not tell us what to do when it comes to that particular debate.

Whether this move will be useful to the methodological naturalist depends on how widespread level dependence turns out to be in scientific methodology. Recall that throughout the earlier chapters of the book I have been happy to allow that scientific methodology does not settle all or even most metaphysical debates. My claim is that the view has significant consequences—not that it has consequences in every single case. If it turns out that level dependence is widespread in scientific methodology, and one chooses to be a quietest about metaphysical debates where different methodologies yield different results, then that would be a worry for how impactful methodological naturalism would turn out to be. I myself see no reason for thinking that level dependence will be all that widespread. But this potential concern is worth keeping in mind insofar as one is attracted to the quietist position.

7.4 Context Dependence More Generally

As a closing thought for this chapter, let me emphasize that level dependence as discussed above is just one way in which the competing methodologies challenge can arise. Suppose, for instance, that you think that the goal of science is at least in part a pragmatic matter. We want theories that work well for creatures like us. And suppose that the kinds of creatures we are can vary in substantial ways. So scientific methodology for a 20th-century human may be different from the scientific methodology for a 22nd-century genetically enhanced human with dramatically improved computing power. Or perhaps you think that the methodology of science is value-laden, and that at least some of the relevant values vary from culture to culture.[26] On the former view scientific methodology will be time-dependent; on the latter it will be culturally dependent. And at least in principle, the relevant kind of context dependence in each case might give rise to the competing methodologies challenge.

In each of these cases, the options available to the metaphysician will mirror the options discussed above. First, you can try to argue that one of the relevant methodologies is in fact the correct methodology. (This corresponds to choosing, say, physical methodological naturalism over biological and psychological methodological naturalism.) Alternatively one can adopt a pluralist view that corresponds to the multi-level metaphysics position described above. On this kind of view, there will be distinct sub-fields of metaphysics that mirror each of the distinct contexts that give rise to a distinct scientific methodology. There will be a metaphysics for 20th-century humans and a metaphysics for 22nd-century humans, for instance, or a metaphysics for each cultural context. I myself don't find either of these types of metaphysical pluralism attractive. But it is worth noting that metaphysical pluralism can extend to a wider range of cases, besides the multi-level view discussed above. Third, and finally, one can be a quietist about the cases where different scientific methodologies conflict.

The goal in this chapter has been to discuss the ways in which scientific methodology might be context-dependent, to what extent various kinds of context dependence in scientific methodology might raise issues for

---

[26] For a nearby account consider Larry Laudan's (1984) *reticulated model of scientific rationality*, according to which scientific methods change over time as desired ends change. (This view involves an even more wholesale pragmatism than the kind that I am describing in the main body of the text.)

methodological naturalism, and how the methodological naturalist might respond to those worries. There hasn't been a single, straightforward conclusion, in large part because the concrete proposals for ways in which scientific methodology is context-dependent do not themselves give rise to the competing methodologies worry. As a result, much of the discussion has focused on a hypothetical way in which simplicity might be level-dependent as a way of illustrating the options available to the methodological naturalist. Taken as a whole, the discussion above has established that there is no reason for thinking that context dependence is going to create insurmountable difficulties for methodological naturalism or make the view in any way unimportant or uninteresting. Certainly, if scientific methodology is indeed context-dependent, it may make developing methodological naturalism in detail more challenging, but there was never any promise that the view wouldn't face challenges—and indeed the kinds of challenges that arise as a result of context dependence appear to be the kinds that give rise to interesting and exciting philosophical investigations. The methodological naturalist should embrace this result.

8
Metaphysics Unmoored?

In the first two chapters of this book, I argued that if one is a content naturalist, then one should also be a methodological naturalist. I also argued both that the vast majority of metaphysicians endorsed content naturalism and that they were justified in doing so; content naturalism ought to be the default view with respect to the relationship between metaphysics and science. For the rest of the book, up until this point, I have been assuming that we should be content naturalists and that therefore we should also be methodological naturalists.

In this chapter, I want to investigate what would happen if one instead decides to reject methodological naturalism. Maybe one finds some of the specific conclusions I arrived at in the case studies in Chapters 4–6 untenable. Or maybe one has bigger-picture concerns about the justification and role of extra-empirical reasoning in determining what the world is like. In any case, it remains an open option, given everything I have said so far, to reject methodological naturalism. Let us examine what would happen if one does so.

First and foremost, given the argument in Chapter 1, if one rejects methodological naturalism, then one ought to reject content naturalism as well. Let us call an approach to metaphysics that rejects both content and methodological naturalism *unmoored metaphysics*.[1] Unmoored metaphysics is not tied to either the content of our best scientific theories or the methodology that produces those theories. It floats free from both. Indeed it could float quite far from any scientific influence at all.

Note that the 'could' in the previous sentence is important. There is nothing in the definition of unmoored metaphysics that requires metaphysicians to adopt a methodology that differs substantially from scientific methodology or to put forward theories that conflict substantially with our best scientific

---

[1] Note that I am explicitly avoiding calling a view that rejects methodological naturalism and content naturalism "non-naturalistic," since such a view might still satisfy very minimal notions of naturalism.

theories. Unmoored metaphysics as defined above *might* hew quite closely to science, but there is no in principle reason to expect it to do so. Once one's metaphysics is unmoored, it is an open possibility to respond to apparent conflicts with science by simply embracing those conflicts.

For this reason, as I argued in Chapter 1, to reject content naturalism is to think that metaphysics should be practiced in a quite different way from what we see in the current philosophical literature. If we adopt unmoored metaphysics, then we should be at least open to metaphysical views that appear to conflict with science. These views will be fair game in a way that currently they are not. Recall from Chapter 1 that even those philosophers who currently defend views that seem to conflict with our best science, like Markosian or Merricks, tend to do so by arguing for a reinterpretation of the relevant science. If metaphysics were unmoored, then no such reinterpretation is necessary. Markosian, for instance, could simply reject or ignore special relativity when formulating his favored theory of time. Were we to recognize this as a legitimate option, whole swaths of the metaphysics literature should be rewritten.

To sharpen the point, note that contemporary metaphysics is a field that involves both little consensus and little sense of anything like straightforward progress. As a result, if there are metaphysical views that are legitimate but have seen little attention to date, surely they ought to be explored. Indeed one of the few points on which there seems to be lasting and widespread consensus among metaphysicians is with respect to content naturalism. If we give up that consensus, it is hard to predict how the field will develop.

All that by way of arguing that unmoored metaphysics is potentially a highly revisionary view. If we were to adopt such an approach, metaphysics has the potential to look quite different than it currently does. As a corollary, there will also very likely be important differences between unmoored metaphysics, as it is defined here, and the swaths of actual current metaphysics that are assumed to be not sufficiently naturalistic and that come in for critique from philosophers like Ladyman and Ross (2007), Maclaurin and Dyke (2012), Bryant (2020), and many others. The latter category—the category of actual current metaphysics which naturalistically inclined philosophers like to target as not sufficiently naturalistic—goes by a range of different labels, including 'analytic' metaphysics, 'free range' metaphysics, 'fantasy' metaphysics, 'neo-scholastic' metaphysics, 'a priori' metaphysics, and more. I'm going to call it *armchair metaphysics*. The key charge against this kind of metaphysics is that it is done from the armchair, i.e., without sufficient information about and engagement with science.

What I have been arguing above is that currently existing armchair metaphysics is not truly unmoored. Even paradigm examples of armchair metaphysicians take seriously potential conflicts with science. Unmoored metaphysics, therefore, is a practice that does not currently exist. And there is no reason, therefore, that a truly unmoored metaphysics needs to look anything like armchair metaphysics as it is currently practiced and currently critiqued. There is no reason to assume, moreover, that the objections that target armchair metaphysics will extend to unmoored metaphysics.

So should we adopt an unmoored metaphysics? As readers who have hung in there this far into the book can probably guess, I myself am not especially inclined to unmoor. Insofar as one either needs to accept both content and methodological naturalism, or reject both, I think the best option would be to accept both. But I don't think that it is an open-and-shut case. The question of how to proceed here is connected in interesting and nuanced ways to a range of important philosophical questions that have only begun to be explored in the preceding pages. As such, it is worth exploring the possible ways of understanding unmoored metaphysics in more detail.

8.1 Unmoored Metaphysics without Genuine Conflicts

Let's begin by introducing a key choice point that will help structure the discussion of different types of unmoored metaphysics. This choice point involves whether the unmoored metaphysician adopts the following principle:

Genuine conflicts. Apparent conflicts between scientific theories and metaphysical theories are, in general, genuine conflicts.

It is compatible with genuine conflicts that on occasion an apparent conflict between a scientific theory and a metaphysical theory can be avoided by revising our understanding of one of the theories. But there is no systematic way of avoiding conflicts by claiming, for instance, that scientific theories describe scientific aspects of the world while metaphysical theories describe metaphysical aspects of the world, or that scientific theories are describing the world from a scientific perspective, while metaphysical theories are describing the world from a metaphysical perspective, or anything along those lines.

Let's focus first on what unmoored metaphysics might look like insofar as we reject genuine conflicts. On this view, there is a systematic reason for thinking that apparent conflicts between science and metaphysics are not genuine conflicts. Note that it might at first appear that if one were to reject genuine conflicts, that would amount to *accepting* content naturalism—for content naturalism would turn out to be trivially true. And that therefore to reject genuine conflicts should not be described as a version of unmoored metaphysics. To some extent this is a terminological issue, but here's why I think that rejecting genuine conflicts should in fact count as a version of unmoored metaphysics. Recall from section 1.1 that one of the key assumptions that informed our understanding of content naturalism was the assumption that apparently conflicts between scientific theories and metaphysical theories were (at least sometimes) genuine. Genuine conflicts, then, was built in as an assumption underlying content naturalism, and to reject genuine conflict, therefore, is to reject content naturalism as it has been understood throughout the book. Of course one could still argue that someone who rejects genuine conflicts can still accept a nearby, trivially true version of content naturalism, but this hardly yields the result that their view doesn't count as a version of unmoored metaphysics. If content naturalism is only trivially true, then (a) it places no constraints on our metaphysical theorizing and (b) its being trivial undermines the argument for the content-methodology link. So to reject genuine conflicts is to accept a view on which there are no constraints placed on our metaphysical theorizing by either the content or the methodology of science. That is enough for a view to count as unmoored.

There are two relatively straightforward ways of spelling out unmoored metaphysics that involve rejecting genuine conflicts. On the one hand, one can reject genuine conflicts and adopt some kind of pluralism or relativism about what the world is like. There's what the world is like in some scientific sense, and there's what the world is like in some metaphysical sense, and those are two different, non-overlapping aspects of the world. Let's call this *unmoored pluralist metaphysics*. On the other hand, one can reject genuine conflicts and avoid pluralism by revising one's view about what the goal of metaphysical theorizing is in the first place. On this view, metaphysics isn't about what the world is like in a straightforward sense; there's something else going on. Let's call this *unmoored revisionary metaphysics*.

In the next two subsections, I investigate each of these versions of unmoored metaphysics in turn, before going on to discuss what unmoored metaphysics might look like insofar as one hangs onto genuine conflicts.

Unmoored Pluralist Metaphysics

According to unmoored pluralist metaphysics, we should reject both content and methodological naturalism, and furthermore we should not be bothered by apparent conflicts between science and metaphysics, for when putting forward theories about what the world is like, metaphysicians are doing something importantly different from what scientists are doing. Metaphysicians are putting forward theories about the metaphysical aspects of the world, while scientists are putting forward theories about the scientific aspects of the world, and the metaphysical and scientific aspects of the world are two distinct things.

As a concrete example of a view that can reasonably be interpreted as a version of unmoored pluralist metaphysics, consider a Kantian-inspired dualism according to which there are the *phenomena*, which are the aspects of things that we can access through empirical investigation, and the *noumena*, which are things in themselves.[2] On this view, there is what the world is like with respect to the phenomena and there is what the world is like with respect to the noumena, and those are two distinct things. Suppose we claim, further, that science is the study of the phenomena while metaphysics is the study of the noumena. Then one cannot straightforwardly object to a metaphysical theory by claiming that it conflicts with some physical theory. For the way the world is with respect to the noumena might well be different from the way the world is with respect to the phenomena.

Obviously, this example is a dramatic over-simplification of Kant's views. And it is not in any obvious sense a view that many contemporary philosophers hold. Nonetheless it can be used to illustrate a couple of important points that will apply quite generally to unmoored metaphysical pluralist views. Note, for instance, that this way of understanding Kantian-inspired dualism involves putting forward a story about what metaphysics and science are that is quite different from what contemporary philosophers think metaphysics and science are. As I have said before, what it means to be able

---

[2] I'm especially thankful to Michaela McSweeney for helpful discussion of these ideas.

to access something through empirical investigation is itself a vexed question, but on any natural understanding of this criteria, contemporary science is often concerned with entities that we cannot access directly through empirical investigation (fundamental particles, black holes, dark energy, and so on). And on any natural understanding of what it means to be able to access something through empirical investigation, metaphysics often involves entities that we can so access (hallucinations and illusions, for instance, or the experience of time passing). So the Kantian-inspired dualist will almost certainly end up being fairly revisionary about what counts as science and what counts as metaphysics.

Indeed, there is good reason to think that this kind of concern will end up applying to unmoored metaphysical pluralists quite generally. As has been discussed several times in earlier chapters, it is difficult, if not impossible, to draw a clear distinction between what counts as science and what counts as metaphysics.[3] Since the unmoored pluralist wants to claim that there is an important distinction between science and metaphysics, they will have to force a sharp distinction where one does not antecedently exist and will therefore likely have to classify some debates as metaphysics or as science in a way that seems at odds with the way we standardly think about those debates.

Here is a second point that the Kantian-inspired dualist version of unmoored pluralist metaphysics illustrates. In order to evaluate just how far metaphysical theories can "float" from science on this view, we need a clear story about whether and how the noumena and the phenomena are related. Do the noumena "give rise to" the phenomena? If so, what are the restrictions on the relevant "giving rise to" relation? This will also be an open question for any version of unmoored pluralist metaphysics. Given that there are different aspects to what the world is like, it is natural to wonder how, if at all, those aspects are connected.

Finally, note that the version of unmoored pluralist metaphysics under consideration here faces a quite serious concern about epistemic justification. What reason do we have for thinking that unmoored metaphysical theories are likely to be good theories about what the world is like? Given that the unmoored metaphysician has rejected content and methodological naturalism, we can't point to the success of science to help justify unmoored metaphysical theories. And the farther apart the scientific aspects of the world are from the metaphysical aspects of the world, the less of a clear grip we seem to

---

[3] See Chakravartty (2017) for more on how challenging it is to draw this distinction.

have on what the latter is or how to go about investigating it. Moreover, given that there is a lot of disagreement and not a lot of progress in metaphysics, there doesn't seem to be any internal standard of success within metaphysics that could justify any degree of confidence here.[4]

Of course, in order to really make this epistemic worry for unmoored metaphysical pluralism precise, we would need to specify what the methodology of this approach might be. But we can potentially take at least some cues here from recent criticisms of armchair metaphysics as it is actually practiced. A prominent recent example of this kind of objection is due to Amanda Bryant (2020). Bryant argues that armchair metaphysics (what she calls "free range metaphysics") is constrained only by (a) simplicity, (b) consistency, and (c) intuitive plausibility.[5] And, Byrant argues, these constraints, even taken in conjunction, fail in two ways. First, they are not *robust*, where "robustness is a function of how much theoretical content the constraint permits into the theory" (2020, 1872). Second, they fail to secure *epistemic warrant*, because "they permit into the theory both demonstrable falsehoods and claims that we have little reason to accept" (1871). Insofar as one finds this critique of armchair metaphysics compelling one should also try to ensure that whatever methodology one adopts for one's unmoored metaphysics does not run into similar issues with respect to robustness and epistemic warrant. But at least on the face of it, this will leave the methodology of unmoored metaphysics vastly underdetermined. And this reinvigorates the broader epistemic worry outlined above: Why think that whatever particular methodology the pluralist adopts is going to yield successful theories if there is so little that constrains that methodology?

Ultimately, then, I don't think that unmoored pluralistic metaphysics is a very attractive way of proceeding, although it's important to recognize that the concerns raised above are less objections than they are potential worries. To a large extent, what we can say about unmoored pluralistic metaphysics will depend on the way in which the view is developed.

---

[4] This worry seems especially notable if we want to be realists about unmoored metaphysics, and therefore want our unmoored metaphysical theories to be true theories about what the world is like. It is potentially less of a worry if you are merely a pragmatist about unmoored metaphysics, and therefore looking only for metaphysical theories that are useful to creatures like us. (Although most existing metaphysical theories probably don't qualify as especially useful for creatures like us, I see no reason why a fully unmoored metaphysics could not produce such theories.)

[5] Bryant initially considers explanatory power as a distinct constraint but ends up arguing that the explanatory power constraint devolves into the intuitive plausibility constraint. The details of that argument are nuanced. In any case, none of what I say here will change if we add 'explanatory power' as a distinct fourth constraint.

Unmoored Revisionary Metaphysics

The second version of unmoored metaphysics that involves a rejection of genuine conflicts between metaphysics and science is unmoored revisionary metaphysics. According to this approach, metaphysicians should not endorse either content or methodological naturalism, but there is no reason to be concerned about conflicts between metaphysics and science because metaphysics is not in the business of investigating what the world is like; it is doing something else.

There may be many different ways of pursuing this line of thinking, but the one that I will focus on here is the prescriptive conceptual approach first discussed in Chapter 1. Recall from that chapter that according to the descriptive conceptual approach, the goal of metaphysical theorizing is conceptual analysis—specifically the analysis of our actually existing conceptual scheme. It is the role of the metaphysician to identify the rules that govern our conceptual scheme and the relations that hold between various concepts. According to the prescriptive conceptual approach, the goal of metaphysical theorizing is to determine what conceptual scheme we *should* have—to identify the rules that govern that conceptual scheme and what relations hold between the concepts within it.

On the prescriptive approach, disagreements that seem to be about the nature of reality turn out to actually be disagreements about our conceptual schemes—specifically about which scheme we should adopt.[6] As a result, as I understand it, the prescriptive conceptual approach is a revisionary account. At least at first glance, this is a view on which metaphysics is not the study of what the world is like. It is the study of what the world should be like.

For this reason, it is at least somewhat plausible to imagine an advocate of prescriptive conceptual analysis adopting an unmoored approach to metaphysics. After all, metaphysics, on this view, seems to not be about what the world is like. But surely that is what science *is* about. So why should the metaphysician qua prescriptive conceptual analyzer care if her views conflict with science?

I have two main concerns about this way of making sense of an unmoored approach to metaphysics. The first is just that it isn't at all obvious that what the world is like is wholly irrelevant to what conceptual schemes we should

---

[6] Plunkett (2015) (following Plunkett and Sandell 2013) calls these disagreements *metalinguistic negotiations* and argues that at least some paradigmatically metaphysical disputes can be interpreted in this way.

adopt. Perhaps what the world is like will not *fully* answer questions about what conceptual schemes we should adopt (especially insofar as those conceptual schemes concern socially important entities), but it still seems that what the world is like will be relevant, if only because what the world is like places important constraints on what we can do and how successful our interactions with the world are likely to be. Once we acknowledge this, maybe it makes sense to think that even those with a prescriptive conceptual analysis approach should be content naturalists.

One might think that we could look to philosophers who actually practice prescriptive conceptual analysis to help us understand how their views interact with content naturalism, but, as I said in Chapter 1, the current literature is not at all clear on this question. Sally Haslanger, for instance, writes that "the world by itself can't tell us what gender is, or what race is" (2012, 224). But this quote alone doesn't settle the question of whether someone who endorses Haslanger's approach should be a content naturalist. It might be that what science tells us about the world must be respected, but we are allowed to—and indeed plausibly need to—go beyond what we are so told. Or it might be that what science tells us about the world is just irrelevant. With respect to terms that play a role in scientific laws, Amie Thomasson explicitly acknowledges, "Since these terms have the function of serving in explanatory and predictive scientific theories, which in turn aim to predict and explain, there are worldly constraints on what concepts we ought to adopt" (2020, 450). This suggests that she might be a content naturalist—though of course quite a bit depends on how she understands 'worldly constraints' and also on the extent to which she thinks these constraints extend to other terms (even if, when it comes to other terms, our best scientific theories are largely silent).

In any case, the point is that for all that has been said so far—both here and in the literature—it may be that philosophers who endorse the prescriptive conceptual approach should in fact endorse content naturalism. In which case they should also, given the argument in Chapter 1, endorse methodological naturalism, and unmoored metaphysics is off the table.

Here is a second point that may undermine the hope that one can build a respectable version of unmoored metaphysics by appealing to the literature on the prescriptive conceptual approach. The prescriptive conceptual analysis is fairly plausible as a way of understanding higher-level metaphysical debates, like debates about the nature of race and gender, or social entities. But as a view about *all* of metaphysical theorizing, this is a fairly radical claim. Can we really interpret metaphysical debates about the nature of time or laws of nature as merely debates about the conceptual schemes that we should have?

This point becomes even more substantive if we recall the concerns mentioned above regarding there being no clear demarcation between debates that count as metaphysics and debates that count as science. This means that if we try to interpret *all* metaphysical theorizing as some form of prescriptive conceptual analysis, we will almost certainly end up counting at least some scientific theorizing as also being prescriptive conceptual analysis. Perhaps this is all things considered the right way to think about science, but it is a fairly revisionary way to think about it.

8.2 Unmoored Metaphysics with Genuine Conflicts

Let us turn now to the question of what unmoored metaphysics might look like insofar as we retain a commitment to apparent conflicts between metaphysics and science being (in general) genuine conflicts. Here again I think there are two versions of this approach. On the one hand, one might think that when there is a genuine conflict between metaphysics and science, we should adopt the metaphysical view. This view combines unmoored metaphysics with a claim about the primacy of metaphysics. On the other hand, one might think that when there is a genuine conflict between metaphysics and science, the scientific view should trump the metaphysical view. This view combines unmoored metaphysics with a claim about the primacy of science.

With respect to the view that unmoored metaphysical views trump scientific views, I won't say very much here. The key challenge for any such view is to spell out the epistemic justification for taking metaphysical views to be better than scientific theories as theories about what the world is like. Given the success of science, anyone who takes this route has their work cut out for them.

More can and should be said, however, about a version of unmoored metaphysics that says that there are genuine conflicts between science and metaphysics and that science trumps metaphysics. This view, which I will call, for reasons that will become clear in a moment, *instrumental unmoored metaphysics*, faces an immediate challenge. What reason could we have for doing metaphysics that does not adhere to content naturalism or methodological naturalism, but that also maintains that there are genuine conflicts between science and metaphysics and that science trumps metaphysics when those conflicts arise? One cannot, it seems, justify the practice of this kind of unmoored metaphysics on straightforward epistemic grounds. Instead this kind of approach is most plausible insofar as we have some sort of alternative justification for metaphysical theorizing.

The idea that actual armchair metaphysics has important collateral benefits that make it worth pursuing even if it is unlikely to secure epistemic justification was present in early critiques of Ladyman and Ross (2007). Cian Dorr, for instance, in his review of *Every Thing Must Go*, claimed that Ladyman and Ross "have missed what is best and most distinctive about the tradition they set themselves against: its gradual raising of the standards of clarity and explicitness in the statement of metaphysical claims" (2010, n.p.). And Katherine Hawley, in her review, argued:

> Much of what has lasting value in the metaphysical literature, as in many areas of philosophy, consists in the careful, detailed work of distinguishing conflated questions and issues, investigating the space of possible theories, and establishing relationships of confirmation or even entailment between different claims. (2010, 176)

Both of these authors are suggesting that there is something valuable about armchair metaphysics that at least in principle comes apart from the question of whether the practice brings us any straightforward epistemic benefits in the sense of giving us true theories about what the world is like.

A second instrumental approach, which has been defended in recent work by Michaela McSweeney, is that metaphysics, however unmoored, is valuable because it expands our imaginative capacities (2023, 83). In this way, metaphysics is like art. As McSweeney notes, her view obviously pulls science and metaphysics apart. There is no reason, once one adopts it, to feel any pull at all toward naturalism: "If metaphysics is more like art than science—if it is essentially imaginative and (at least in part) 'up to us'—then there is no reason that it should be *like* science" (88).

By far the most developed view along these lines, however, is due to Steven French and Kerry McKenzie.[7] Because this is one of the most promising ways

---

[7] Note that of course different instrumental approaches could be combined. There is no reason why there must be only one instrumental benefit of doing metaphysics.

of understanding unmoored metaphysics, it is worth going through in some detail.

Metaphysics as a Toolbox

French and McKenzie (2012, 2016) argue that armchair metaphysics can serve an important role as a toolbox for philosophers of science and naturalistic metaphysicians. "The products of analytic metaphysics," they say, "can be regarded as available for plundering by philosophers of science in order that we might exploit them for our own purposes" (2012, 44). In this view they are shaped by their experience as advocates of a particular version of structural realism—ontic structural realism. The latter view, they write,

> has had to deploy a great deal of involved metaphysical theory in order to articulate its core claims . . . The growing literature on ontological dependence, for example, is proving useful in expressing the core metaphysical claim of ontic structuralism, namely, that physical objects are ontologically secondary to structures. (French and McKenzie 2012, 44)

One way of understanding this view, French and McKenzie say, is that metaphysics stands to philosophy of science as mathematics stands to physics: "Just as it was useful to Einstein that the theory of non-Euclidean geometry was there for the taking when the moment arose, so it is useful to eliminative structuralists that there has been developed a theory of dependence compatible with the elimination of the dependent entity" (2012, 44).

French and McKenzie call their view the *heuristic approach* to analytic metaphysics. It's worth emphasizing that, as they spell it out, the heuristic approach says that analytic metaphysics is a toolbox for other *philosophers*—philosophers of science or naturalistic metaphysicians. But others have pointed out that the toolbox might also be used by scientists themselves. At the beginning of his book *Philosophy of Biology*, for instance Peter Godfrey-Smith describes what he calls philosophy's *incubator* role with respect to the sciences.[8] He writes "philosophy has often also functioned as an 'incubator'

---

[8] The idea that scientists might deploy a metaphysical toolbox is of course connected to the idea that science in some sense "presupposes" metaphysics as discussed in section 2.1. See Kuhn (1962), Chang (2008), and Paul (2012), among many others.

of theoretical ideas, a place where they can be developed in a speculative way while they are in a form that cannot be tested empirically" (2014, 1).[9]

An especially telling example of metaphysics playing a toolbox role in contemporary physics (and philosophy of physics) comes from recent debates about quantum ontology. The key question of quantum ontology is what the wavefunction represents. It has been repeatedly observed, at least since Erwin Schrödinger developed his formalism for quantum mechanics, that a natural interpretation of the wavefunction is that it represents a field. But Schrödinger, and almost everyone who followed him for the next 75 years, thought that view was a non-starter. The reason was that the wavefunction is defined on an extremely high-dimensional space—a space that is dramatically different from ordinary three-dimensional space.

This was the state of play in quantum ontology up until the 2000s. But then *wavefunction realism* (the name for the view that the wavefunction represents a physical field) took off. Why was this? Another thing happening around the same time was a sudden surge of interest in philosophical theories of grounding, and various ways in which one thing can give rise to another. Today, discussions of wavefunction realism are deeply engaged with philosophical work on the notions of parthood, dependence, supervenience, and more.[10]

It is worth emphasizing that the toolbox view is especially powerful when it is paired with a certain kind of epistemic humility with respect to the nature of future science. Suppose, for instance, that one endorses something like the following principle:

Future science humility. We have little, if any, knowledge of what form future science will take.

---

[9] Baron (2018) argues that philosophy plays a similar role. Bihan and Barton (2021) discuss a number of examples of this view. Maclaurin and Dyke (2012) critique the toolbox view (as it applies to science).

[10] See Ney (2021). To take another example that draws on the same observations that French and McKenzie make about ontic structural realism, consider the current debate among physicists about quantum gravity. One of the key features of any of the current candidates for understanding quantum gravity is that time does not appear to be a feature of the fundamental theory. Instead time is somehow emergent. Whatever else one has to say about this theory, it seems clear that it will need to make use of elements of the analytic philosophy toolbox—indeed it seems clear that it will need to make use of some of the very same elements that the ontic structural realist already has started to "plunder," including notions like ontological dependence, fundamentality, and emergence.

Then virtually any metaphysical theory, no matter how strange, fantastic, or utterly divorced from current science it may be, has the potential to contribute to the toolbox. Consider, for instance, the following complaint from Maclaurin and Dyke about metaphysical theorizing about the nature of properties:

> Scientists are interested in how various properties are distributed across the world. But . . . the question of what the metaphysical nature of properties is has no bearing whatsoever on the actual instances of properties out there in the world. Suppose, *per impossibile*, that we discovered that properties really are universals. Such a conclusion would have no effect on the scientists' investigations into the properties that are actually instantiated in the world. (2012, 304)

Someone who adopts the toolbox view in combination with future science humility can straightforwardly dismiss this kind of concern. Sure, it is hard to imagine how a choice between an analysis of properties as universals, tropes, or mere resemblances would impact future science. But then it would have been quite hard 30 years ago to anticipate the ways in which arguments about fundamentality would impact debates about ontic structural realism, or quantum ontology. Even if it is not obvious how debates about the nature of properties might impact future science—it still might. And that is enough to make investigation into these theories worthwhile.

Indeed, if one takes the toolbox approach, one should think that even metaphysical theories that wholly conflict with current science are worth pursuing—maybe not *as* worth pursuing as theories that are compatible with current science, but worth pursuing nonetheless. As French and McKenzie write, "The reason for this is that, ultimately, we have only the dimmest idea of what changes in physics lie ahead of us. How, then, do we know that the current metaphysical models, even though they seem to be in contradiction with actual physics and problematic for that reason, might not themselves come to be useful in the course of time?" (2016, 44).

French and McKenzie are themselves "aghast" at this result and at the prospect of the "metaphysical-free-for-all" that they worry will result from this observation. But ultimately they accept it. They think that any metaphysical theory whatsoever can be valued because of the toolbox potential.[11] Of course, someone who is an unmoored metaphysician, on the other hand, has

---

[11] They do try to rein things in somewhat by noting that the value accorded to analytic metaphysics by the heuristic approach is highly conditional. Bihan and Barton (2021) think there is no reason to

already given up content naturalism, and with it any concerns about metaphysical theories that are not compatible with our best science. So she will likely take heart from this result. For it means that no matter how far from science her theory floats, it is still worth pursuing because it still has the potential to contribute to the toolbox.

To those who are inclined toward unmoored metaphysics, therefore, I recommend the toolbox approach as a justification for continuing metaphysical theorizing despite that theorizing becoming unmoored.

It is worth emphasizing, however, that many metaphysicians will be uncomfortable with this view. Barbara Vetter, for instance, writes that the toolbox approach is "rather devastating to the mainstream metaphysician who strives to participate directly in the pursuit of truth" (2018, 233). McKenzie herself calls it a "position of last resort." She writes, "[I]n metaphysics, generally we do not conduct ourselves in a fashion that suggests we don't believe there's something for us to be right about" (2020, 25). But it's worth noting that these kinds of concerns are concerns about the general maneuver of providing a justification for unmoored metaphysics that is purely instrumental. They aren't concerns about the toolbox view in particular. The heart of the issue here is that most of us who think of ourselves as metaphysicians are not developing theories solely with the hope that someday to someone they might prove useful. Most of us, myself included, are genuinely interested in figuring out what the world is like. Insofar as we are, no instrumental approach—the toolbox approach included—will be satisfying.

8.3 Fine-Grained Naturalism

Throughout this chapter, and indeed throughout the book as a whole, I have been talking as though one has to have "a view" about what metaphysical theorizing consists in and what kinds of metaphysical theories we should be aiming for. On the one hand, I have argued, one can accept both content naturalism and methodological naturalism. On the other hand, one can reject both and adopt either the pluralist, the revisionary, or the instrumental versions of unmoored metaphysics. This is all, however, an oversimplification.

---

qualify the result and draw and analogy between the heuristic approach to analytic metaphysics and an instrumental approach to mathematics.

One can of course adopt a more fine-grained view, according to which for some areas of metaphysics, one should be both a content and a methodological naturalist, and for other areas one should be neither.

On the face of it, this seems like a very plausible approach. On the one hand, we have metaphysical debates that are clearly adjacent to science, like debates over time or laws or probability. On the other hand, we have metaphysical debates that seem wholly distinct, like debates about social ontology. Surely we can be naturalists about the former and not about the latter. But I want to end on a note of caution. For defending fine-grained naturalism will take some serious work. The key thing to notice is that nothing that has been said above has called into question the content-methodology link. And, as the discussion throughout the book has shown, the methodology of science has a far broader reach than the content of science. So just because the content of our best science seems irrelevant to a particular debate, that does not automatically mean that there are no scientific considerations that are relevant. Someone who wishes to argue that there are no scientific considerations that are relevant to, for instance, debates about social ontology needs to address the question of whether a conflict with our best science would be disqualifying for candidate theories in the relevant debate—even if in fact there does not seem to be any such conflict. If such a conflict would be disqualifying, then this philosopher is still committed to content naturalism and thus to methodological naturalism. And if such a conflict would not be disqualifying, they owe us some story about why: Is it that there are no genuine conflicts between the social domain and the scientific domain? Why not?

As a last point, let me also note that very little has been said above about what the standards of success are for various types of unmoored metaphysics. This has been by design, for I think that unmoored metaphysics of any of these types—once it is explicitly acknowledged as unmoored—can be developed in a wide range of different ways. But at least as of yet, I see little reason to think that the means by which we judge these different types of metaphysics as successful (or not) will be similar. And therefore it will be of the utmost importance for the fine-grained naturalist to state explicitly what it is they take themselves to be doing when they undertake a particular metaphysical project. It is of the utmost importance, in other words, that one be clear as to whether one is:

Putting forward a theory about what the world is like that is supposed to be in keeping with both the content and methodology of our best science.

Putting forward a theory about the metaphysical aspects of what the world is like (where the metaphysical aspects and the scientific aspects of the world are importantly distinct).

Putting forward a theory about the conceptual scheme that we use or ought to be using.

Putting forward a theory about what the world is like that is (hopefully!) useful in some way, regardless of its truth.

Insofar as these aims are not stated clearly we can only expect ongoing confusion about both the goals to which we are aiming and the degree of success which we have achieved.

Conclusion

On the last day of my undergraduate courses in metaphysics I often read my students a passage from Timothy Williamson's *The Philosophy of Philosophy*. Over the course of the semester we have investigated all sorts of questions about what the world is like. What makes someone the same person over time, even when many of their characteristics change? Do possible worlds exist? What kinds of things are they? Is the future open? What does that mean? When do two things compose a third thing? All of these questions are abstract. Some seem to be wholly divorced from other areas of inquiry. The techniques that have been deployed in the papers we've read have ranged from formal logic proofs to loose gestures toward the intuitive results of various thought experiments. As the semester comes to a close, and we take a moment to reflect, I often have the impression that my students find themselves a little lost. There are the diehards, of course, who are discussing the nuances of counterpart theory for hours in the lounge after class. But there are also quite a few who, as soon as we take a step back and try to understand what we've been doing in a larger context, seem to be struck by a case of intellectual vertigo.

Here is the passage that I read my students from Williamson:

> Imagine a philosophy conference in Presocratic Greece. The hot question is: what are things made of? Followers of Thales say that everything is made of water, followers of Anaximenes that everything is made of air, and followers of Heraclitus that everything is made of fire. Nobody is quite clear what these claims mean; some question whether the founders of the respective schools ever made them. But among the groupies there is a buzz about all the recent exciting progress. The mockers and doubters make plenty of noise too. They point out that no resolution of the dispute between the schools is in sight. They diagnose Thales, Anaximenes, and Heraclitus as suffering from a tendency to over-generalize. We can intelligibly ask what

bread is made of, or what houses are made of, but to ask what *things in general* are made of is senseless, some suggest, because the question is posed without any conception of how to verify an answer; language has gone on holiday. Paleo-pragmatists invite everyone to relax, forget their futile pseudo-inquiries, and do something useful instead.

The mockers and doubters had it easy, but we know now that in at least one important respect they were wrong. With however much confusion, Thales and the rest were asking one of the best questions ever to have been asked, a question that has painfully led to much of modern science. To have abandoned it two and a half thousand years ago on grounds of its conceptual incoherence or whatever would have been a feeble and unnecessary surrender to despair, philistinism, cowardice, or indolence. (2007, 280)

I like this way of ending class. It encourages optimism without risking hubris. But as with the definition of metaphysics that I give students on the first day of class, what I am telling my students here about the underlying reason for thinking that metaphysical inquiry is legitimate is not the whole of what I think. Yes, it's hard to tell in advance what sorts of inquiry will be important or worthwhile. And yes, that means that we should approach even those fields where the practical payoffs are far from obvious with an open mind. And perhaps that's good enough for my students, or for those who are just investigating philosophy for the first time. But those of us who are professional philosophers must do more.

For here is an important difference between contemporary metaphysicians and Thales and the rest. We contemporary metaphysicians are operating in a context where we aren't the only ones asking what the world is like. We are asking these questions at a time when there also exists a robust, intellectually respectable and enormously successful field (or set of fields) that is wholly devoted to this type of inquiry—namely science. This gives rise to a special challenge, one that all of us who today ask philosophical questions about what the world is like must face. We must figure out how to think about what we are doing in relation to what scientists are doing.

This is the project that I have taken up in this book. One of the key claims that I have made is that while metaphysicians have of course been aware that they need to have something to say about how their views related to science, they haven't been as clear as they need to be about what they are saying and the consequences that follow. In particular, I have argued that while virtually all contemporary metaphysicians appear to be committed to content naturalism, few of them recognize that if one is a content naturalist then one should also be a methodological naturalist. Nor have they examined in much detail the consequences of the latter view. These consequences, I have argued, via the case studies that form the core of the book, are both significant and surprising. Methodological naturalism has the potential to significantly impact seemingly intransigent metaphysical debates, including in areas of metaphysics that seem, at least on the face of it, to have little if anything to do with science.

Of course, none of this shows that one has to be a naturalist, of either the content or the methodological variety. One might instead choose to reject both views. This is not my own preferred view, for reasons outlined in Chapter 8, but it is a viable option.

The central upshot of this book, therefore, is that whether you choose to accept both content naturalism and methodological naturalism or to reject both, you will need to revisit some of the central assumptions of your current metaphysical theorizing. If the conclusions I have been arguing for here are fully internalized, metaphysical inquiry will look quite different than in currently does.

Of course, in order to know what metaphysical inquiry should look like, whether it involves the rejection of content naturalism or the acceptance of methodological naturalism, quite a bit more work needs to be done. In particular, if the implications of methodological naturalism are going to be fully understood there needs to be significant further research into the extra-empirical aspects of scientific theorizing. Most importantly, we need to think more about the possible ways in which extra-empirical reasoning influences scientific theorizing, in both general and specific terms. I argued that in at least some cases, scientists use extra-empirical principles like the pattern-explanation principle (Chapter 4), the principle of minimal divergence (Chapter 5), and the excess structure principle (Chapter 6). What other extra-empirical principles are part of standard scientific practice? And how do these extra-empirical principles interact, when more than one of them is relevant?[1]

---

[1] The discussion above was especially inconclusive with respect to the role of simplicity and inference to the best explanation (insofar as it goes beyond the pattern-explanation principle), both of which are often mentioned as playing an important role in scientific theory choice. One often also hears discussion of the role of various aesthetic values in scientific theory choice (including by scientists; see the overview in Ivanova 2017). All of these would be excellent starting points for further research into applications of methodological naturalism.

We also need further investigation into the general framework in which methodological naturalism takes place. Are there other ways in which extra-empirical reasoning influences scientific theorizing besides the kinds of extra-empirical principles that I have focused on here? What are these other ways? Does extra-empirical reasoning shape what we take the data to be? It seems to be at least sometimes deployed via Bayesian confirmation theory. Can all instances of extra-empirical reasoning be modeled in this way? When and how is the extra-empirical reasoning that is deployed in science context-dependent, and what are the relationships between these different contexts?

Ultimately, this research needs to be done jointly by philosophers of science, scientists, and metaphysicians. Without this research, we cannot fully understand the potential implications of methodological naturalism on a wide range of philosophical debates. Nor can we decide, ultimately, whether to be methodological naturalists. Either way, metaphysical theorizing should look quite different than it currently does. That much has already been established. But it would be nice to know, with more certainty, what it should in fact look like. This is the broader project for which this book has merely laid the groundwork.

References

Acuña, P. (2014). On the Empirical Equivalence between Special Relativity and Lorentz's Ether Theory. *Studies in History and Philosophy of Science Part B: Studies in History and Philosophy of Modern Physics, 46*, 283–302. https://doi.org/10.1016/j.shpsb.2014.01.002.

Allori, V. (2013). Primitive Ontology and the Structure of Fundamental Physical Theories. In A. Ney and D. Z. Albert (Eds.), *The Wave Function: Essays in the Metaphysics of Quantum Mechanics* (168–183). Oxford University Press.

Andreasen, R. O. (1998). A New Perspective on the Race Debate. *British Journal for the Philosophy of Science, 49*(2), 199–225.

Andreasen, R. O. (2000). Race: Biological Reality or Social Construct? *Philosophy of Science, 67*, S653–S666.

Appiah, K. A. (1996). Race, Culture, Identity: Misunderstood Connections. *Tanner Lectures on Human Values, 17*, 51–136.

Armstrong, D. M. (1983). *What Is a Law of Nature?* Cambridge University Press.

Armstrong, D. M. (1996). *A World of States of Affairs*. Cambridge University Press.

Audi, P. (2012). Grounding: Toward a Theory of the In-Virtue-Of Relation. *Journal of Philosophy, 109*(12), 685–711.

Baker, A. (2016). Simplicity. In E. N. Zalta (Ed.), *The Stanford Encyclopedia of Philosophy* (Winter 2016). Metaphysics Research Lab, Stanford University. https://plato.stanford.edu/archives/win2016/entries/simplicity/.

Balaguer, M. (ms). How to Make Presentism Consistent with Special Relativity. Unpublished manuscript.

Balashov, Y., and M. Janssen. (2003). Presentism and Relativity. *British Journal for the Philosophy of Science, 54*(2), 327–346.

Barnes, E. (2014). Going Beyond the Fundamental: Feminism in Contemporary Metaphysics. *Proceedings of the Aristotelian Society, 114*(3, pt. 3), 335–351. https://doi.org/10.1111/j.1467-9264.2014.00376.x.

Baron, S. (2018). A Formal Apology for Metaphysics. *Ergo, an Open Access Journal of Philosophy, 5*. https://doi.org/10.3998/ergo.12405314.0005.039.

Bealer, G. (1996). A Priori Knowledge and the Scope of Philosophy. *Philosophical Studies, 81*(2–3), 121–142.

Beebe, J. R. (2009). The Abductivist Reply to Skepticism. *Philosophy and Phenomenological Research, 79*(3), 605–636. https://doi.org/10.1111/j.1933-1592.2009.00295.x.

Beebee, H. (2000). The Non-Governing Conception of Laws of Nature. *Philosophy and Phenomenological Research, 61*(3), 571–594.

Beebee, H. (2018). I—The Presidential Address: Philosophical Scepticism and the Aims of Philosophy. *Proceedings of the Aristotelian Society, 118*(1), 1–24. https://doi.org/10.1093/arisoc/aox017.

Belot, G. (2013). Symmetry and Equivalence. In R. Batterman (Ed.), *The Oxford Handbook of Philosophy of Physics* (318–339). Oxford University Press.

Belot, G. (2015). Down to Earth Underdetermination. *Philosophy and Phenomenological Research*, 91(2), 456–464.

Bennett, K. (2009). Composition, Colocation, and Metaontology. In D. J. Chalmers, D. Manley, and R. Wasserman (Eds.), *Metametaphysics: New Essays on the Foundations of Ontology* (38). Oxford University Press.

Bhogal, H. (ms). What Motivates Humeanism?

Bihan, B. L., and A. Barton. (2021). Analytic Metaphysics versus Naturalized Metaphysics: The Relevance of Applied Ontology. *Erkenntnis*, 86(1), 21–37. https://doi.org/10.1007/s10670-018-0091-8.

Bird, A. (2007). Inference to the Only Explanation. *Philosophy and Phenomenological Research*, 74(2), 424–432. https://doi.org/10.1111/j.1933-1592.2007.00028.x.

Bonk, T. (2008). *Underdetermination: An Essay on Evidence and the Limits of Natural Knowledge*. Springer.

Bostrom, N. (2003). Are We Living in a Computer Simulation? *Philosophical Quarterly*, 53(211), 243–255.

Bourget, D., and D. J. Chalmers. (Forthcoming). "Philosophers on Philosophy: The PhilPapers 2020 Survey." *Philosophers' Imprint*.

Bourne, C. (2006). *A Future for Presentism*. Oxford University Press.

Brenner, A. (2017). Simplicity as a Criterion of Theory Choice in Metaphysics. *Philosophical Studies*, 174(11), 2687–2707.

Bricker, P. (2006). Absolute Actuality and the Plurality of Worlds. *Philosophical Perspectives*, 20(1), 41–76.

Bricker, P. (2008). Concrete Possible Worlds. In T. Sider, J. Hawthorne, and D. W. Zimmerman (Eds.), *Contemporary Debates in Metaphysics* (111–134). Blackwell.

Bricker, P. (2020). *Modal Matters: Essays in Metaphysics*. Oxford University Press.

Brown, L. (1978). The Idea of the Neutrino. *Physics Today*, 31(9), 23–28.

Bryant, A. (2020). Keep the Chickens Cooped: The Epistemic Inadequacy of Free Range Metaphysics. *Synthese*, 197(5), 1867–1887.

Bueno, O., and S. A. Shalkowski. (2020). Troubles with Theoretical Virtues: Resisting Theoretical Utility Arguments in Metaphysics. *Philosophy and Phenomenological Research*, 101(2), 456–469.

Burge, T. (2005). Disjunctivism and Perceptual Psychology. *Philosophical Topics*, 33(1), 1–78. https://doi.org/10.5840/philtopics20053311.

Burge, T. (2011). Disjunctivism Again. *Philosophical Explorations*, 14(1), 43–80. https://doi.org/10.1080/13869795.2011.544400.

Burgess, A., and D. Plunkett. (2013a). Conceptual Ethics I. *Philosophy Compass*, 8(12), 1091–1101. https://doi.org/10.1111/phc3.12086.

Burgess, A., and D. Plunkett. (2013b). Conceptual Ethics II. *Philosophy Compass*, 8(12), 1102–1110. https://doi.org/10.1111/phc3.12085.

Busse, R. (2009). Properties in Nature: A Nominalist Account of Fundamental Properties. Habilitation, University of Regensburg.

Callender, C. (2000). Shedding Light on Time. *Philosophy of Science*, 67(3), 599.

Callender, C. (2011). Philosophy of Science and Metaphysics. In S. French and J. Saatsi (Eds.), *Bloomsbury Companion to the Philosophy of Science* (33–54). Continuum.

Cappelen, H., and D. Plunkett. (2020). Introduction: A Guided Tour of Conceptual Engineering and Conceptual Ethics. In H. Cappelen, D. Plunkett, and A. Burgess (Eds.), *Conceptual Engineering and Conceptual Ethics* (1–34). Oxford University Press. https://doi.org/10.1093/oso/9780198801856.003.0001.

Carmichael, C. (2015). Toward a Commonsense Answer to the Special Composition Question. *Australasian Journal of Philosophy, 93*(3), 475–490.

Caro, M. D., and D. Macarthur. (2004). *Naturalism in Question*. Harvard University Press.

Carroll, J. W. (1994). *Laws of Nature*. Cambridge University Press.

Carroll, J. W. (2016). Laws of Nature. In E. N. Zalta (Ed.), *The Stanford Encyclopedia of Philosophy* (Winter 2016). Metaphysics Research Lab, Stanford University. https://plato.stanford.edu/archives/win2020/entries/laws-of-nature/.

Carroll, S. (2007). *Dark Matter, Dark Energy: The Dark Side of the Universe*. The Teaching Company.

Chakravartty, A. (2008). What You Don't Know Can't Hurt You: Realism and the Unconceived. *Philosophical Studies, 137*(1), 149–158. https://doi.org/10.1007/s11098-007-9173-1.

Chakravartty, A. (2017). *Scientific Ontology: Integrating Naturalized Metaphysics and Voluntarist Epistemology*. Oxford University Press.

Chang, H. (2008). Contingent Transcendental Arguments for Metaphysical Principles 1. *Royal Institute of Philosophy Supplements, 63*, 113–133.

Close, F. (2012). *Neutrino*. Oxford University Press.

Cohen, I. B. (1985). *The Birth of a New Physics*. W. W. Norton.

Craig, W. L. (2000). *The Tenseless Theory of Time: A Critical Examination* (Vol. 294). Springer.

Dardashti, R., R. Dawid, and K. Thébault. (2019). *Why Trust a Theory? Epistemology of Fundamental Physics*. Cambridge University Press.

Dasgupta, S. (2016). Symmetry as an Epistemic Notion. *British Journal for the Philosophy of Science, 67*(3), 837–878.

Dawid, R. (2013). *String Theory and the Scientific Method*. Cambridge University Press.

Dawid, R. (2022). Meta-empirical Confirmation: Addressing Three Points of Criticism. *Studies in History and Philosophy of Science, 93*, 66–71. https://doi.org/10.1016/j.shpsa.2022.02.006.

Dawid, R., S. Hartmann, and J. Sprenger. (2015). The No Alternatives Argument. *British Journal for the Philosophy of Science, 66*(1), 213–234. https://doi.org/10.1093/bjps/axt045.

Day, T., and H. Kincaid. (1994). Putting Inference to the Best Explanation in Its Place. *Synthese, 98*(2), 271–295.

Descartes, R. ([1647] 1983). *Principles of Philosophy* (V. R. Miller and R. P. Miller, Trans.). Reidel.

Dorr, C. (2005). What We Disagree About When We Disagree About Ontology. In M. E. Kalderon (Ed.), *Fictionalism in Metaphysics* (234–286). Oxford University Press.

Dorr, C. (2010). Review of James Ladyman and Don Ross, Every Thing Must Go: Metaphysics Naturalized. *Notre Dame Philosophical Reviews, 2010*(6).

Dorst, C. (2019). Towards a Best Predictive System Account of Laws of Nature. *British Journal for the Philosophy of Science, 70*(3), 877–900. https://doi.org/10.1093/bjps/axy016.

Dupré, J. (2002). The Lure of the Simplistic. *Philosophy of Science, 69*(S3), S284–S293. https://doi.org/10.1086/341852.

Earman, J. (1989). *World Enough and Spacetime*. MIT Press.

Earman, J. (1993). Underdetermination, Realism, and Reason. *Midwest Studies in Philosophy, 18*(1), 19–38.

Emery, N. (2015). Chance, Possibility, and Explanation. *British Journal for the Philosophy of Science*, 66(1), 95–120. https://doi.org/10.1093/bjps/axt041.

Emery, N. (2017a). Against Radical Quantum Ontologies. *Philosophy and Phenomenological Research*, 95(3), 564–591.

Emery, N. (2017b). A Naturalist's Guide to Objective Chance. *Philosophy of Science*, 84(3), 480–499.

Emery, N. (2017c). Temporal Ersatzism. *Philosophy Compass*, 12(9), e12441.

Emery, N. (2019). Laws and Their Instances. *Philosophical Studies*, 176(6), 1535–1561.

Emery, N. (2021). Temporal Ersatzism and Relativity. *Australasian Journal of Philosophy*, 99(3), 490–503. https://doi.org/10.1080/00048402.2020.1780621.

Emery, N. (2022). Quantum Correlations and the Explanatory Power of Radical Metaphysical Hypotheses. *Philosophical Studies*, 179(7), 2391–2414. https://doi.org/10.1007/s11098-021-01769-z.

Esfeld, M. (2018). Metaphysics of Science as Naturalized Metaphysics. In A. Barberousse, D. Bonnay, and M. Cozic (Eds.), *The Philosophy of Science: A Companion* (142–170). Oxford University Press.

Fairchild, M., and J. Hawthorne. (2018). Against Conservatism in Metaphysics. *Royal Institute of Philosophy Supplement*, 82, 45–75.

Faraday, M. (1852). On the Physical Character of the Lines of Magnetic Force. *London, Edinburgh, and Dublin Philosophical Magazine and Journal of Science*, 3(29), 401–428.

Feyerabend, P. K. (1962). Explanation, Reduction and Empiricism. In H. Feigl and G. Maxwell (Eds.), *Scientific Explanation, Space, and Time (Minnesota Studies in Philosophy of Science, Volume III)* (28–95). University of Minnesota Press.

Feynman, R. P., R. B. Leighton, and M. Sands. (1963). *Feynman Lectures on Physics* (Vol. 1). Addison-Wesley.

Fine, K. (2001). The Question of Realism. *Philosophers' Imprint*, 1, 1–30.

Fish, W. (2021). Perceptual Paradigms. In H. Logue and L. Richardson (Eds.), *Purpose and Procedure in Philosophy of Perception* (23–42). Oxford University Press. https://doi.org/10.1093/oso/9780198853534.003.0002.

French, S. (1998). On the Withering Away of Physical Objects. In E. Castellani (Ed.), *Interpreting Bodies* (93–113). Princeton University Press.

French, S. (2000). Identity and Individuality in Quantum Theory. In E. N. Zalta (Ed.), *Stanford Encyclopedia of Philosophy (Winter 2019)*. Metaphysics Research Lab, Stanford University. https://plato.stanford.edu/archives/win2019/entries/qt-idind/

French, S. (2020). *There Are No Such Things as Theories*. Oxford University Press.

French, S., and K. McKenzie. (2012). Thinking Outside the Toolbox: Towards a More Productive Engagement Between Metaphysics and Philosophy of Physics. *European Journal of Analytic Philosophy*, 8(1), 42–59.

French, S., and K. McKenzie. (2016). Rethinking Outside the Toolbox. In T. Bigaj and C. Wüthrich (Eds.), *The Metaphysics of Contemporary Physics* (Poznan Studies in Philosophy of Science and the Humanities vol. 104) (25–54). Brill.

Friedman, M. (2001). *Dynamics of Reason: The 1999 Kant Lectures at Stanford University*. CSLI.

Geroch, R. (1981). *General Relativity from A to B*. University of Chicago Press. https://press.uchicago.edu/ucp/books/book/chicago/G/bo25841687.html.

Gilmore, C. (2018). Location and Mereology. In E. N. Zalta (Ed.), *The Stanford Encyclopedia of Philosophy* (Fall 2018). Metaphysics Research Lab, Stanford University. https://plato.stanford.edu/archives/fall2018/entries/location-mereology/.

Glasgow, J., S. Haslanger, C. Jeffers, and Q. Spencer. (2019). *What Is Race? Four Philosophical Views*. Oxford University Press.
Godfrey-Smith, P. (2014). *Philosophy of Biology*. Princeton University Press.
Gould, B. A. (1850). Report on the History of the Discovery of Neptune. Smithsonian Institute. http://archive.org/details/reportonhistoryo00goulrich.
Guay, A., and T. Pradeu. (2020). Right Out of the Box: How to Situate Metaphysics of Science in Relation to Other Metaphysical Approaches. *Synthese*, 197(5), 1847–1866. https://doi.org/10.1007/s11229-017-1576-8.
Hall, E. (Forthcoming). Humean Reductionism about Essence. In M. T. Hicks, S. Jaag, and C. Loew (Eds.), *Humean Laws for Human Agents*. Oxford University Press.
Hanson, N. (1962). Leverrier: The Zenith and Nadir of Newtonian Mechanics. *Isis*, 53, 359–378. https://doi.org/10.1086/349597.
Harman, P. M. (1982). *Energy, Force and Matter: The Conceptual Development of Nineteenth-Century Physics*. Cambridge University Press.
Haslanger, S. (2000). Gender and Race: (What) Are They? (What) Do We Want Them to Be? *Noûs*, 34(1), 31–55. https://doi.org/10.1111/0029-4624.00201.
Haslanger, S. (2006). What Good Are Our Intuitions: Philosophical Analysis and Social Kinds. *Aristotelian Society Supplementary Volume*, 80(1), 89–118. https://doi.org/10.1111/j.1467-8349.2006.00139.x.
Haslanger, S. (2012). *Resisting Reality: Social Construction and Social Critique*. Oxford University Press.
Hawley, K. (2006). Science as a Guide to Metaphysics? *Synthese*, 149(3), 451–470.
Hawley, K. (2009). Metaphysics and Relativity. In R. L. Poidevin, P. Simons, R. Cameron, and A. McGonigal (Eds.), *The Routledge Companion to Metaphysics* (507–516). Routledge.
Hawley, K. (2010). Critical Notice of Every Thing Must Go. *Metascience*, 19(2), 174–179.
Hawthorne, J., and G. Uzquiano. (2011). How Many Angels Can Dance on the Point of a Needle? Transcendental Theology Meets Modal Metaphysics. *Mind*, 120(477), 53–81.
Henderson, L. (2014). Bayesianism and Inference to the Best Explanation. *British Journal for the Philosophy of Science*, 65(4), 687–715. https://doi.org/10.1093/bjps/axt020.
Hesse, M. (1961). *Forces and Fields: The Concept of Action at a Distance in the History of Physics*. Philosophical Library.
Hicks, M. T. (2021). Breaking the Explanatory Circle. *Philosophical Studies*, 178(2), 533–557. https://doi.org/10.1007/s11098-020-01444-9.
Hicks, M. T., and P. van Elswyk. (2015). Humean Laws and Circular Explanation. *Philosophical Studies*, 172(2), 433–443.
Hicks, M. T., S. Jaag, and C. Loew (Eds.). (Forthcoming). *Humean Laws for Human Agents*. Oxford University Press.
Hildebrand, T. (2019). Scientific Practice and the Epistemology of Governing Laws. *Journal of the American Philosophical Association*, 5(2), 174–188.
Hinchliff, M. (2000). A Defense of Presentism in Relativistic Setting. *Philosophy of Science*, 67(3), S575.
Hofweber, T., and M. Lange. (2017). Fine's Fragmentalist Interpretation of Special Relativity. *Noûs*, 51(4), 871–883.
Huemer, M. (2001). *Skepticism and the Veil of Perception*. Rowman & Littlefield.
Huemer, M. (2009). When Is Parsimony a Virtue? *Philosophical Quarterly*, 59(235), 216–236.

Huemer, M. (2016). Serious Theories and Skeptical Theories: Why You Are Probably Not a Brain in a Vat. *Philosophical Studies, 173*(4), 1031–1052.

Huemer, M. (2017). There Is No Pure Empirical Reasoning. *Philosophy and Phenomenological Research, 95*(3), 592–613.

Humphreys, P. (2013). Scientific Ontology and Speculative Ontology. In D. Ross, J. Ladyman, and H. Kincaid (Eds.), *Scientific Metaphysics* (51–78). Oxford University Press.

Ismael, J. T. (2009). Probability in Deterministic Physics. *Journal of Philosophy, 106*(2), 89–108. https://doi.org/10.5840/jphil2009106214.

Ivanova, M. (2017). Aesthetic Values in Science. *Philosophy Compass, 12*(10).

Ivanova, M., and M. Farr. (2020). Methods in Science and Metaphysics. In R. Bliss and J. T. M. Miller (Eds.), *The Routledge Handbook of Metametaphysics* (447–458). Routledge.

Jansson, L., and J. Tallant. (2017). Quantitative Parsimony: Probably for the Better. *British Journal for the Philosophy of Science, 68*(3), 781–803. https://doi.org/10.1093/bjps/axv064.

Jeffers, C. (2019). Cultural Constructionism. In J. Glasgow, S. Haslanger, C. Jeffers, and Q. Spencer, *What Is Race?* (38–72). Oxford University Press.

Khalifa, K., J. A. Millson, and M. Risjord. (2017). Inference to the Best Explanation: Fundamentalism's Failures. In K. McCain and T. Poston (Eds.), *Best Explanations: New Essays on Inference to the Best Explanation* (80–96). Oxford University Press.

Kincaid, H. (2013). Introduction: Pursuing a Naturalist Metaphysics. In D. Ross, J. Ladyman, and H. Kincaid (Eds.), *Scientific Metaphysics* (1–26). Oxford University Press.

Kitcher, P. (1999). Race, Ethnicity, Biology, Culture. In L. Harris (Ed.), *Racism* (87–120). Humanity Books.

Korman, D. Z. (2015). *Objects: Nothing Out of the Ordinary*. Oxford University Press.

Kuhn, T. S. (1962). *The Structure of Scientific Revolutions*. University of Chicago Press.

Kuhn, T. S. (1977). Objectivity, Value Judgment, and Theory Choice. In T.S. Kuhn (Ed.), *The Essential Tension: Selected Studies in Scientific Tradition and Change* (320–339). University of Chicago Press.

Kukla, A. (1996). Does Every Theory Have Empirically Equivalent Rivals? *Erkenntnis, 44*(2), 137–166. https://doi.org/10.1007/BF00166499.

Ladyman, J. (1998). What Is Structural Realism? *Studies in History and Philosophy of Science Part A, 29*(3), 409–424.

Ladyman, J. (2007). Does Physics Answer Metaphysical Questions? *Royal Institute of Philosophy Supplements, 61*, 179–201.

Ladyman, J. (2012). Science, Metaphysics and Method. *Philosophical Studies, 160*(1), 31–51.

Ladyman, J., and D. Ross. (2007). *Every Thing Must Go*. Oxford University Press.

Lange, M. (2013). Grounding, Scientific Explanation, and Humean Laws. *Philosophical Studies, 164*(1), 255–261.

Laudan, L. (1981). A Confutation of Convergent Realism. *Philosophy of Science, 48*(1), 19–49. https://doi.org/10.1086/288975.

Laudan, L. (1984). *Science and Values: The Aims of Science and Their Role in Scientific Debate*. University of California Press.

Laudan, L., and J. Leplin. (1991). Empirical Equivalence and Underdetermination. *Journal of Philosophy, 88*(9), 449–472.

Lewis, D. (1986). *On the Plurality of Worlds*. Wiley-Blackwell.

Lewis, D. (1994). Humean Supervenience Debugged. *Mind*, *103*(412), 473–490.
Lipton, P. (2004). *Inference to the Best Explanation*. Routledge.
Liston, M. (2007). Review of Penelope Maddy, Second Philosophy: A Naturalistic Method. *Notre Dame Philosophical Reviews*, *2007*(12).
Loew, C., S. Jaag, and M. T. Hicks. (Forthcoming). *Humean Laws for Human Agents*. Oxford University Press.
Loewer, B. (1996). Humean Supervenience. *Philosophical Topics*, *24*(1), 101–127.
Loewer, B. (2007). Laws and Natural Properties. *Philosophical Topics*, *35*(1–2), 313–328.
Loewer, B. (2012). Two Accounts of Laws and Time. *Philosophical Studies*, *160*(1), 115–137.
Longino, H. E. (1996). Cognitive and Non-Cognitive Values in Science: Rethinking the Dichotomy. In L. H. Nelson and J. Nelson (Eds.), *Feminism, Science, and the Philosophy of Science* (39–58). Kluwer Academic.
Longino, H. E. (2001). *The Fate of Knowledge*. Princeton University Press.
Lowe, E. J. (1998). *The Possibility of Metaphysics: Substance, Identity, and Time*. Clarendon Press.
Lowe, E. J. (2002). *A Survey of Metaphysics*. Oxford University Press.
Lowe, E. J. (2003). In Defense of Moderate-Sized Specimens of Dry Goods. *Philosophy and Phenomenological Research*, *67*(3), 704–710.
Lowe, E. J. (2011). The Rationality of Metaphysics. *Synthese*, *178*(1), 99–109. https://doi.org/10.1007/s11229-009-9514-z.
Ludwig, D. (2015). Ontological Choices and the Value-Free Ideal. *Erkenntnis*, *6*, 1–20. https://doi.org/10.1007/s10670-015-9793-3.
Maclaurin, J., and H. Dyke. (2012). What Is Analytic Metaphysics For? *Australasian Journal of Philosophy*, *90*(2), 291–306. https://doi.org/10.1080/00048402.2011.587439.
Maddy, P. (2001). Naturalism: Friends and Foes. *Noûs*, *35*(s15), 37–67.
Maddy, P. (2007). *Second Philosophy: A Naturalistic Method*. Clarendon Press.
Mallon, R. (2006). "Race": Normative, Not Metaphysical or Semantic. *Ethics*, *116*(3), 525–551.
Markosian, N. (1998). Brutal Composition. *Philosophical Studies*, *92*(3), 211–249.
Markosian, N. (2001). Critical Studies: Robin le Poidevin (Ed.), Questions of Time and Tense. *Noûs*, *35*(4), 616–629.
Markosian, N. (2004). A Defense of Presentism. In D. W. Zimmerman (Ed.), *Oxford Studies in Metaphysics* (Vol. 1, 47–82). Oxford University Press.
Markosian, N. (2014). A Spatial Approach to Mereology. In S. Kleinschmidt (Ed.), *Mereology and Location* (69–90). Oxford University Press. https://doi.org/10.1093/acprof:oso/9780199593828.003.0005.
Marshall, D. G. (2015). Humean Laws and Explanation. *Philosophical Studies*, *172*(12), 3145–3165.
Maudlin, T. (2007). *The Metaphysics Within Physics*. Oxford University Press.
Maxwell, J. C. (1861). On Physical Lines of Force. Part I. *London, Edinburgh, and Dublin Philosophical Magazine and Journal of Science*, *4*, 161–175.
McDaniel, K. (2004). Modal Realism with Overlap. *Australasian Journal of Philosophy*, *82*(1), 137–152.
McDowell, J. (2010). Tyler Burge on Disjunctivism. *Philosophical Explorations*, *13*(3), 243–255. https://doi.org/10.1080/13869795.2010.501905.
McDowell, J. (2013). Tyler Burge on Disjunctivism II. *Philosophical Explorations*, *16*(3), 259–279. https://doi.org/10.1080/13869795.2013.808693.

McKenzie, K. (2011). Arguing against Fundamentality. *Studies in History and Philosophy of Science Part B: Studies in History and Philosophy of Modern Physics, 42*(4), 244–255. https://doi.org/10.1016/j.shpsb.2011.09.002.

McKenzie, K. (2020). A Curse on Both Houses: Naturalistic versus a Priori Metaphysics and the Problem of Progress. *Res Philosophica, 97*(1), 1–29. https://doi.org/10.11612/resphil.1868.

McSweeney, M. (2023). Metaphysics as Essentially Imaginative and Aiming at Understanding. *American Philosophical Quarterly, 60*(1), 83–97.

Menzies, P. (1993). Laws, Modality, and Humean Supervenience. In J. Bacon, K. Campbell, and L. Reinhardt (Eds.), *Ontology, Causality and Mind: Essays in Honour of D. M. Armstrong* (195–224). Cambridge University Press.

Mermin, N. D. (2009). *It's About Time: Understanding Einstein's Relativity*. Princeton University Press.

Merricks, T. (2001). *Objects and Persons*. Oxford University Press.

Merricks, T. (Ed.). (2003). Replies. *Philosophy and Phenomenological Research, 67*(3), 727–744.

Miller, E. (2015). Humean Scientific Explanation. *Philosophical Studies, 172*(5), 1311–1332.

Mills, C. W. (1998). *Blackness Visible: Essays on Philosophy and Race*. Cornell University Press.

Monton, B. (2001). Presentism and Quantum Gravity. In D. Dieks (Ed.), *The Ontology of Spacetime* (263–280). Elsevier.

Monton, B. (2006). Quantum Mechanics and 3 N-Dimensional Space. *Philosophy of Science, 73*(5), 778–789.

Monton, B. (2011). Prolegomena to Any Future Physics-Based Metaphysics. In J. L. Kvanvig (Ed.), *Oxford Studies in Philosophy of Religion: Vol. 3* (142–165). Oxford University Press.

Morganti, M. (2013). *Combining Science and Metaphysics*. Palgrave Macmillan. https://doi.org/10.1057/9781137002693.

Myrvold, W. C. (2017). On the Evidential Import of Unification. *Philosophy of Science, 84*(1), 92–114. https://doi.org/10.1086/688937.

NASA Science. 2023. Dark Energy, Dark Matter. January 3. https://science.nasa.gov/astrophysics/focus-areas/what-is-dark-energy.

Newton, I. (1999). *The Principia: Mathematical Principles of Natural Philosophy* (I. B. Cohen and A. Whitman, Trans.). University of California Press.

Ney, A. (2012). Neo-Positivist Metaphysics. *Philosophical Studies, 160*(1), 53–78. https://doi.org/10.1007/s11098-012-9912-9.

Ney, A. (2021). *The World in the Wave Function: A Metaphysics for Quantum Physics*. Oxford University Press.

Nolan, D. (1997). Quantitative Parsimony. *British Journal for the Philosophy of Science, 48*, 329–343.

North, J. (2009). The "Structure" of Physics: A Case Study. *Journal of Philosophy, 106*(2), 57–88.

Norton, J. D. (2000). What Can We Learn About the Ontology of Space and Time from the Theory of Relativity? In L. Sklar (Ed.), *Physical Theory: Method and Interpretation* (185–228). Oxford University Press.

Norton, J. D. (2003). A Material Theory of Induction. *Philosophy of Science, 70*(4), 647–670. https://doi.org/10.1086/378858.

Norton, J. D. (2021). *Material Induction*. University of Calgary Press.

Okasha, S. (2000). The Underdetermination of Theory by Data and the "Strong Programme" in the Sociology of Knowledge. *International Studies in the Philosophy of Science*, 14(3), 283–297. https://doi.org/10.1080/026985900437782.

Pais, A. (1986). *Inward Bound: Of Matter and Forces in the Physical World*. Oxford University Press.

Papineau, D. (2021). Naturalism. In E. N. Zalta (Ed.), *The Stanford Encyclopedia of Philosophy* (Summer 2021). Metaphysics Research Lab, Stanford University. https://plato.stanford.edu/entries/naturalism/.

Paul, L. A. (2010). Temporal Experience. *Journal of Philosophy*, 107(7), 333–359. https://doi.org/10.5840/jphil2010107727.

Paul, L. A. (2012). Metaphysics as Modeling: The Handmaiden's Tale. *Philosophical Studies*, 160(1), 1–29.

Paul, L. A., and N. Hall. (2013). *Causation: A User's Guide*. Oxford University Press.

Pettigrew, R. (2021). On the Pragmatic and Epistemic Virtues of Inference to the Best Explanation. *Synthese*, 199(5–6), 12407–12438. https://doi.org/10.1007/s11229-021-03338-7.

Plunkett, D. (2015). Which Concepts Should We Use? Metalinguistic Negotiations and the Methodology of Philosophy. *Inquiry: An Interdisciplinary Journal of Philosophy*, 58(7–8), 828–874. https://doi.org/10.1080/0020174X.2015.1080184.

Plunkett, D., and T. Sundell. (2013). Disagreement and the Semantics of Normative and Evaluative Terms. *Philosophers' Imprint*, 13(23), 1–37.

Popper, K. (1959). The Logic of Scientific Discovery. *British Journal for the Philosophy of Science*, 10(37), 55–57.

Potochnik, A. (2021). Our World Isn't Organized into Levels. In J. DiFrisco, W. C. Wimsatt, and D. S. Brooks (Eds.), *Levels of Organization in the Biological Sciences* (61–76). MIT Press.

Psillos, S. (1999). *Scientific Realism: How Science Tracks Truth*. Psychology Press.

Putnam, H. (1967). Time and Physical Geometry. *Journal of Philosophy*, 64(8), 240–247.

Putnam, H. (1975). *Mathematics, Matter and Method*. Cambridge University Press.

Quine, W. V. O. (1951). Two Dogmas of Empiricism. *Philosophical Review*, 60(1), 20–43.

Quine, W. V. (1953). On What There Is. In W. V. Quine (Ed.), *From a Logical Point of View* (1–19). Harvard University Press.

Rabin, S. (2019). Nicolaus Copernicus. In E. N. Zalta (Ed.), *The Stanford Encyclopedia of Philosophy* (Fall 2019). Metaphysics Research Lab, Stanford University. https://plato.stanford.edu/entries/copernicus/.

Reiss, J., and J. Sprenger. (2020). Scientific Objectivity. In E. N. Zalta (Ed.), *The Stanford Encyclopedia of Philosophy* (Winter 2020). Metaphysics Research Lab, Stanford University. https://plato.stanford.edu/archives/win2020/entries/scientific-objectivity/.

Rettler, B. (2018). Mereological Nihilism and Puzzles About Material Objects. *Pacific Philosophical Quarterly*, 99(4), 842–868.

Robus, O. M. (2015). Does Science License Metaphysics? *Philosophy of Science*, 82(5), 845–855.

Rosen, G. (2010). Metaphysical Dependence: Grounding and Reduction. In B. Hale and A. Hoffmann (Eds.), *Modality: Metaphysics, Logic, and Epistemology* (109–136). Oxford University Press.

Rosenkrantz, R. (1977). *Inference, Method and Decision*. D. Reidel.

Roski, S. (2018). Grounding and the Explanatory Role of Generalizations. *Philosophical Studies, 175*(8), 1985–2003.

Rueger, A., and P. McGivern. (2010). Hierarchies and Levels of Reality. *Synthese, 176*(3), 379–397. https://doi.org/10.1007/s11229-009-9572-2.

Saatsi, J. (2017). Explanation and Explanationism in Science and Metaphysics. In M. Slater and Z. Yudell (Eds.), *Metaphysics and Philosophy of Science: New Essays* (163–192). Oxford University Press.

Saunders, S. (2002). How Relativity Contradicts Presentism. *Royal Institute of Philosophy Supplement, 50*, 277–292.

Savitt, S. F. (2000). There's No Time Like the Present. *Philosophy of Science, 67*(3), 574. https://doi.org/10.1086/392846.

Schaffer, J. (2008). Causation and Laws of Nature: Reductionism. In T. Sider, J. Hawthorne, and D. W. Zimmerman (Eds.), *Contemporary Debates in Metaphysics* (82–107). Blackwell.

Schaffer, J. (2009a). On What Grounds What. In D. Manley, D. J. Chalmers, and R. Wasserman (Eds.), *Metametaphysics: New Essays on the Foundations of Ontology* (347–383). Oxford University Press.

Schaffer, J. (2009b). Spacetime the One Substance. *Philosophical Studies: An International Journal for Philosophy in the Analytic Tradition, 145*(1), 131–148.

Schaffer, J. (2016). Grounding in the Image of Causation. *Philosophical Studies, 173*(1), 49–100.

Schindler, S. (2018). *Theoretical Virtues in Science: Uncovering Reality Through Theory.* Cambridge University Press.

Schindler, S. (2022). Theoretical Virtues: Do Scientists Think What Philosophers Think They Ought to Think? *Philosophy of Science, 89*(3), 542–564. https://doi.org/10.1017/psa.2021.40.

Schwarz, G. (1978). Estimating the Dimension of a Model. *Annals of Statistics, 6*, 461–464.

Sellars, W. (1963). *Science, Perception and Reality.* Humanities Press.

Sider, T. (2001). *Four Dimensionalism: An Ontology of Persistence and Time.* Oxford University Press.

Sider, T. (2011). *Writing the Book of the World.* Oxford University Press.

Sider, T. (2013). Against Parthood. *Oxford Studies in Metaphysics, 8*, 237–293.

Sider, T., J. Hawthorne, and D. W. Zimmerman. (2008). Introduction. In T. Sider, J. Hawthorne, and D. W. Zimmerman (Eds.), *Contemporary Debates in Metaphysics* (8). Blackwell.

Sklar, L. (1981). Time, Reality, and Relativity. In R. Healey (Ed.), *Reduction, Time, and Relativity* (129–142). Cambridge University Press.

Skow, B. (2015). *Objective Becoming.* Oxford University Press.

Slater, M. (2017). Naturalized Metaphysics and the Study of Species. In M. Slater and Z. Yudell (Eds.), *Metaphysics and the Philosophy of Science* (55–80). Oxford University Press.

Sober, E. (1990). Explanation in Biology: Let's Razor Ockham's Razor. *Royal Institute of Philosophy Supplement, 27*, 73–93. https://doi.org/10.1017/S1358246100005051.

Sober, E. (2009). Parsimony Arguments in Science and Philosophy—A Test Case for Naturalism. *Proceedings and Addresses of the American Philosophical Association, 83*(2), 117–155.

Sober, E. (2010). Evolutionary Theory and the Reality of Macro Probabilities. In E. Eells and J. H. Fetzer (Eds.), *The Place of Probability in Science* (133–160). Springer.

Sober, E. (2015). *Ockham's Razors: A User's Manual.* Cambridge University Press.

Sober, E. (2022). Parsimony Arguments in Science and Metaphysics, and Their Connection with Unification, Fundamentality, and Epistemological Holism. In S. Ioannidis, G. Vishne, M. Hemmo, and O. Shenker (Eds.), *Levels of Reality in Science and Philosophy* (229–260). Springer International. https://doi.org/10.1007/978-3-030-99425-9_13.

Spencer, Q. (2019). How to Be a Biological Racial Realist. In J. Glasgow, S. Haslanger, C. Jeffers, and Q. Spencer, *What Is Race?* (73–110). Oxford University Press.

Stanford, K. (2006). *Exceeding Our Grasp: Science, History, and the Problem of Unconceived Alternatives*. Oxford University Press.

Stanford, K. (2017). Underdetermination of Scientific Theory. In E. N. Zalta (Ed.), *The Stanford Encyclopedia of Philosophy* (Winter 2017). Metaphysics Research Lab, Stanford University. https://plato.stanford.edu/archives/win2017/entries/scientific-underdetermination/.

Stein, H. (1991). On Relativity Theory and Openness of the Future. *Philosophy of Science*, 58(2), 147–167. https://doi.org/10.1086/289609.

Strevens, M. (2008). *Depth*. Harvard University Press.

Sugunasiri, S. H. J. (1995). The Whole Body, Not Heart, as "Seat of Consciousness": The Buddha's View. *Philosophy East and West*, 45(3), 409.

Suppes, P. (1960). A Comparison of the Meaning and Uses of Models in Mathematics and the Empirical Sciences. *Synthese*, 12(2–3), 287–301.

Swoyer, C. (1983). Realism and Explanation. *Philosophical Inquiry*, 5(1), 14–28.

Swoyer, C. (2008). Abstract Entities. In T. Sider, J. Hawthorne, and D. W. Zimmerman (Eds.), *Contemporary Debates in Metaphysics* (11–31). Blackwell.

Tallant, J. (2013). Quantitative Parsimony and the Metaphysics of Time: Motivating Presentism. *Philosophy and Phenomenological Research*, 87(3), 688–705. https://doi.org/10.1111/j.1933-1592.2012.00617.x.

Taylor, E. (2018). Against Explanatory Realism. *Philosophical Studies*, 175(1), 197–219. https://doi.org/10.1007/s11098-017-0862-0.

Thomasson, A. L. (2017). What Can We Do, When We Do Metaphysics? In G. D'Oro and S. Overgaard (Eds.), *The Cambridge Companion to Philosophical Methodology* (101–121). Cambridge University Press. https://doi.org/10.1017/9781316344118.007.

Thomasson, A. L. (2020). A Pragmatic Method for Normative Conceptual Work. In D. Plunkett, H. Cappelen, and A. Burgess (Eds.), *Conceptual Engineering and Conceptual Ethics* (435–458). Oxford University Press. https://doi.org/10.1093/oso/9780198801856.003.0021.

Thomasson, A. L. (ms). Should Ontology Be Explanatory. In *The Question of Ontology*.

Thomson, J. J. (1998). The Statue and the Clay. *Noûs*, 32(2), 149–173.

Tobin, E. (2010). Crosscutting Natural Kinds and the Hierarchy Thesis. In H. Beebee and N. Sabbarton-Leary (Eds.), *The Semantics and Metaphysics of Natural Kinds* (179–191). Routledge.

Tooley, M. (1977). The Nature of Laws. *Canadian Journal of Philosophy*, 7(4), 667–698.

Tooley, M. (2012). Against Presentism, Two Very Different Types of Objection. In A. Bardon (Ed.), *The Future of Philosophy of Time* (25–40). Routledge.

Turner, M. (2000). Dark Matter and Energy in the Universe. In L. Bergstrom, C. Fransson, and P. Carlson (Eds.), *Particle Physics and the Universe* (210–220). Physica Scripta.

van Cleve, J. (2008). The Moon and Sixpence: A Defense of Mereological Universalism. In T. Sider, J. Hawthorne, and D. W. Zimmerman (Eds.), *Contemporary Debates in Metaphysics* (321–340). Blackwell.

van Fraassen, B. (1980). *The Scientific Image*. Clarendon Press.

van Fraassen, B. (1989). *Laws and Symmetry*. Oxford University Press.
van Inwagen, P. (1990). *Material Beings*. Cornell University Press.
Vetter, B. (2018). Digging Deeper: Why Metaphysics Is More Than a Toolbox. *Journal for General Philosophy of Science*, 49(2), 231–241. https://doi.org/10.1007/s10838-017-9387-7.
Vogel, J. (1990). Cartesian Skepticism and Inference to the Best Explanation. *Journal of Philosophy*, 87(11,), 658–666.
Weisberg, J. (2009). Locating IBE in the Bayesian Framework. *Synthese*, 167(1), 125–143. https://doi.org/10.1007/s11229-008-9305-y.
Willard, M. B. (2014). Against Simplicity. *Philosophical Studies*, 167(1), 165–181.
Williamson, T. (2002). Necessary Existents. In A. O'Hear (Ed.), *Logic, Thought, and Language* (233–251). Cambridge University Press.
Williamson, T. (2007). *The Philosophy of Philosophy*. Wiley-Blackwell.
Wilson, F. L. (1968). Fermi's Theory of Beta Decay. *American Journal of Physics*, 36(12), 1150–1160.
Woodward, J. (2003). *Making Things Happen: A Theory of Causal Explanation*. Oxford University Press.
Worrall, J. (1989). Structural Realism: The Best of Both Worlds? *Dialectica*, 43(1–2), 99–124.
Wüthrich, C. (2010). No Presentism in Quantum Gravity. In V. Petkov (Ed.), *Space, Time, and Spacetime: Physical and Philosophical Implications of Minkowski's Unification of Space and Time* (257–280). Springer.
Wüthrich, C. (2011). The Fate of Presentism in Modern Physics. In R. Ciuni, K. Miller, and G. Torrengo (Eds.), *New Papers on the Present: Focus on Presentism* (92–133). Philosophia Verlag.
Zack, N. (2002). *Philosophy of Science and Race*. Routledge.
Zimmerman, D. (2008). The Privileged Present: Defending an "A-Theory" of Time. In T. Sider, J. Hawthorne, and D. W. Zimmerman (Eds.), *Contemporary Debates in Metaphysics* (211–225). Blackwell.

Index

For the benefit of digital users, indexed terms that span two pages (e.g., 52–53) may, on occasion, appear on only one of those pages.

a priori metaphysics. *See* metaphysics: a priori
abstract (or non-concrete) objects, 115–16n.19, 155
actualism, 153–79
　radical versus ersatz or proxy, 155
analytic metaphysics. *See* metaphysics: analytic
anti-parsimony, 194
arbitrary privilege principles, 177–78. *See also* disagreement
assumption of positive correlation, 188–89

background assumptions, playing a role in theoretical virtues, 184–92
background-sensitive likelihood principle, 189
background sensitive methodology, 189–90
Bayes' theorem, 95–98
Bayesian confirmation theory, 95–98
Bayesianism
　subjective, 97n.35
Boltzmann Brains, 71–72, 134, 135–36, 138, 142–44, 149
brain-in-a-vat hypothesis, 134, 137–38, 142–44, 149

classical physics, 161
common sense, 19, 128–30. *See also* Mooreanism
competing methodologies challenge, the, 40–41, 180–81, 182–83, 186–89, 202–4
composition, 4–5, 8–9, 10–44, 63–64, 85n.23, 91–92
　conservatism about, 146–50

brute conservatism, 146
　dynamical conservatism, 147–50
　principled conservatism, 146–50
nihilism about, 23, 81–82, 87, 144–51
　radical versus nuanced nihilism, 145
universalism about, 85n.23, 145n.24, 146, 150n.32
conceptual analysis, 30–32, 212–14
　descriptive versus prescriptive, 30–10
confirmation theory, 73n.10, 95–98
content-methodology link, the, 26–43, 58–65, 100, 192n.17, 197, 220
　weak version, 44
　worries about, 33–43
content, of scientific theories, 17–26, 72, 144n.22
　empirical versus extra-empirical content, 19, –84, 209–10
　relativized approach to, 24–26, 208
　structural content, 57–59, 63–64
　as underdetermining metaphysics, 51–52
content of experience (modal and temporal), 173–75
content naturalism, 10–26, 45–65, 90–91
　biological content naturalism, 196–99
　definition of, 10
　domain-dependent content naturalism, 35–37
　as involving non-fundamental science, 198–99
　level-relative content naturalism, 40, 199–202
　limited content naturalism, 35–37, 58–65
　modality-restricted, 53–47
　non-IBE content naturalism, 60

content naturalism *(cont.)*
  overlapping content naturalism, 35–37
  physical content naturalism, 192n.17, 196–99
  psychological content naturalism, 196–99
  radical, 22–24, 49–50
  relation to scientific realism, 54–58
  restricted to a particular science, 196–99
  simple case for, 46
  strategies for rejecting, 205–21
  structural content naturalism, 57, 58–59
  worries about, 47–54
context dependence
  relative to cultures, 203–4
  relative to level, 26–27, 39–41, 192–96
  scientific methodology as context dependent, 26–27, 39–41, 180–204
  simplicity as context dependent, 184–96
conventionality of actuality, 164
conventionality of presentness, the, 13, 20–21, 157–59
conventionality of simultaneity, 13, 19–21, 68–69, 156, 158–60, 162–63, 165–66, 178
Copernicus, Nicolaus 67–68, 74–75, 77

dark energy, 89, 106–7, 111, 113–14, 117, 126, 209–10
data
  collection of as context-dependent, 193n.19
  as theory-laden, 92–95, 150–51
  as thick, 92–95, 131–32n.6
  as underdetermining scientific theories, 4–5, 6, 20–21, 66, 67–16, 73n.10, 80–87, 92–95
degree of epistemic commitment, 56, 83
determinate existence, 13–14, 158–59, 164–65
disagreement
  between modal perspectives, 167
  between reference frames, 165–67, 175–78
domains
  of science versus metaphysics, 33–37, 46, 52–54, 182–83

electromagnetic field, 89, 105–3, 113–14, 117–18
electromagnetism, 85n.23, *See also* electromagnetic field
emergence, 217
empirical adequacy, 19, 67–68, 69, 70, 71, 72–55, 75, 76–56, 79, 81–61, 93–95, 102, 131–32
  definition of, 19
empirical equivalence, 70n.8, 97n.34, 190
empirical vetting, 80–84
epiphenomenalism, 195–96
eternalism, 153
evil demon hypothesis, 70–72, 73, 86, 134, 137, 149
evolution, 85n.23, 187–88, 198–99
excess structure principle, 166–73
explanation, theories of, 108–11
  causal explanation, 201
  as involving pattern subsumption, 108, 108n.13, 110–75, 113
  metaphysically robust, 109–11, 113–14, 120–21, 122–23, 126
explanationism, 59–60, 114–18
explanatory power. *See* inference to the best explanation
extra-empirical principles, 4–5, 7, 48–49n.7
  as context dependent, 181–96
  general form, 73–74
  in metaphysics, 78–92
  in science, 72–78, 80–91
  worries about, 100
  See also theoretical virtues
extra-empirical reasoning, 4–5, 72–98
  as involving confirmation theory, 95–98
  as involving interpretation of the data, 92–95
  See also extra-empirical principles

Faraday, Michael, 105–6, 113–14, 117
fecundity, as a theoretical virtue, 75
fine-grained naturalism, 37, 219–21
free-range metaphysics, 206–7, 211
fundamentality, 192–93, 197, 217n.10, 218

Galileo Galilei, 67–68, 73, 74–75, 140–41, 160–61

general relativity, 69n.7, 155, 157n.7
genuine conflicts (between metaphysics and science), 24–26, 207–8
geology, 11, 18, 69–70, 86, 192
governance relation, the, 122–27
governing accounts of laws, 101, 111–14, 118–27
gravimetry, 69, 86
grounding, 217
  as an analysis of governance, 122–26
  as an analysis of Humeanism, 121–22
  as playing a role in explanation, 108, 109

heliocentric model, the, 67–68, 73, 74–75, 140–41
heuristic approach, the. *See* toolbox view, the
Humeanism about laws of nature, 118–22

indeterminacy, 156n.6
indeterminism, 17–18, 123–25
individuals, 51, 201–2
inference to the best explanation, 6–7, 37–38, 59–62, 74, 76–77, 79, 81, 96, 97, 102n.1, 114–18, 137–38, 183, 211n.5, 224n.1
inference to the existence of an explanation, 114–15. *See also* pattern explanation principle
intuition, 13, 42–43, 77–78, 128–29, 211

Kant, Immanuel, 48, 209–10

law neutrality principle, the, 166–73
law of likelihood, the, 187–89
laws of nature, 55n.18, 101–2, 110, 111–2, 201, 213–14
levels in science. *See* science: levels of
level-relative content naturalism. *See* content naturalism: level-relative
level-relative methodological naturalism. *See* methodological naturalism: level-relative
Le Verrier, Urbain, 184–85, 193–94
Lewis, David, 23, 85n.23, 121–22, 130n.3, 163n.17, 163n.18
likelihood paradigm of parsimony, the, 187–92

manifest image, 131–33, 135, 136–37, 139–40, 145–47, 145n.24, 149–51
Maxwell, James Clerk, 105–6
mental causation, 195–96, 199–200
mereology, 53. *See also* composition
metaphysics
  analytic metaphysics, 91–92, 206–7
  armchair metaphysics, 206–7, 211, 215
  as broken into sub-fields, 37, 54, 203
  as conceptual analysis (*see* conceptual analysis)
  definition of, 1–2
  as distinct from science, 46, 50 (*see also* domains)
  as distinct from other fields of philosophy, 1, 9
  distinction between a priori and naturalistic, 91, 206–7
  multi-level metaphysics, 199–202
  A priori metaphysics, 91, 206–7
  progress in, 206, 210–11
  realist versus pragmatist approaches, 55
  structural realism about, 57
  as the study of the possible, 52–54
  as subservient to science, 47–54
  as underdetermined by science, 51–52
methodological naturalism
  biological methodological naturalism, 196–99
  definition of, 10
  domain-dependent, 36–37
  as impactful in metaphysics, 66–100
  as initially plausible, 4–7
  level-relative methodological naturalism, 200
  limited methodological naturalism, 59
  modality restricted version of, 46–48
  non-IBE methodological naturalism, 61–62
  physical methodological naturalism, 196–99
  psychological methodological naturalism, 196–99
  structural methodological naturalism, 59
  worries about, 33–39 (*see also* competing methodologies challenges; no applicability challenge)

methodology of metaphysics
   alternative versus supplemental, 42–43, 189n.14
   as involving extra-empirical principles, 78–92
methodology of science. *See* scientific methodology
minimal divergence, principle of, 131–33
   argument for, 133–38
modal perspective, 163–71
   definition of, 159
modal realism, 85n.23
modal relativism
   definition of, 163
model selection paradigm, the, 187, 193–94, 195
Mooreanism, 128–31, 146n.25
   in metaphysics, 128–30
multi-level metaphysics. *See* metaphysics: multi-level

naturalism
   as coming in degrees, 3–4
   definition of, 3
   See also content naturalism; fine grained naturalism; methodological naturalism
Neptune, postulation of, 184–85, 193–94
neutrino
   introduction of, 89, 103–5, 113–14, 116, 117–18, 168, 185, 193–94
   tomography, 69–70
Newtonian mechanics, 73, 77, 92–93, 112–14, 120, 168n.25, *See also* classical physics
Newtonian parsimony, 184–85, 187, 193–94, 195, 202
nihilism, compositional. *See* composition: nihilism about
no applicability challenge, the, 182–84
no privileged modal perspective, 163, 165–71
no privileged reference frame, 20–21, 24–25, 159–63, 165–71

parsimony
   ideological, 148–49
   ontological, 61–62
   quantitative, 184n.5

pattern explanation principle, the
   application to laws of nature, 111–14
   argument for, 103–7
   final version of, 109
   initial version of, 102
Pauli, Wolfgang, 103–5, 113–14, 116, 117, 185, 193–94
perception, 16–17, 173
personal identity, 2, 4–5, 91–92, 128
pluralism
   as a response to conflicts between metaphysics and science, 208–11
   as a response to context dependence, 203 (*see also* multi-level metaphysics)
possibilism, 153
possible worlds, 1, 2, 4–5, 8–9, 52, 63–64, 172–73
   as concrete, 87–88, 128, 155n.3 (*see also* modal realism)
pragmatism
   about metaphysics, 29, 55, 211n.4
   about science, 54–55, 203
   about theoretical virtues, 37–38, 90–91
presentism, 12–14, 20–21, 25–26, 52, 153–63, 169–70, 175, 178–79
   definition, of, 153
   radical versus ersatz and proxy, 155
problem of evil, 190–92

quantum mechanics, 17–18, 51, 76–77, 85–86, 129n.2, 136n.14, 217
quietism, as a response to the competing methodologies challenge, 202

race, metaphysics of, 14–16, 199–200
radical metaphysical hypotheses, 133–44
realism
   about metaphysics (*see* metaphysics: realist versus pragmatist approaches)
   configuration space realism, 142n.20
   restricted versions of, 55–57
   scientific, 46n.1, 46–47n.4, 54–58, 73n.11, 100n.37
   structural, 56, 216, 218
   wavefunction, 217

reduction
    between scientific or metaphysical
        levels, 200–1
reference frame, 20–22, 24–25, 68–69,
        86n.26, 142n.20, 159–63, 165–79
    definition of, 160
    nomological, 161–63
relativity principle, 160n.13
robustness, as a characteristic of scientific
        theories, 87–90

science
    as distinct from metaphysics, 46
    as involving metaphysics
        presuppositions, 48–50
    levels of, 39–41, 47–48, 192–202
    predictions about the future
        development of, 217–18
scientific methodology
    actual versus ideal, 39
    as about the fundamental, 198
    as context dependent, 39–42, 180–204
    as involving extra-empirical principles,
        72–78, 80–91
    as minimal, 41–42
    as separable or non-separable, 58–65
    structural versus extra-structural, 58
    as value laden (*see* values in science)
scientific realism. *See* realism: scientific
semantic view, the, 88
simplicity, 6–7, 37–39, 74–78, 79, 81, 84,
        97–98, 100n.37, 137–38, 153, 183,
        184–96, 211, 224n.1
    See also parsimony
skepticism, 70–72, 133–38, 142–44
solipsism, 134, 134n.10, 135–36, 137, 138, 149
spacelike separated pairs of events, 157

spacetime-specific principles, 171–73
special relativity, 12–14, 19–22, 68–69, 73,
        86n.26, 94–95, 137–38, 142n.20,
        153–63, 165–79, 206
structural realism. *See* realism: structural

temporal ontology. *See* eternalism;
        presentism
theoretical virtues, 37–38, 74, 76–78, 79,
        81, 83–84, 90–91, 97, 99, 182–83
theories as models. *See* semantic view, the
toolbox view, the, 216–19

underdetermination
    in actual scientific practice, 67–70
    as an argument for scientific realism,
        73n.11, 100n.37
    of metaphysics by science, 51–52
    philosophical arguments for, 70–72
    and unconceived alternatives, 73n.11
    weak versus strong, 84–87
undetectable features principle, the, 167–69
universalism, about composition. *See*
        composition: universalism about
unmoored metaphysics
    definition of, 205–6
    as distinct from armchair
        metaphysics, 206–7
    with genuine conflicts, 207–14
    instrumentalist, 214–19
    pluralist, 209–11
    revisionary, 212–14
    without genuine conflicts, 214–19

vagueness
    ontic, 158n.8
values in science, 37–39, 197, 203